Extra-regional Powers in Latin America in the 21st Century

Studies in Critical Social Sciences Book Series

Haymarket Books is proud to be working with Brill Academic Publishers (www.brill.nl) to republish the *Studies in Critical Social Sciences* book series in paperback editions. This peer-reviewed book series offers insights into our current reality by exploring the content and consequences of power relationships under capitalism, and by considering the spaces of opposition and resistance to these changes that have been defining our new age. Our full catalog of *SCSS* volumes can be viewed at https://www.haymarketbooks.org/series_collections/4-studies-in-critical-social-sciences.

Series Editor
David Fasenfest (York University, Canada)

Editorial Board
Eduardo Bonilla-Silva (Duke University)
Chris Chase-Dunn (University of California–Riverside)
William Carroll (University of Victoria)
Raewyn Connell (University of Sydney)
Kimberlé W. Crenshaw (University of California–LA and Columbia University)
Raju Das (York University, Canada)
Heidi Gottfried (Wayne State University)
Alfredo Saad-Filho (Queen's University Belfast)
Chizuko Ueno (University of Tokyo)
Sylvia Walby (Royal Holloway, University of London)

Extra-regional Powers in Latin America in the 21st Century

The Impact of the US, EU, China, and Russia

Ekaterina Kosevich

Haymarket Books
Chicago, IL

First published in 2024 by Brill Academic Publishers, The Netherlands
© 2024 Koninklijke Brill NV, Leiden, The Netherlands

Published in paperback in 2025 by
Haymarket Books
P.O. Box 180165
Chicago, IL 60618
773-583-7884
www.haymarketbooks.org

ISBN: 979-8-8889-056-23

Distributed to the trade in the US through Consortium Book Sales and Distribution (www.cbsd.com) and internationally through Ingram Publisher Services International (www.ingramcontent.com).

This book was published with the generous support of Lannan Foundation, Wallace Action Fund, and the Marguerite Casey Foundation.

Special discounts are available for bulk purchases by organizations and institutions. Please call 773-583-7884 or email info@haymarketbooks.org for more information.

Cover design by Jamie Kerry and Ragina Johnson.

Printed in the United States.

Library of Congress Cataloging-in-Publication data is available.

Contents

Acknowledgments VII
List of Figures and Tables VIII

Introduction 1

1 **Latin America in the System of International Relations: the Evolution of Theoretical Concepts** 7
  1   Understanding the Theoretical Basis of the Foreign Policy of Latin American Countries 7
      1.1   *1950–1970: a Realist Approach to Autonomy and Integration* 9
      1.2   *Autonomy and Integration in the 1980s: Development from Within* 15
      1.3   *1990s: the Primacy of the Relational Approach* 19
      1.4   *The Beginning of the 21st Century: a Clash of Two Trends* 23
      1.5   *World Order 2.0: Liquid Autonomy and Niche Integration* 28
  2   Latin America's Approaches to Multipolarity 31
      2.1   *Latin America: Multipolarity through the Lens of Autonomy and Integration* 34

2 **Inter-American Relations at the Beginning of the 21st Century** 42
  1   US Foreign Policy in LAC at the Beginning of the 21st Century: Innovation and Continuity 42
  2   US Security and Defense Policy toward Latin America: Ensuring an Enduring Influence 64
      2.1   *Tracing the Evolution of the US Security and Defense Policy toward Latin America* 65
      2.2   *The Biden Presidency* 84

3 **China and LAC in the New Global Context** 92
  1   "Fast and Furious" Strategy: Chinese Foreign Policy in LAC 92
      1.1   *History of the China–LAC Relationship* 94
      1.2   *The Institutionalization of Cooperation* 106
      1.3   *Military-Technical Cooperation* 111
  2   Chinese Trade and Investment Presence in LAC: Main Spheres of Influence 118
      2.1   *Trade* 119
      2.2   *Investment* 124

2.3 The Belt and Road Initiative and LAC 132
2.4 China's Current Investment Presence in LAC 135

4 The European Union as a Player in Latin America 142
1 Three Institutions for Multilateral Cooperation in EU-LAC Relations 142
   1.1 Political Dialogue 143
   1.2 Assistance 148
   1.3 Trade 151
   1.4 Cooperation during New Global Challenges 154
   1.5 Perception of the EU's Regional Policy by Residents of Latin America 156
2 EU–LAC Relations: the Priority of Economics over Politics 159
   2.1 Trade and Economic Relations between the EU and LAC 161
   2.2 The EU, Mexico, and Chile 162
   2.3 The EU, Colombia, Peru, and Ecuador 164
   2.4 The EU and the Caribbean 166
   2.5 The EU and Central America 169
   2.6 The EU–MERCOSUR Agreement 171

5 Russia and LAC 180
1 The Place of Latin America in Russia's Foreign Policy Interests at the Beginning of the 21st Century 180
   1.1 Political Dialogue 181
   1.2 Defense and Security Cooperation 187
   1.3 Trade Relations 188
   1.4 Cultural and Humanistic Cooperation 192
   1.5 Russia–Latin America Relations in the Context of the Ongoing Global Systemic Transition 196
2 Russia's Zones of Political and Economic Activity in LAC 199
   2.1 Traditional Partners 201
   2.2 Ideological Allies 206
   2.3 Trade Partners 211
   2.4 Low Priority Countries 222

6 Where Are the Extra-regional Powers in Latin America Going? 230

References 237
Index 250

Acknowledgments

I would like to express my appreciation to my parents Larissa and Yury, as well as my husband Atrem, who have always helped and supported me throughout the building of my academic career.

I want to thank my four-year-old son Ivan, my muse, who always motivates me to appreciate every free minute of time.

I would like to especially thank Dr. Alexander Lukin, my current supervisor, for providing me with excellent conditions to conduct my research.

I also express my appreciation to my editor Dr. David Fasenfest, who made it possible to publish my research for a wide English-speaking audience.

I also want to give special thanks to my proofreader David Connolly, who edited all the English in my book, as well as the entire team of the Academic Writing Center of HSE University.

Figures and Tables

Figures

1 US foreign military financing to Venezuela 1991–2021, US dollars   69
2 US arms sales to Latin America and the Caribbean, US dollars, thousands   74
3 US foreign military assistance to Latin America and the Caribbean, US dollars, millions   77
4 Volumes of official development assistance (ODA) provided by the EU and its member states to LAC countries in the period 1990–2020, EUR, billions   150
5 EU imports from LAC and EU exports to LAC, 2000–2021, EUR, billions   152
6 Assessment of the presence and influence of the EU, China and the US in certain areas through the eyes of Latin Americans, % of the number of respondents (results of a Latinobarómetro survey conducted at the end of 2021)   158

Tables

1 Volume of US trade turnover with Latin American countries (US dollars, billions)   61
2 Data on US exports and imports to Latin American countries (US dollars, billions) and place among all trading partners of the country in terms of export and import volumes   62
3 US foreign military sales to Latin America and the Caribbean, US dollars   73
4 The top 10 recipients of US foreign military assistance   89
5 Volume of trade turnover between China and Latin American countries (US dollars, billions)   119
6 Assessment of the presence and influence of the EU and the US in certain areas through the eyes of Latin Americans, % of the number of respondents (Results of a Latinobarómetro survey conducted in 2004)   157
7 Volumes of mutual trade in 2021 within the framework of the main interregional agreements in the field of trade   176

Introduction

> And remember: you must never, under any circumstances, despair. To hope and to act, these are our duties in misfortune. To do nothing and to despair is to neglect our duty.
> BORIS PASTERNAK, *Doctor Zhivago* (1957)

∴

The beginning of the 21st century, marked by several conflicts in different regions of the world, confirmed the tendency towards increased resistance to the unipolar world order on the part of states that found themselves subordinate to industrialized countries and the increasing desire to reduce the influence of the US in world politics. The complex combination of political conflicts and interstate crises has once again drawn attention to understanding the concept of a multipolar world from a progressive point of view. The growing confrontation between the non-West and the West, especially aggravated after the outbreak of the military conflict between Russia and Ukraine in February 2022, has forced the entire planet to believe that the struggle between unipolarity and multipolarity is the main universal contradiction, which only a global restructuring and new alliances can overcome. The proactive foreign policy actions of Russia, whose government insists that it will continue to defend its autonomy by force from Western aggression, have led to greater attention from the world community to the idea of uniting progressive political forces as an important step towards strengthening the foundations of a multipolar world, which has been a response to the weaknesses of imperialism and globalism, seen as the main sources of the destruction of humanistic social structures and moral values.

The idea of building multipolarity has come to be seen by progressive governments, and in particular those of Latin America and the Caribbean (LAC), as a unique context in which the negative impact of imperialist aggression is mitigated, thereby allowing them to focus on internal transformation in favor of national interests. In the context of the crisis of a unipolar world, the debate that multipolarity, as a reality, is capable of ensuring the sustainable existence and progressive development of states, and multipolarity, as a doctrine, is no longer a utopia, but an entirely achievable goal, has acquired particular importance.

In the summer of 2023, at the BRICS (Brazil, Russia, India, China and South Africa) Summit, which has already become a symbol of the "new world", where developing countries have more opportunities to influence world affairs, a landmark decision for world politics was made to expand the bloc. More than 40 countries have expressed their desire to join at different times. On the eve of the Summit, the South African Ministry of Foreign Affairs approved a list of 23 states that have applied for membership. Of the countries representing the Latin American region, their desire to join the bloc five have been officially confirmed: Argentina, Bolivia, Venezuela, Honduras, and Cuba. Their governments declared solidarity with the principles of BRICS and advocated expanding cooperation through the Global South line.

Despite the fact that only Argentina received an invitation to join the group from January 1, 2024, at the South American Summit, further steps cannot be ruled out to intensify relations with BRICS on the part of other LAC partners with the prospect of their full entry. Argentina's decision to join BRICS was ultimately adjusted not only by global economic conditions, but also factors related to internal political processes: Buenos Aires abandoned this opportunity as a result of the change in politics after the presidential elections held at the end of 2023.

BRICS has become an important interstate union, symbolizing the idea of building a multipolar world in the 21st century embodied in reality, questioning the priority of interaction between developing states and the countries of the developed North. The growing popularity of BRICS among the states of the Global non-West confirmed that the Western political worldview is rapidly losing its influence in a world where developing countries are ready to fight to preserve their own civilizational uniqueness, culture, and identity, denying Western development models. Against the backdrop of the changing balance of forces on the world stage, the desire of the LAC region, as a new player in world politics, to more actively participate in international affairs has become increasingly clear.

By the 2020s, LAC states were forced to face the consequences of a number of shocks that significantly worsened their internal economic situation and investment and production conditions: the global financial crisis, economic tensions between the main poles of the world economy, the COVID-19 pandemic, armed conflict between Russia and Ukraine, the Israel–Hamas war, and the uncontrolled growth of inflation. This situation was further aggravated by environmental problems, which became even more urgent with the implementation of energy and digital transition strategies by LAC countries.

The whole range of crises and challenges faced by LAC countries in the 21st century has worsened the ideological crisis in this region, revealing the gap between the "top" and the "bottom" in individual LAC countries, and the isolation between the countries of the "first", the "second" and the "third" echelon of modernization.

The belief that developing countries should strive to follow the example of the countries of the West, which were traditionally seen as positive examples in matters of foreign policy and domestic political development, was shaken.

This led to another revision of the paradigm of the global system of international relations and the place of the LAC countries in it, and of theoretical approaches to understand the ongoing global transformations.

For LAC, 2013–2023 was not just a bad economic cycle, but a period marked by high inequality, weak institutions, poor governance, and a middle-income trap that significantly hampered economic growth. Annual growth rates in the region averaged no more than 0.9%. This figure was the worst indicator even in comparison to the notorious "lost decade" of the 1980s, which featured an acute debt crisis, stagnation of integration processes, authoritarian sentiments, and the institutional weakness of states.

Over the past decades, LAC countries have accumulated many unresolved problems that hinder their development, from which not only the poor and vulnerable segments of the population suffer, but also the middle class. Residents of LAC countries, no longer willing to hide their dissatisfaction, expect newly elected governments to fulfill their election promises, and to do so in the near future. Latin Americans want to see real positive results that will impact their daily lives. The LAC socio-political panorama is characterized by a general state of impatient anticipation of change for the better with an extremely low level of trust in the institutions of government.

The low growth rates of LAC economies, characteristic of the early 2020s, cannot contribute to creating new jobs. They do not allow governments to create a competitive financial space in which the interests of citizens and companies will be taken into account, while promoting investment in education and creating the tools for the effective adaptation and integration of migration flows. Under these circumstances, the LAC region once again faces a high risk of widespread social protests. In this difficult regional context, a sharp increase in interest in LAC by the most important players in the international system is increasingly evident. This interest is multifaceted and multidimensional: from economic expansion and the extension of diplomatic interaction to the manifestation of geostrategic ambitions. Been partly the result of the gradual decline in the dominant role of the US in the region, which began at the turn of the millennium, the rapid expansion of extra-regional actors in LAC has led to a significant weakening of traditional Western influence.

By the beginning of the 2020s the expanded presence of non-traditional actors in the LAC has become visible, persistent, and constant. LAC countries were able to build a multi-level system of external relations, which involved a whole range of extra-regional players who occupied a prominent place in the system of relations with the Americas. The reorganization of the global and regional international systems has led to an expansion of the confrontation between the powers already established in LAC and the newly emerged players who have successfully expanded their presence in this space. The dynamic transformations in the system of international relations in LAC in the struggle for leadership and increasing competition between extra-regional and regional actors are creating new uncertainties and reinforcing several pre-existing trends.

China already plays a dominant role in the global economy, politics, and the balance of power in international relations. Eurasia and the Indo-Pacific region, especially as part of the strategic confrontation between the US and China, are becoming zones of acute tension, the echoes of which affect other distant regions, in particular LAC. China is becoming the most important economic partner for a number of countries in LAC, in some cases surpassing the US.

Back in 1999, Beijing began implementing a strategy for the global expansion of Chinese business, called "Going Outward," which involved a sharp increase in investment activity abroad in order to acquire raw materials and technological assets, and expand its presence in new markets. LAC has become an important direction in the priorities of this new Chinese diplomacy.

Over time, the intensifying strategic competition between Washington and Beijing at the diplomatic, economic, and technological levels began to increasingly affect LAC. Washington's foreign policy priorities, key among them migration, drug trafficking, and trade, have gradually become a source of conflict rather than cooperation.

The EU is seeking to take a leading role in the interregional energy and digital transition, which could partially restore the EU's already shaky status as an important actor in LAC.

Russia, which still views LAC as the "backyard" of the US, has noticeably intensified its presence in the region, managing to expand political ties with a number of countries in the region in addition to its traditional partners, which since Soviet times have been Cuba and Nicaragua. The LAC direction of Russian foreign policy is still extremely uncertain, due to the lack of thought through conceptual issues.

By the 2020s, the dynamics of the global economy had changed radically, which led to the fact that the rules of interstate and interregional interaction in the context of the previously built "North-South hierarchy" ceased to apply. As part of the new international order, LAC countries are seeking to develop a pragmatic foreign policy, trying to play on the contradictions in the increasing competition for influence in the Americas among the main actors of global politics.

This study provides a comprehensive analysis of the key trends in the system of international relations in LAC. The work, for the first time in global studies, provides an up-to-date and multilateral assessment of the relations of LAC countries with their most important extra-regional partners at the beginning of the 21st century: the US, China, the EU, and Russia.

The book presents a comprehensive analysis of the evolution of the presence and influence of global players in LAC at the beginning of the 21st century, opening up for readers new multilateral perspectives on the role of this region in global processes in the interaction and confrontation between the worldviews of the West and the non-West.

The fact that the author is from Eastern Europe brings a fresh perspective on the dynamics and ongoing transformations of geopolitical processes in LAC, considering her extensive research experience.

The main questions addressed in this work are: What role do the extra-regional actors the US, China, the EU, and Russia play in the modern system of international relations formed in LAC? What are the essential characteristics of the foreign policy and foreign economic strategies of the extra-regional partners of LAC countries, which are gradually changing under the pressure of global economic and political transformations? What are the main trends in the domestic and foreign policies of individual LAC countries, and the prospects for intraregional and interregional relations? How exactly can the unfolding scenario improve or worsen the long-term prospects of LAC countries?

The answers to these questions determined the structure of the text. The first chapter is devoted to the study of the theoretical and methodological foundations of foreign policy, the definition of basic concepts and notions necessary for the subsequent study of the modern foreign policy course of LAC countries. From a historical perspective, the theoretical and conceptual content of "multipolarity" in LAC is analyzed. In this part of the work, the author examines the main theoretical concepts of international relations that dominate among Latin American researchers.

The second chapter studies the features and dynamics of the development of the political landscape in the Americas at the beginning of the 21st century, where attention is paid to the analysis of the foreign policy and security policy of the US toward LAC countries.

The third chapter examines the main stages, features, and results of the "Fast and furious" strategy of China, which, for the first time, has become an important player in the LAC economy and, to a lesser extent, in its politics.

The fourth chapter studies the evolution of the EU's strategy in LAC and gives a comprehensive study of the main mechanisms of political, trade, and investment cooperation formed between the EU and LAC.

The fifth chapter studies the place of Latin America in Russia's foreign policy. A comprehensive analysis of the bilateral relations of Russia with LAC countries identifying four levels of interstate interaction.

The author did not set herself the task of giving an accurate forecast of where the new system of foreign policy and foreign economic relations will lead LAC. Her main aims are to identify key trends towards rapprochement with the Western world, with its promising and tempting prospects for development according to Western patterns, and unity with the non-West, based on the idea of challenging the Western-centric perspective that has traditionally dominated the political and public discourse of LAC countries.

CHAPTER 1

Latin America in the System of International Relations: the Evolution of Theoretical Concepts

1   Understanding the Theoretical Basis of the Foreign Policy of Latin American Countries

The foreign policy strategies of Latin American and Caribbean (LAC) states have traditionally sought to achieve greater autonomy from more powerful countries (Bernal-Meza, 2005; Colacrai, 2005; Kosevich, 2023). The search for ways to expand autonomy noticeably intensified in the second half of the 20th century, the impetus for which was the strengthening of US hegemony in the Western Hemisphere, which occurred against the backdrop of the flaring up of the Cold War and the opposition of North and South (Kosevich, 2020; Kosevich, 2023).

As Marcos Kaplan noted, since the late 1940s, LAC and most of the "third world" have joined the new international system, characterized by a pronounced hierarchy of "dominance-subordination", formed, on the one hand, by developed countries, and on the other, by developing countries (Kaplan, 1983). This system was, among other things, characterized by the hegemony of the US and the USSR—two opposing superpowers that supported an imperial condominium. As Kaplan emphasizes, LAC countries found themselves embedded in a new system of relations, which has a *three-dimensional structure of dominance-dependence-uneven development*, which led to a decrease in their autonomy in matters of choosing models of economic and social development, and the independent management of their foreign policy.

According to Kaplan, LAC states participated in dialogue with the North primarily to discuss three issues within the framework of the established "order of assumptions and conditions": regarding the global concentration of power, the new global division of labor, the choice of development models, and modernization (Kaplan, 1983: 186). Representatives of the North had exclusive powers and privileges in relation to the LAC, whose foreign policy was strongly influenced by the trade and economic interests of the "northern hegemons". The model of flexible relations with open discussion of key issues on the global and regional agenda, including the adoption of common solutions to emerging problems, was categorically excluded.[1] As a result, problems in inter-American relations worsened, pushing the LAC states to build new foreign policy strategies in which the concept of autonomy occupied a significant place (Briceño Ruiz, 2017).[2]

This chapter distinguishes between the concepts of "autonomy" and "sovereignty". The latter appeals, first of all, to the dominance of a specific political entity over a specific territory, being implemented in the legal plane. Latin American authors tend to understand sovereignty as a representation of the total power of the state, which emphasizes its superiority over any other variation of domestic political power. This definition contains the modality of the invalidity of any enemy of state power, which acts as a guarantor of a sovereign state. Autonomy should be understood as the ability of a people to achieve independence, self-sufficiency, self-determination, and also to implement an independent foreign policy. It is autonomy that contributes to the formation of fully managed intranational and interethnic relations, while allowing them to be effectively controlled from within. Unlike sovereignty, autonomy is interpreted in terms of independence and adherence to rules that are fundamental for a particular society.

In this regard, researchers agree that it was the theory of autonomy that became the basis for the formation of all modern Latin American concepts of international relations (Santana, 2013; Simonoff, 2019). The key factor for achieving autonomy has traditionally been integration, which in a broad sense is understood as a special process consisting of combining parts into a single whole, and which also acts as an additional dimension of autonomy.

This introductory first section of the book examines the main stages of development that the concept of autonomy has gone through within the framework of theories of international relations developed by Latin American researchers. The changing role and essential characteristics of integration are also considered as a process that modifies its direction under the pressure of various external and internal circumstances. The author identifies five key stages in the development of the concept of autonomy, which are correlated

---

1 These observations were confirmed, in particular, by the fact that the Organization of American States (OAS), created in 1948 as a political forum for multilateral dialogue and American integration, during the Cold War, in most conflict situations, invariably supported the position taken by Washington.
2 The word of "concept" in this work is considered by the author from the point of view of a broad theoretical and philosophical approach. In this regard, the "concept of autonomy" is an idea that contains specific semantic content at each individual stage of its development, which, in turn, is associated with the concept of "integration".

with real historical events, each of which is interconnected in its own way with the concept of integration. All this allows us to take a fresh look at the place of extra-regional actors in the foreign policy priorities of LAC countries in the 21st century.

1.1   1950–1970: a Realist Approach to Autonomy and Integration

Awareness of the need to expand autonomy in LAC strengthened in the second half of the 20th century under the influence of endogenous models of economic growth.[3] Since the late 1940s, the foreign policy of the states in the region was focused on finding a response to the next rise of the North American hegemony, as well as mechanisms for intraregional dialogue in the changing ideological landscape (Hofman, 2000). The system of international relations that emerged in the second half of the 20th century predetermined the pronounced asymmetry in the interaction of the LAC states with developed countries. This led to the fact that three directions became the priorities of the foreign policy of Latin American countries: expansion of autonomy, economic development, and the inclusion in the global economy and politics as more prominent players.

All this predetermined the formation of the new concept of autonomy. It could be achieved in LAC only through structural changes, mainly in internal politics, which correlated with the endogenous type of economic growth model prevailing in LAC during this period of time. Based on the fact that the choice of economic management model relates to the internal policy of government bodies, the countries of the region were inclined to abandon capitalism in favor of a different model of the economic system of production and distribution with a different hierarchy of power and authority.

In the 1960s and 1970s, Latin American countries simultaneously gave the concept of autonomy supporting (the central task of the international policy of an individual state) and stimulating functions (the ability to direct the interests of all foreign policy actors to achieve the required results) in their foreign policy. The increased importance of rising autonomy in the system of foreign policy priorities was influenced by the intensification of decolonization, and increased attention from the world community to the importance of the peaceful coexistence of states. The Lusaka Conference (1970) also played a significant role, as part of which the states of Latin America, together with the countries of Asia, Africa, and Europe, sharply criticized the policies of

---

3 In endogenous models of economic growth, GDP per capita depends primarily on internal factors, such as capital reserves and productivity, the efficiency of innovation, the quality of the management system and the level of education.

imperialism, emphasizing the importance of the struggle for economic independence and the establishment of mutually beneficial and equal cooperation between states.

After the start of the Cold War, the attention of Latin American theorists was focused on explaining the functioning of the global economic system and its influence on the policies of key players in the region, studied from the perspective of dependency theory[4] (Marini, 1973; Calduch 1981). The theory of autonomy, in turn, has been traditionally associated with the latter: peripheral countries are able to achieve a way out of the vicious circle of center-periphery relations due to greater autonomy from world centers. However, unlike the theory of dependence, the theory of autonomy was designed to put an end to the deterioration in the terms of trade generated by the model of asymmetrical center-periphery relations, changing the very structure of international relations (Lechini, 2009).

It was in the context of growing anti-hegemonic sentiment that Guillermo O'Donnell's seminal work, Modernization and Authoritarianism, was published, which has become a classic of Latin American political thought. The researcher argued that achieving autonomy, the levels of which vary, is possible only through a radical transformation of the internal political hierarchy of dominance-subordination (O'Donnell, 1972). Referring to the Argentine experience of the 1960s and 1970s, in particular the "Argentine Revolution" (1966)[5] and the "El Onganiato" period (1966–1970), he viewed autonomy through the prism of the system of power relations within the state in matters of domination and subordination, where great importance was attached to the "force factor" of the state mechanism and the "inequality factor" of social groups within one nation. In his logic, a state with a sufficient degree of autonomy should try to establish itself as an agent of inclusive and stable capitalism. This strategy will allow it, over time, to appear in the eyes of other subjects of world politics as a significant partner, capable of presenting decisions as fair and

---

4 The theory of dependence or the theory of dependent development is based on the thesis that peripheral countries are not able to overcome their economic backwardness and political instability due to the systematic pressure exerted on them by the developed countries of the center, as well as the outflow of their resources and capital to richer countries.
5 The "Argentine Revolution" is the generally accepted name for the civil-military dictatorship that overthrew the legally elected President AArturo Umberto Illia (1963–1966) in a coup on June 28, 1966. Unlike other successful coups that rocked Argentina in previous years (1930, 1943, 1955 and 1962), the "Argentine Revolution" did not position itself as a "temporary force". On the contrary, it sought to establish itself as a new dictatorial system of a permanent type, subsequently associated with the concept of an "authoritarian-bureaucratic state".

independent of external interests. In this context, O'Donnell puts forward the *concept of specific autonomy*.

> *Specific autonomy (autonomía específica)* is a different vision of autonomy, in which special attention is paid to attempts to partially satisfy the interests of the lowest social strata, which allows for the preservation of the intranational hierarchy of dominance–subordination. These components of the social structure, considered as new instrumental mechanisms of autonomy, were endowed with the ability to increase the level of independence of the state on the world stage.
> O'DONNELL, 1982

The beginning of the 1970s for LAC was a period of emerging hopes for the independent rise of the region. After centuries of dependent relationships, Latin American countries for the first time saw opportunities to gain greater autonomy, achieve sustainable development, and gain a more prominent role in world politics. LAC states were faced with a dilemma regarding the choice of a political course that could bring them closer to these goals: through revolution or through reforms.

The symbol of the *revolutionary path* was the Cuban revolution (1953–1959), as well as the activities of armed anti-government formations, such as the guerrilla struggle of Che Guevara in Bolivia. The standard of the *reformist path* was the "Revolution in Freedom" (Revolución en libertad), which Eduardo Frei (1964–1970) tried to implement in Chile in the period from 1964 to 1969 through the law on agrarian reform (1967), the "Chilenization" of copper (1965–1966),[6] "concerted nationalization" (1969)[7] and other social changes (1968).[8]

The very essence of the inter-American system, characterized by contradictory and complementary relationships between the "two Americas"—the developed US and LAC states, noticeably inferior to its northern neighbor in terms of technical, economic and financial indicators—became a catalyst for the integration aspirations of LAC in the second half of the 20th century. In

---

6 "Chilenization" consisted of the state appropriating 51% of the shares of all copper companies.
7 The "concerted nationalization", the culmination of the "Chilenization" process, consisted of the purchase of most of the mining companies, thereby ensuring full control of them by the Chilean state.
8 Here, first of all, we are talking about the Popular Promotion program (Law No. 16880 of 1968), which changed the forms of collective organization of Chilean society. Thanks to this program, new social organizations were created aimed at improving the lives of marginalized sections of the population.

this context, leading Latin American states began to build their own geopolitical axes, crossing the entire region and even intersecting between each other in some cases. Some countries (mainly Brazil and Argentina) openly competed with each other. Washington's interventionist policies[9] further strengthened centrifugal tendencies, as a result of which the already unbalanced asymmetrical system disintegrated into separate, loosely connected regional coalitions.

As a result, political economic views based on the idea of a "new foreign policy", less dependent on the interests of the US as a hegemonic power, began to prevail in LAC. The realist approach became dominant, prominent representatives of which were Helio Jaguaribe and Juan Carlos Puig. In their studies, they emphasized including Latin America in the international system as an equal participant, addressing the vulnerabilities of weak states. Both authors, albeit each in their own way, defined autonomy and linked it with integration.

According to Jaguaribe, access to autonomy depends on the satisfaction of two conditions: the national viability of the state and international permissibility. The first "at a particular historical moment depends on the extent to which a country has a critical minimum of human and natural resources, including the capacity for international exchange." The second refers to "the extent to which, given a country's geopolitical position and its international relations, it has the conditions to neutralize the risk posed by third countries and also has sufficient resources to exert effective coercion on third countries" (Jaguaribe, 1979: 96–97).

Jaguaribe, back in the late 1960s, argued that in Latin America the necessary and sufficient conditions were not created to achieve autonomy through a revolutionary path. His works noted that the most promising model for the region was autonomy through development. In fact, he equated it with the term autonomous development ("desarrollo autónomo"), which must be combined with regional integration (Jaguaribe, 1969).

Thus, in Jaguaribe's approach, autonomy is the ability to make decisions that meet national interests and are aimed at overcoming the objective conditions of international reality, such as the power and influence of leading powers and transnational companies that form an international oligopoly. An important role was played by the desire of elites in LAC countries to freely choose the economic and political models they consider most suitable to lead their societies

---

9 Washington's growing interventionist sentiments toward the LAC are illustrated by the intensive military exercises of the US Army's 82nd Airborne Division in Panama in the 1950s and 1960s; the US military invasion of the Dominican Republic (1965), undertaken to overthrow the leftist government that came to power as a result of the civil war; and the CIA's repeated covert interventions in Latin American countries in the late 1960s.

along the path of comprehensive development. In this regard, Latin American governments must know exactly what their true position is, measured in terms of individual national viability, and what room to maneuver they have in world politics and economics.

Integration is seen as a necessary support for the process of autonomous development and as a tool that strengthens national vitality by strengthening the position of Latin American states in relation to industrialized countries and within the Western Hemisphere. Integration must be gradual and remain open to the inclusion of all Latin American countries if they have national vitality and are moving towards autonomous development.

In his works, Puig proposed rethinking autonomy through a realist approach, in which the world is perceived as a platform for conflicting interests between strong and weak states (Puig, 1986). Interstate interaction develops according to the rules of a zero-sum game played between dominant and subordinate ones:

> The strategic maneuver that this former committent[10] must set in motion will be successful only to the extent that the political diagnosis relating to the enemy—the dominant force—is correct and, as a consequence, mobilizes the resources of power sufficient to suppress the will of the opponent.
> PUIG, 1984: 44

The elimination of a rigid hierarchical structure characterized by unequal relations is possible only through a change in the policies of peripheral countries pursued by their elites. States are *a priori* endowed with the ability to independently take the path of autonomy. This transition is possible only when the peripheral elites are ready to make decisions that lead to the achievement of national goals. An important support is the stability of the economic system, considered as the viability of the state, which correlates with the Jaguaribe approach.

In the course of studying the world order, autonomy and the possibilities of changing the position of peripheral countries in international processes, Puig identified four models of foreign policy: paracolonial dependence, national dependence, unorthodox autonomy, and separatist autonomy (Puig, 1984). Paracolonial dependence is maintained in cases where the state formally has

---

10   To describe the center-periphery relationship, the researcher uses the terms "commission agent"—as a party that assumes certain obligations to the other party—the "committent".

sovereignty and is not a colony, but in reality the groups with real power are an appendage of the state apparatus of another country. National dependence is inherent in those countries in which groups with real power rationalize dependence. Consequently, they set their own goals, which can lead to the formation of a national project, and they are also ready to extend it to the whole world. It is the presence of a national project that distinguishes this foreign policy model from paracolonial dependence. Unorthodox autonomy is characterized by volatile relations between the center and the periphery. The internal development model of the latter may not coincide with the expectations of the center. A peripheral country is able to take part in international relations if they are not globally strategic, which implies non-participation in military-political alliances and coalitions. The national interests of the dominant power are the starting point for building center–periphery relations. Puig also emphasized that not every policy imposed by a leading power must necessarily be harmful to the subordinate country. Separatist autonomy means a global challenge: a peripheral country cuts the umbilical cord that connected it to the center. The leadership of the peripheral state decides to no longer take into account the interests of the dominant power. Puig himself emphasized that such an approach to foreign policy is very risky, since it depletes national resources, and utopian, since it can lead to a result opposite to expectations.

Puig perceives autonomy as the development of national interests, directly related to the rational use of the available room to maneuver. Such an approach can lead to the construction of a full-fledged national state. Integration can have ambiguous consequences, that is, the assessment of its significance depends on the goal of a particular state.

For Puig, integration is instrumental in nature, its meaning depends on the goal of a particular state, and also has three main characteristics: (1) it is a social phenomenon; (2) it involves not only states, but also any social group, both micro-level (such as organizations, unions and companies) and macro-level (for example, the international community); (3) the main purpose of integration is "to ensure that these "social groups" forego individual action in certain matters in favor of cooperative action with a sense of collective belonging" (Puig, 1986: 41). He is convinced that integration should be the product of societies striving for it. In this aspect, he anticipated many works of the 1990s, when scientists began to analyze civil society as a player in global politics.

In the 1950s to 1970s, Latin American authors viewed autonomy, understood as autonomous development, and integration as the main objectives for the foreign policy of LAC countries, a region that sought to find its own path in world politics. This has led LAC countries to link varying degrees of state autonomy in the face of hegemony in world politics and imbalances in the world economy with changes in the balance of forces in world politics and economics. It was emphasized that peripheral LAC countries should strive for a transition from a nation-state to a region-state, which became the central idea in building an integration initiative based on the idea of solidarity and therefore going beyond the elites promoting it.

1.2 Autonomy and Integration in the 1980s: Development from Within

The UN Economic Commission for Latin America and the Caribbean (ECLAC), which took on the role of leader in shaping development concepts for the region, in the mid-20th century actively promoted the model of "inward development", developed in the 1950s and 1960s and focused on domestic markets (CEPAL, 1951; CEPAL, 1966). The "lost decade" of the 1980s entered the history of the LAC under the signs of an acute debt crisis, the stagnation of integration processes, authoritarian sentiments, and institutional weakness of states. These developments caused disillusionment with the model of "inward development" and led to the search for a new conceptual approach that could provide solutions to the pressing problems of the region. It is in this context that a practical approach to policymaking in peripheral countries, based on the desire to extract direct material benefits from every interstate interaction and focused primarily on meeting current needs and requirements, was becoming increasingly popular in LAC (Tomassini, 1989).

The name of the Argentine researcher Raúl Prebisch is directly connected with Latin American economic thought and ideas about uniting the efforts of the LAC countries. In his works, he emphasized that the centers were never interested in the social effects of the development of the peripheries. The policy of the strong is not aimed at ensuring that the weak cease to be so. Prebisch emphasized that transformation will never come from the outside, either as an idea or as specific events. In his opinion, the countries of Latin America, through their collective actions, can lead to positive changes towards improving the situation of developing countries in socio-economic aspects.

His work covered four areas: the analysis and study of the economic reality of Latin American countries; the creation of a system of institutions that can help resolve the main problems of the region and prevent their aggravation, which subsequently resulted in the independent concept of Latin American structuralism; the preparation of specific proposals for economic policy and domestic reforms; the creation of a theoretical basis for the concept of development of peripheral countries. The latter, as Prebish's most important line of research, led to the creation of the theory of peripheral capitalism (Prebish, 1981). According to this approach, the centripetal nature of developed capitalism is the root cause of retarded development, economic and technological inferiority, and fragmentation of the periphery. Strong centers initiate technological progress, while taking for themselves all the benefits of growing productivity. As a result, the development of the periphery occurs only to the extent of the individualistic interests of stronger powers.

The central place in Prebisch's theory was occupied by the thesis: peripheral development is an integral part of the world system of capitalism, but it is formed and carried out in conditions very different from those in the center. It is assumed that peripheral capitalism is inspired by the centers and tends to develop in their image. The development in the peripheries of the imitative model, which is belated and strictly controlled by the central hegemons, is aggravated by the asymmetrical nature of foreign economic relations. It represents the root of the conflicts and contradictions of peripheral capitalism, which leads to the uneven and spasmodic dynamics of economic growth in weak states.

To overcome this dependent situation, peripheral countries need to develop, through collective thinking, a model of "dynamic redistribution accompanied by other forms of social improvement in response to pressing needs" (Prebish, 1981: 48). Achieving autonomy is directly associated with a high level of democracy, without which autonomy cannot be achieved. Prebisch considered industrialization to be the cornerstone of development and a means of increasing autonomy. In his opinion, autonomy is characterized by industrial integration, understood as the unification of a wide range of industries and an increase in mutual trade.

The most prominent representative of the movement that actively criticized the approaches of ECLAC was the Brazilian researcher Fernando Cardoso (Cardoso, 1977). In his works, he questioned the approach according to which the capitalist development of the periphery is impossible, and its underdevelopment is an inevitable result of the development of the center, due to which the periphery is *a priori* doomed to underdevelopment. Cardoso put forward his own version of dependency theory as an analytical construct to explain capitalist expansion in developing countries. Within this theoretical framework, the expansion of capitalism in peripheral countries is uneven, but quite achievable. Cardoso's dependency theory sought to demonstrate a wide range of international economic processes and their embeddedness in the social structure of LAC countries in terms of existing alliances between ruling elites. He considered the dominant social groups in Latin America to be those that established alliances with the outside world and that, thanks to this cooperation, were able to effectively adapt to economic changes. According to this approach, overcoming barriers to the development of states primarily depends on the alignment of the main political forces, and their interests and international ambitions, rather than on purely economic conditions (Cardoso, 1973).

One of the key arguments Cardoso used to build his version of dependency theory was Weber's thesis about which class should lead social change. Cardoso attached great importance to the circulation of elites, their quality and characteristics. In his opinion, the main enemies of the development of the peripheries are corporatism and the conservative bureaucratic bourgeoisie. Among other things, they significantly limit the country's ability to participate in international negotiations at the new level of dependence generated by technological progress and the new system of international division of labor, which emerged in the 1970s, resulting from the global distribution of industrial production.

The consequences of the "lost decade" became apparent by the mid-1980s when a severe socio-economic crisis hit LAC. The region's real growth rate was less than 2.3%, and poverty levels had increased by 20% since the end of the 1970s. All this took place against the backdrop of capital flight and currency devaluation (CEPAL, 1985). The need to overcome the economic and social consequences of the crisis and the backwardness of the region as a whole, led to the formation of a new theoretical approach. It covered macro- and microeconomic levels and was aimed at achieving quick results in the short term.

The mid-1980s were marked by the research of Chilean authors Fernando Fajnzylber and Osvaldo Sunkel. Their work marked a regional revision of the structuralist paradigm and was called *Latin American neostructuralism*. This approach emphasized the inconsistency of the postulates of classical structuralism for LAC, reflecting attempts to overcome the differentiation of regional development.

The works of Fajnzylber, published in the 1980s, made the greatest contribution to the theoretical understanding of the development of LAC from the point of view of neostructuralism. He analyzed the traditional problems of Latin America from a critical perspective of the limitations faced by industrialization in this part of the world in comparison with other regions. He concluded that the Latin American industrialization model had failed to achieve two key development goals: economic growth and income redistribution.

The region's pressing problems were seen as an "empty box" (in Spanish "casillero vacío"), arising from the lack of sustainable growth and the unequal distribution of national income. Fajnzylber saw a solution to the problems in a new industrialization strategy, which would be centered on accelerated scientific and technological progress and a series of reforms (primarily in the education system) ensuring social stability through active redistribution policies and expanding international participation (Fajnzylber, 1988). His approach was based on the integration of LAC countries into the global economy and strengthening the resource potential of the core of the development of scientific and technological progress and its acceleration—the main conditions for competitive and sustainable entry into world markets.

Sunkel's study, "Development from Within", offered a comprehensive analysis of Latin American development strategies, covering three overlapping dimensions: resources and productive sectors, the international context, and the role of the state (Sunkel, 1991). Agreeing with Fajnzylber's conclusions, Sunkel noted that LAC needs to move away from the development strategy that the region followed in the period 1945–1973, "development going inward" to a new strategy "development coming from within." The researcher criticized the model of pseudo-modern societies that most Latin American countries implemented in 1945–1973, when the problem of economic development was a key topic of discussion in this region, and which was actively abandoning the traditional predominance of rural populations in favor of increasing urban ones. In this regard, Sunkel noted that in the 1970s and 1980s, the process of import-substituting industrialization, which began in the 1930s and intensified during the Second World War, continued to develop in the region, which the countries of the region tried to combine with an orientation towards export development. As a result, by the 1980s, the growing need to achieve sustainable development had, in many cases, transformed into a need for structural change aimed at leaving behind decades of underdevelopment and dependency. The importance of increasing political autonomy was emphasized by new forms of US intervention in the internal affairs of Latin American countries: during the maritime conflicts between the US and Ecuador (1961–1963, 1966–1974), the United States and Peru (the 1960s), and the invasion of Panama by the US in 1989.

In his works, Sunkel developed the ideas of Prebisch, in particular on the analysis of import-substituting industrialization, which was considered as a factor capable of giving impetus to development coming from within. In this regard, Prebisch emphasized the importance of increasing demand, expanding the domestic market, and replacing imports with locally produced goods (Prebisch, 1970; Prebisch, 1981). Sunkel argued that for the "development from within" strategy, supply, not demand, is critical. Supply is formed through a number of factors: the accumulation of capital and improvement in product quality; stimulating scientific and technological progress and social discipline; moderation and prudence in consumption; and dynamic integration into the global economy.

Integration was viewed in terms of a global interdependent and interconnected economy, in which market segments of all countries are involved: the integration of international financial markets began to set the opportunities, connections, and limitations of the economic policy of each individual country. In this case, the principle of communicating vessels operates: the integration processes of some countries lead to the disintegration of others (Sunkel, 1987).

Complementing Fajnzylber's reasoning, Sunkel emphasized the importance of forming an "endogenous core of technological renaissance", which could push the LAC countries to create an effective structure of the national economy. The latter should help them successfully integrate into the world economic system. In contrast to ECLAC concepts, the international context was not seen as an insurmountable factor, but as a complex factor influencing the development trajectories of the peripheries. This approach reflected a new trend in political thought in LAC.

The theoretical ideas formulated in the region in the 1980s first began to be characterized by a loss of radical sentiment and a greater degree of pragmatism in proposing structural reforms compared to previous decades. The political and economic powers of a particular country and region are intertwined and assessed based on their competitiveness in the market environment. The level of autonomy is determined based on the costs of challenging the hegemonic order.

1.3 *1990s: the Primacy of the Relational Approach*

The end of the Cold War led to the formation of a new system of international relations, in which heteronomy determined the position, space for maneuvering, and policies of minor players in the world system. Peripheral states began to take a more pragmatic approach to achieving greater autonomy, seeking to make the most of limited and, as a rule, temporarily acquired opportunities.

By the early 1990s, LAC was already recovering from the "lost decade", which significantly changed the economic landscape of the region. Those countries that previously had enormous weight in the regional subsystem, such as Argentina, Mexico, and Venezuela, had still not fully overcome the negative consequences of the crisis. Previously lagging countries such as Chile, Peru, Colombia, and Brazil came to the fore (CEPAL, 1990). They were distinguished by rapid economic growth and a tangible increase in well-being and quality of life.

In this context, Argentine researcher Carlos Escude proposed the theory of peripheral realism. Within this approach, the foreign policies of peripheral countries are usually structured and implemented in such a way that national interests are defined in terms of development. Confrontation with great powers must be avoided at all costs. Autonomy is understood from the point of view of "possible negative consequences from the use of almost unlimited freedom of maneuver in the sphere of domestic and foreign policy" (Escudé, 1992: 8).

A foreign policy based on peripheral realism should eliminate all forms of external conflict. Disagreements can arise only over material issues that are directly related to the welfare and power base of the peripheral country. Thus, foreign policy strategy should be built in a utilitarian manner and should be based on taking into account the limits of material costs and benefits. The practical application of this approach in foreign policy was the Buenos Aires strategy, which led to the formation of Argentina's special relationship with the US under the administration of Carlos Menem (1989–1999).

Proponents of this utilitarian approach to autonomy, who mostly represented the countries of the Southern Cone,[11] drew attention to the fact that states need to stop being subject to pressure from great powers. This can be achieved by developing pragmatic positions which allow weak peripheral countries to move forward in forming their own values. Country risks can be reduced through calculated and balanced actions, as well as patient dialogue with stronger states.

In the 1990s, autonomy was also considered from the perspective of transnationalism, which entered into widespread scientific circulation. The transnationalist approach emphasized the importance of increasing the interdependence of countries and reducing the autonomy of leading powers in terms of their use of power resources (Portes, Guarnizo, Landlot, 1999). It was in the context of the increasing importance of interconnectedness between nation states, while the economic and social significance of officially established borders was decreasing, that the rise of Latin American integration took place, due to the founding of the Common Market of South America (MERCOSUR), and by enhancing subregional cooperation within the Andean Community (CAN).

The main prerequisites for the creation of MERCOSUR were formed in the previous decade. The failure of the Latin American Free Trade Association initiative, which was replaced in 1980 by the Latin American Integration Association, as well as the creation of other regional associations, laid the foundation for new approaches to the integration of Latin America. The radical transformations that have occurred in global politics (primarily the move away from the confrontation of the Cold War) have gradually led to the negative attitude towards communism in Latin America weakening. This change,

---

11   The Southern Cone includes Chile, Argentina, Uruguay, as well as Paraguay and the southern states of Brazil.

in turn, contributed to the replacement of military governments in the region's two largest countries—Argentina and Brazil—by new democratic regimes.

Internal political changes contributed to overcoming tensions in bilateral relations and the development of interstate cooperation. Under the new regional and international conditions, in 1985, Argentina and Brazil signed the Foz de Iguaçu Declaration.[12] Their integration agreements laid the foundations for what would become MERCOSUR six years later. The main objectives of the Declaration were the elimination of all forms of economic, political, and military rivalry between the two countries; the gradual and balanced opening of bilateral trade; and the intensification of industrial and technological development. Thanks to this document, the outlines of a future common market, characterized by closer cooperation and gradually covering all countries of the Southern Cone, were outlined. It marked the beginning of a new stage of Latin American integration, the distinctive feature of which can be called the fusion of political and economic aspects which play complementary roles in the development of integration.

The 1990s in LAC countries were marked by slow economic growth, the complete discredit of development models promoted by ECLAC, and the democratic transition which had begun in the previous decade. Against this background, the recipes of the "Washington consensus" managed to captivate the new political elites of the region, which led to the emergence of neoliberal convergence, expressed in reforms aimed at denationalization and opening up economies (Delgado, 2010). The 1990s, in LAC were marked by the "Washington Consensus," neoliberalism, representative democracy, and a focus on human rights (Aranda, 2011).

The active inclusion of the region in the transnationalized neoliberal economy, which was one of the consequences of the implementation of the recommendations enshrined in the "Washington Consensus," allowed states that were not themselves hegemons to gradually acquire nascent and limited autonomy in world politics. A number of LAC countries, most notably Brazil, Venezuela, Ecuador, Chile, Argentina, Mexico, and Peru, have benefited from their growing subregional influence, by the adoption of foreign policy strategies based on open regionalism, and the availability of mineral resources in strong demand from largest world economies.

At the turn of the millennium, the *concept of relative autonomy*, created by the Argentines Juan Gabriel Tokatlian and Roberto Russell, gained the greatest popularity. This approach made the case for the relevance of a foreign policy

---

12   https://www.cancilleria.gob.ar/es/actualidad/noticias/declaracion-de-iguazu-1985.

strategy which abandons the idea of autonomy as confrontation or isolation in favor of ensuring more regular and systematic interaction between Latin American states. Autonomy was no longer considered as a tool for achieving specific material benefits, but as:

> the ability of an individual country to act independently in world politics, as well as to develop external relations with other states thoughtfully, to treat its obligations responsibly and conscientiously. ... Foreign policy practice, international organizations and theoretical approaches are created and developed within the framework of relationships in which the "other", instead of being the opposite, begins to be an integral part of a common and unified system.
> TOKATLIAN, 2002: 179

Foreign policy based on relative autonomy is aimed at expanding interstate interaction and participation in the development of international norms and rules, especially in the field of constitutive elements of international law (those rules of law which define the basic principles, and which must guide any international action). Autonomy is no longer determined by the country's ability to control external processes and events, but by the ability to influence world events, international organizations, and cooperation mechanisms.

In LAC countries, an important role was assigned to the construction of a collective Latin American identity around the coordinated involvement of the countries of the region in the emerging system of international relations. To this should be added the intensification of regional integration processes, which traditionally occur in the region in an extremely fragmented manner:

> Latin America should view integration as a regional strategy that can be used as a political tool to strengthen its bargaining position with other external players.
> TOKATLIAN, 2002: 182

The popularity of this approach in Latin America quickly yielded results. By the end of the 1990s, discussions and consultations noticeably intensified at the intraregional and extra-regional levels. De facto, they represented the practical implementation of Latin American foreign policy based on the concept of relative autonomy.

For the Latin American region, the 1990s passed under the auspices of the concept of relative autonomy, defined in terms of the increasing interdependence of states, which leads to the need to distribute the costs of globalization among all elements of the mosaic of the modern world system. The change in the structure of the world system contributed to increasing the importance of international institutions in states achieving sustainable development and stable cooperation in the short and medium term. In this regard, relative autonomy was characterized by the active participation of Latin American countries in international organizations and by the limitation of unidirectional policies beneficial only to the individualistic interests of a single country.

1.4 The Beginning of the 21st Century: a Clash of Two Trends

In the early 2000s, the LAC region was swept by a powerful wave of change, preparing fertile ground for the ideologies of economic self-sufficiency and the political identity of the region. Several factors contributed to the changes taking place. First of all, the results of the "lost five years" for Latin America, covering the period 1999–2003,[13] led to disillusionment with the neoliberal model promoted by the US (Neoliberalismo, 2015). An important factor was the fact that after 2001, the US began to lose allies in Latin America due to the initiation of the "global war against terrorism." It was accompanied by such unacceptable actions for the states of the region as the invasion of other countries and violation of their sovereignty.

Once consensus was reached in LAC countries to deepen regional integration in the 21st century, the overall challenge for the countries became the creation of institutionalized policy mechanisms. They were understood as general principles and values guiding the behavior of the Latin American community within various integration platforms, especially MERCOSUR and CAN. The fulfillment of this task made it possible to determine the limit of autonomy in this region in relation to the initiative to create the Free Trade Area of the Americas (FTAA). The latter was promoted by Washington and quickly became synonymous with the "framework" for the actions of Latin American states in their domestic and foreign policies.

The failure of the FTAA initiative in 2005 led to the US adjusting its approach to interaction with countries in the region in favor of bilateral trade cooperation. In short order, the US signed a series of free trade agreements with Chile, Peru, and Colombia. The consequence of this targeted policy was the destruction of the core of Latin American integration and the erosion of the vision of autonomy as a guideline for the foreign policy of Latin American countries. The attention of LAC was focused on the concept of autonomy, based

---

13 Period 1999–2003 was marked by zero growth in GDP per capita for the entire LAC region.

on integration around common values, the manifestation of which was the formation of permanent regional blocs.

Thus, two trends competed in the region in the 2000s. The first boiled down to maintaining neoliberal options for international integration, as was the case in Chile, Peru, and Colombia. The second referred to a multidimensional form of integration, characterized by strong social, geopolitical, and anti-imperialist orientations. In this regard, the examples of Venezuela, Bolivia, and Ecuador were the most instructive. Some countries were at the intersection of these trends. In particular, Brazil actively promoted the emergence of strong alternatives to the FTAA initiative, first through the formation of the South American Community of Nations and then the Union of South American Nations (UNASUR).[14] The emergence of these initiatives was interconnected with Brasília's ambition to become a regional leader of LAC, which was achieved by increasing Brazilian influence in regional trade, as a result of increasing its exports and investments. This nimble strategy also helped Brazil raise its profile in global politics as a major new player, maintain its status as a competitive industrial powerhouse established in the 1960s, and increase the presence of Brazilian corporations throughout Latin America.

Although Brasília's initiatives had a more modest geographic scope than the FTAA project promoted by Washington, they addressed similar problems: the increase of trade and partnership, which are the keys to achieving leadership status in the region. This strategy covered all LAC countries, regardless of their political ideology, but priority was given to South American states. In this regard, Brazilian researchers Tullo Vigevani and Gabriel Cepaluni presented their own classification of three subtypes of autonomy of a peripheral state, which can explain the evolution of Brazilian foreign policy at the beginning of the 21st century.

Autonomy at a distance—the country opposes the great powers, striving for isolation and self-sufficient development; *Participatory autonomy*—foreign policy is based on a commitment to global governance and multilateral institutions; *Autonomy through diversification*—foreign policy is focused on developing relations with the Global South (Vigevani, Cepaluni, 2007). The authors emphasize that it is the concept of autonomy through diversification that is more applicable to explain the main changes that occurred in Brazilian foreign policy in the period from the 1980s to the mid-2000s, compared to the concepts of autonomy at a distance and participatory autonomy.

---

14 Union of South American Nations (UNASUR) is a South American integration organization, created in 2008 that includes 12 South American countries (Argentina, Bolivia, Brazil, Colombia, Chile, Ecuador, Guyana, Paraguay, Peru, Suriname, Uruguay, and Venezuela).

The trend towards a multidimensional form of integration, covering not only economics and trade, but also a wide range of other aspects of cooperation (for example, ecology, healthcare, energy, food, and sports), was set by Venezuela. In this country, the state and society began to change radically in 1999 with the coming to power of Hugo Chavez. Caracas' new strategy was based on the desire to reduce US influence. Having started on its territory, the Venezuelan government hoped to then extend this process to the rest of Latin America. It assigned a key role to the search for new forms of economic integration of LAC which is an important step towards building a multipolar world.

Since 2001, active discussions began on the creation of the Bolivarian Alliance for the Peoples of Our America (ALBA),[15] which took place against the backdrop of post-neoliberal processes that were gaining strength in the region. ALBA promoted the values, methods, and formats of regional organizations, which laid the foundations for a new mechanism of interstate interaction with wider regional coverage. This process included not only South America, but also the countries of Central America and the Caribbean.

This integration association was aimed at deepening cooperation between the participating countries, especially in the financial, energy and telecommunications fields. Its main task was to increase the level of social justice while maintaining traditional economic and political autonomy. Gradually, the states that made up ALBA began to diverge more openly from the US on a number of issues.

The updated foreign policy, and new options for "alternative development" in various areas (economics, ecology, indigenous peoples) adopted by individual countries, made it clear that LAC states began to condemn the categorical imposition of decisions on them that meet the interests of Washington. It was in this context that the reformatting of Latin American foreign policy took place, where the *concept of separatist autonomy* was taken as a basis. The latter was most evident in the policies pursued by Venezuela and Bolivia, which directly opposed the US on issues such as security, military cooperation, economics, and trade.

Integration was given an important place in new foreign policy strategies. The idea of creating a centralized republic, put forward by Simon Bolivar, came to the fore, which was called the "Nation of Republics" (Spanish: Nación de Repúblicas). Within this approach, it was Latin America's deep

---

15   Bolivarian Alliance for the Peoples of Our America (ALBA) is an international regional organization, was established in 2004. It includes Cuba, Venezuela, Antigua and Barbuda, Bolivia, Dominica, Ecuador, Nicaragua, Saint Lucia, Saint Vincent, and the Grenadines, Grenada, and Saint Kitts and Nevis.

integration, as well as the active diversification of international relations, that determined the prosperous future of the LAC. At the same time, it was planned to develop the so-called solidary integration.

Solidary integration is understood as a tool for ensuring the sustainability of socio-economic development of the Latin American region.[16] This concept is based on the idea of creating a springboard for a cooperative, social and solidarity economy, designed to replace a system of relations, which is built on the basis that national, regional, subregional and continental space performs the functions of a market transferred to the hands of transnational corporations and private investors. In this regard, particularly important importance is attached to the preservation of national identity.

The Latin American and Caribbean Meetings on Solidarity Economy and Fair Trade (Spanish: Encuentro Latinoamericano y Caribe de Economía Solidaria y Comercio Justo) played a fundamental role in the development of this approach. Since 2005, they have been carried out by the Intercontinental Network for the Promotion of the Social Solidarity Economy of Latin America and the Caribbean (Spanish: Red Intercontinental de Promoción de la Economía Social Solidaria—Latinoamérica y Caribe, RIPESS LAC).[17]

Solidary integration was supposed to supplant integration, the central unifying factor of which was economic and trade relations. To stimulate it, the "Southern Energy Ring" was formed in LAC (2005)[18] and Bank of the South, which jointly promoted the format of the region's independent energy and financial agendas.

In the 2000s, an alternative national post-neoliberalism, which was based on autonomous integration, began to actively develop in Latin America. It was built through the intensification of processes to restore popular, national, energy, and territorial sovereignty. This approach was also distinguished by its multidimensional scope and the LAC countries' rejection of the late 20th century model of relations with the US (Ceceña, 2008).

As a result, a new post-neoliberal direction was formed, incorporating Latin American countries, in whose foreign policy a tendency towards *separatist*

---

16   https://publications.iadb.org/es/publicacion/16489/integracion-solidaria-para-la-com petitividad-global-hacia-el-fortalecimiento-de.

17   Since the creation of the format of the Latin American and Caribbean Meetings on Solidarity Economy and Fair Trade, a total of seven such events have been organized, which took place in different cities of the LAC. Links to final documents from past meetings: http://www.ripess.org/redes-continentales/america-latina-y-caribe/?lang=es.

18   The Southern Energy Ring project includes a gas pipeline that begins in the Camisea region, in northern Peru, with the goal of transporting gas to northern Chile. Supplies, although in much smaller quantities, are also made to Argentina, Brazil and Uruguay.

autonomy was increasingly evident. The separatist autonomy emphasized the need for rapid changes in the region that could provide a higher level of independence in relation to the centers of global economic and political influence. Public demand has emerged for a new social model of development that meets the requirements of a fair society, with greater individual participation, and the removal of traditional political elites from power. This trend was most pronounced in Venezuela, Bolivia, Ecuador, Nicaragua, and Cuba. The transformations taking place in these countries in the 2000s took place under the motto of "Socialism of the 21st century":

> the main task of Socialism of the 21st century was "to build a new culture and a new type of society, characterized by the abolition of all forms of oppression and exploitation, the primacy of solidarity…".
> BORÓN, 2009: 103

The complex transformations taking place in LAC countries reflected attempts to create a new system of relations in the region, independent from external forces but not opposed to existing institutions. Against this background, new regional mechanisms of coordination, cooperation and ideological rapprochement of countries emerged, such as Petrocaribe. The emergence of ALBA, UNASUR and the Community of Latin American and Caribbean States (CELAC) represented an important milestone in the construction of a new world order that did not accept relations of domination and subordination.

By the beginning of the 21st century, great importance in the updated interpretation of the concept of autonomy again belonged to regional integration, which was perceived by Latin American researchers as a central element of LAC autonomy:

> Integration is considered, on the one hand, as a stage of comprehensive and solidary development of peoples who have recognized a common origin and destiny; on the other hand, as a systemic tool for overcoming the factors of maintaining a dependent position that prevent countries from achieving full political autonomy.
> BERNAL-MEZA, 2013

In these conditions, Latin American authors especially noted the importance of creating new regional integration initiatives based on the principles of solidarity and social demands. These elements, displacing capitalist logic, were considered as prerequisites for achieving world equilibrium (Spanish: *el equilibrio del mundo*). This approach became a direct reference to the concept of world balance, put forward by José Martí as one of the ways to ensure equality of states. The idea proposed by the Martí is capable of taking into account the interests of all LAC countries, considered as "Our America".[19] It is through joint efforts that Latin America is paving its way to a brighter future (Martí, 1894).

The importance of creating a multipolar world ran through Latin American foreign policy discourse, which emphasized that the post-Cold War global order, characterized by US hegemony, ultimately led to an imbalance in international relations. The creation of "alternative poles of power" would make it possible to restore the lost world balance. According to Chavez's concept, it is South America that can become a new pole of power to counter the unipolar world led by Washington (Ellner, 2009).

The emergence in 2011 of the Pacific Alliance (PA)—a new integration project to create a free trade zone—once again fueled the neoliberal invariants of international integration, in which a relative approach to autonomy dominated. The PA contributed to the creation of a "regional balance" through the development of relations with two competing powers—the United States and China (Correa, 2016), which gradually led to another revision of the concept of autonomy.

During the first two decades of the 21st century, the prevailing view in LAC was that integration, based on shared values and involving the formation of new regional alliances and blocs, was the engine of autonomy. The autonomy of LAC could be achieved due to its strong inclusion in the world economy, and through economic self-sufficiency and the uniqueness of its political culture. An important distinguishing feature of this new form of integration was its multidimensional scope—in addition to the economic sphere, it included such important aspects of public life as culture, education, sports, healthcare, social communications and human rights in a broad sense.

1.5   *World Order 2.0: Liquid Autonomy and Niche Integration*

By the start of the 2020s, LAC found itself between two fires: on the one hand there was a relative decline in US influence in the Western Hemisphere, and while Washington's return to the policy of imposing its dominance on the countries of the region was noticeable. On the other hand, the worsening rivalry between China and the US became a characteristic feature of the 21st century in comparison with previous cycles of the intensification of US hegemony.

---

19   José Martí formulated the concept of "Our America," which became one of the key ones in his political teachings, in which he included all states located south of the river Rio Grande.

The confrontation between the two powers intensified against the background of the confrontation between two global trends that determined the normative contours of the system of international relations. Interaction at the level of states, where the importance of protecting borders, territories, and sovereignty was emphasized, came into conflict with localized, transnational interaction, where the concept of borders is blurred, and an important role is assigned to new actors in world politics. This gave rise to geopolitical competition, increased international tension and, as a result, the emergence of new challenges to the autonomy of states.

Since the late 2010s, LAC has become politically fragmented, which was confirmed by the stagnation and weakening of the main regional integration initiatives—MERCOSUR, CAN, PA, ALBA, CELAC and UNASUR. In this regard, it is indicative that in 2019, at the initiative of the presidents of Colombia and Chile, a new integration bloc was created—The Forum for the Progress and Integration of South America (PROSUR), designed to replace UNASUR, which was paralyzed by internal conflicts. This association was presented as a South American coordination mechanism for public policy in defense of democracy, political independence in foreign and domestic policy, market economy, and the social agenda.

The early 2020s were marked by the largest economic downturn in the region's recent history, caused by the COVID-19 pandemic and the economic and ideological disintegration of LAC. At the same time, there was a sharp change in the ideological map of Latin America, in which the "new left" governments began to dominate.

As a result, the LAC countries gradually moved away from the predictable, relatively constant model of intraregional relations with specific principles of interstate interaction. This was replaced by unstable, fragmented relationships, devoid of behavioral regularity. These processes contrasted with the ideas of uniting the forces of all Latin American countries that prevailed in previous historical periods. As another decline in the region's economy became increasingly obvious, its vulnerability to external interference increased.

As a result, a new concept of liquid autonomy was formed in LAC. It was based on the idea of maintaining an equidistant position in relation to the US and China—two opposing powers on which the sustainable development of the region depended. The emergence of freedom and independence in foreign policy was associated both with the fragility of the global and regional situation and with the ability of states to anticipate problems and to be resilient in the face of unexpected events, which allows them to reduce any future risks.

> The "liquid autonomy" is autonomy that implies proactivity, variability and flexibility in the face of new challenges and opportunities created by the Westphalia and Globalization scenarios. This concept also signifies a certain type of defensive pragmatism, which consists of offering concessions on specific issues that are functional to gain room for maneuver in other future confrontations. Today we are not talking about "autonomy in resistance", but about "autonomy in resilience". Integration has taken the form of niche cooperation with historically related countries, which is seen as a tool that can increase negotiation potential and strengthen the ability to counter global risks.
> ACTIS and MALACALZA, 2021

The term "niche cooperation" explains the special nature of the new system of international relations, where the capabilities of its subjects are limited by their targeting of a certain circle of subjects, considered primarily as consumers. The Mexico-Argentina Strategic Alliance for COVID-19 Vaccine Production (2020)[20] and the Argentine-Brazilian Center for Biotechnology (2019), which was later joined by Uruguay (2021),[21] are examples of regional niche programs.

In order to maintain autonomy and limit maximum interference from outside, the foreign policy of Latin American countries should complement participation in integration associations by forming a list of new strategic partnerships with different countries, embodied in various joint programs. Autonomous enclaves must be formed based on shared priorities and through niche diplomacy, renewed 3-M (multidimensional, multilateral, and multilevel) diplomacy, which involves not only governments, but also local authorities, civil society actors, scientists, businessmen, and ordinary citizens.[22]

∴

The author distinguishes five main stages in the development of the concepts of autonomy and integration in the modern foreign policy of Latin American

---

20 Gobierno de México. México anuncia alianza estratégica para la producción de la vacuna contra COVID-19. https://www.gob.mx/sre/articulos/mexico-anuncia-alianza-estrateg ica-para-la-produccion-de-la-vacuna-contra-covid-19-250178?idiom=es#:~:text=En%20e ste%20acuerdo%20participan%20un,incluye%20una%20transferencia%20de%20t ecnolog%C3%ADa.
21 CABBIO. https://www.cabbio.uy/.
22 *Hacia una gobernanza regional 3M: multilateral, multinivel y multiactoral.* Working paper. Foro Global Colabora. 2021.

countries. The first stage occurred in the period 1950–1970, which was characterized by the prevalence of the realist approach. The second stage, spanning the 1980s, was marked by the rise of the "development from within" strategy. The third stage affected the 1990s, during which the concept of relative autonomy dominated. The fourth stage (from the beginning of the 21st century) was characterized by the dominance of two approaches: separatist and relative. The fifth stage (late 2010s—early 2020s) became another crisis test for LAC, which led to the emergence of the concept of liquid autonomy: mobile autonomy, which is in a state of opportunistic drift.

LAC is characterized by sharp and spasmodic but, at the same time, cyclical development. This suggests that the concept of autonomy and the role of integration will not only continue to change, but will also re-elevate traditional approaches to these concepts, endowing them with heuristic potential for analyzing regional and global dynamics.

2   Latin America's Approaches to Multipolarity

The Russia-Ukraine conflict, which entered an acute phase in February 2022, is already having a noticeable impact on the international order and world politics: from powerful negative impacts on the global food, energy, and financial systems to the increased polarization of the world's major powers, resulting in negative consequences affecting not only the world's leading countries, but also peripheral regions such as LAC. The escalating confrontation, which has already divided the world into several camps, has begun to be seen by political leaders and the academic community as one of the stages towards a multipolar world, designed to eliminate the unipolar world led by the US, which was entrenched after the Cold War.

In the context of the ongoing global systemic transition, when the latest manifestation of multipolarity has not yet been fully formed, the analysis of the concept of a multipolar world in the academic discourse of Latin America acquires special significance and relevance.

The Russia-Ukraine conflict demonstrated that most Latin American countries, in particular Brazil, Argentina, Nicaragua, Cuba, and Venezuela, which are included in the "first level" priority groups for the Kremlin, are not following the policy of Western sanctions on Russia (Kosevich, 2022). Despite the fact that throughout its history, LAC has repeatedly faced international interventions and all kinds of external interference, most LAC governments have not condemned the Kremlin for its invasion, have not justified Russian policies, and have not supported Ukrainian President Volodymyr Zelensky, diligently maintaining a position of neutrality. Kyiv's attempts to change this approach did not find a wide response in Latin America.

This was confirmed by the rejection by MERCOSUR of the request of the Ukrainian president to speak at the summit of its leaders, which took place in July 2022 in Paraguay, despite the fact that since the outbreak of hostilities in Ukraine, Zelensky has spoken at various international forums, in NATO, G7, UN, and World Economic Forum. In the context of this indifference, a video conference was held in Chile in August 2022, at which Zelensky spoke. This event was the first address of the Ukrainian president to LAC after the intensification of the Russia-Ukraine conflict,[23] in which Zelensky called on the entire region to provide humanitarian and security assistance to Ukraine, as well as to isolate the Russian economy. Notably, the organizer was not a government, as is the case in most such events, but the Pontifical Catholic University of Chile. The absence of Chilean President Gabriel Boric and Foreign Minister Antonia Urrejola at the conference, citing a busy work schedule, as well as questions to Zelensky from conference participants representing various LAC countries, confirmed that this region chose to remain indifferent to the conflict.

At the time of this work's publication, the only Latin American president to have visited Ukraine and offer token support, at the time of writing, is Guatemalan President Alejandro Giammattei, who met with Zelensky in the summer of 2022. A manifestation of support for Kyiv was the regional initiative 'Aguanta Ucrania', led by former High Commissioner of Peace, Sergio Jaramillo, which aims to assist Ukrainian people in LAC. The ideologies of this project appeal to the fact that it is precisely the struggle against attacks by a stronger power against a weaker one that is an idea that traditionally unites the LAC population.

The division of LAC countries into several conditional groups that hold different positions on this crisis manifested at the first regional reaction to the Kremlin's actions in Ukraine: on February 25, OAS approved a declaration in which it "strongly condemned the illegal, unjustified, and unprovoked invasion of the Russian Federation into Ukraine", as well as Russia's recognition of the separatist territories of the Donetsk and Luhansk regions.[24] The declaration "The situation in Ukraine", supported by most of LAC, was never signed by the delegations of Argentina, Brazil or Bolivia, despite the fact that their

---

23   The Russian authorities define the Russia-Ukraine conflict, which began on February 24, 2022, as a "special military operation." The Russian government has introduced a ban on the use of the words "war" and "invasion" in publicly published materials concerning this crisis, which is assessed as an unreliable presentation of the essence of the ongoing military operation and discrediting the actions of the Russian government abroad.

24   Declaración "Situación en Urania". OAE/Ser G. CP/INF.9293/22 rev. 31/ 27 de Febrero 2022.

representatives expressed an absolute rejection of aggression and violence. CELAC, whose relations with Russia are developing with the aim of building a multipolar and multilateral world, only adopted an initiative to create a Regional Advisory Assistance Network to coordinate the repatriation of citizens of LAC countries from Ukraine, given that not all the countries of the region have diplomatic missions there.

With the escalation of the Russian-Ukrainian conflict, and the strengthening of Western sanctions and pressure on Russia, a group of countries has formed within LAC that have taken a position of "active neutrality". Cuba, Bolivia, Nicaragua, Venezuela, and El Salvador abstained from voting on the most important resolutions concerning the Russia-Ukraine conflict at the UN.[25]

Bolivia, Cuba, Nicaragua, and Venezuela became conditional "allies" of the Kremlin in LAC. This was facilitated by the transition to a new level of their bilateral relations with Moscow, which took place at the beginning of the 21st century (Kosevich, 2022). Several Latin American governments are trying to adhere to a policy of omnibalancing in terms of the Ukrainian crisis. In particular, Mexican President Obrador openly calls Washington's support for the Ukrainian government a big mistake, while avoiding criticism of the Kremlin's actions, which ensures him the Kremlin's sympathy. Obrador, on occasion, condemns the US for providing military funding to Kyiv faster than economic assistance to the countries of Central America.[26] Brazilian President Lula da Silva said in an interview that Putin and Zelensky share equal responsibility for this conflict.[27] Emphasizing the maintenance of international peace, as a traditional priority of Brazilian foreign policy, Lula da Silva declared that he would create a special international mechanism consisting of states which are influential but not involved in the conflict in Ukraine, such as Brazil, which have the best chance of becoming mediators and concluding a peace agreement.[28] The Paraguayan authorities called on Kyiv to meet Moscow, carry out demilitarization, and abandon plans to join NATO.[29]

---

25   https://www.ohchr.org/en/press-releases/2022/03/human-rights-council-establishes-independent-international-commission; https://digitallibrary.un.org/record/3990673; https://digitallibrary.un.org/record/3966630?ln=en; https://news.un.org/en/story/2023/02/1133847.
26   https://www.telemundo52.com/noticias/mexico/amlo-lopez-obrador-eeuu-ayuda-ucrania-centroamerica/2291733/.
27   https://www.latribuna.hn/2023/03/20/el-arsenal/.
28   https://www.cnnbrasil.com.br/internacional/decisao-da-guerra-foi-tomada-por-dois-paises-diz-lula-sobre-conflito-na-ucrania/.
29   https://www.adndigital.com.py/canciller-sobre-invasion-a-ucrania-paraguay-debe-defender-principios/?amp.

The governments of Argentina, Colombia, Brazil, and Mexico refused to send military equipment to Ukraine, explaining their position by the fact that this would lead to an even greater escalation of the conflict. The head of Colombia, Gustavo Petro, explained his decision by recourse to the Colombian constitution, which stipulates that "peace is order in the international arena".[30] Recall that Bogota, regarding the US invasion of Iraq in 2003, supported Washington without hesitation, despite the fairly strong opposition that had developed throughout the LAC. In 2023, LAC did not support the economic sanctions that the US and the EU imposed on Russia: the countries of the region continue their trade relations with Moscow, albeit at a very modest level.

All this suggests that LAC, seeking to move out of the category of secondary actors in world politics, is trying to form a more pragmatic approach to the concept of multipolarity. Such a policy is especially curious given the fact that for the countries of this region, now divided ideologically and economically, there are no more important principles of international law than respect for sovereignty, which was the result of the history of Latin American countries. At the beginning of the 21st century, LAC recognized the importance of the world moving towards multipolarity, where anti-Americanism periodically flares up, appealing to the need for a radical transformation of the inter-American system (Ellner, 2012). It was the formation of a multipolar system of the world that turned into an ideological narrative of the foreign policy of the Putin regime, the apogee of which was the Ukraine conflict.

In this section, the author outlines the key approaches to the theory of multipolarity, tracing its evolution in LAC in chronological order. For LAC, which is traditionally characterized by social, political, and cultural heterogeneity, the author sought to identify the most popular approaches to the concept of a multipolar world which reflect the diversity of this region.

2.1   Latin America: Multipolarity through the Lens of Autonomy and Integration

Key theoretical approaches and concepts of international relations developed in LAC have traditionally been based on the idea of achieving greater autonomy from stronger countries (Bernal-Meza, 2005). This led to multipolarity being interpreted precisely through the prism of autonomy, which was broadly understood as the ability of the people to achieve independence,

---

30   https://www.infobae.com/colombia/2023/01/25/el-presidente-petro-no-le-jalo-al-llamado-de-estados-unidos-para-enviar-armamento-de-fabricacion-rusa-a-ucrania/.

self-sufficiency, self-determination, and control over any inter-territorial relations without outside interference.

The concept of multipolarity was addressed in the studies of Juan Puig, who connected the formation of a multipolar world, first of all, with the onset of that very "moment" for including LAC in the international system as an equal participant and eliminating the vulnerabilities of weak states in general (Puig, 1986). He emphasized that global multipolarity in itself is a factor in the development of autonomy, substantiating the importance for LAC countries to build a pragmatic foreign policy, based on a realistic approach, in which the world was seen as a platform for conflicting interests between strong and weak states.

The end of the 20th century in LAC academic discourse on the development of a new world order was marked by a cultural-civilizational approach. In this context, Alarcón considered the doctrine of multipolarity through the prism of civilizational development, which defines the contours of cooperation of the emerging poles of influence, lining up around "living cultures", and not ideologies and nation-states (Alarcón, 1990).

In 1999, José Luis León hypothesized that the process of creating a multipolar world could be led by China, which would act as a regional power that balances other forces. The author connects the concept of a multipolar world with a relational structure of power, within which the state has the ability to influence the behavior of other international actors. Based on this, the author argues that China has great opportunities to become a new pole of power, although the potential rise of India and Russia cannot be ruled out (León, 1999).

Gradually, the importance of creating a multipolar world became a common thread in the Latin American academic discourse in the late 20th and early 21st centuries, dedicated to the reconfiguration of the global system of international relations and the foreign policy of LAC countries. In the context of world turbulence, an important role was assigned to the search for new forms of economic integration for LAC, which was considered an important step towards building a multipolar system. Multipolarity was understood as an equitable international order, characterized by democratization and the diversification of the entire system of international relations, jointly guaranteeing the effective deterrence of strong powers (Le-Fort, 2006). In the process of forming a multipolar world, it was the transition of LAC countries to an independent foreign policy that played an important role, where great importance was attached to the diversification of ties, the development of new extra-regional relations, and the intensification of South-South cooperation. The Mexican researcher, Marcos Cueva Perús, highlights that the formation of a multipolar world would mean that the powers emerging countries, if they really are, manage to distance themselves from the US (Cueva Perús, 2010).

It was these three elements together that were supposed to help LAC turn into an "alternative pole of power" and escape the influence of the US. For LAC, international institutions, especially multilateral forums, play a key role in shaping its foreign policy in the context of moving towards a multipolar world, since through active participation in them the region compensates for its still limited economic and military potential (Gálvez, 2010). In this regard, according to Magnotta (2011), the most obvious sign of an emerging and strengthening multipolarity is the growth of the "peripheral world", in particular, through their participation in BRICS and the G20. It is the emergence of important new players representing the developing world that is seen as a clear confirmation of the beginning of a transition to a probable "post-American" world, which is identified with the beginning of the active formation of a multipolar system.

Many researchers expressed solidarity with the position that multipolarity was associated with the transformations that occur as a result of crises. In particular, Dussel views multipolarity through the lens of the Latin American philosophy of liberation, analyzing the structures of colonialism, imperialism, and globalization and linking them with the experience of exploitation and alienation of the countries of the global periphery. He concludes that decolonization, globalization, and multipolarity are components of geopolitics, within which it is crisis situations that move towards polarization and territorial endogeneity (Dussel, 2007). In this context, it was emphasized that the US, as the unspoken "empire" of the late 20th century, did not pass the test for crises. It was the global financial crisis of 2008–2009 which made an important contribution to the process of its destruction (Palma, 2009). Gradually, the opinion began to prevail that the US had already moved from a leading position to an intermediate one. Washington is still distinguished by its military and economic potential, but its direct competitors, primarily China, and the new towering giants, Brazil and India, have already appeared on the world map. The vision of multipolarity through the prism of global crises was reflected in the works published in the next decade (Mejía Jiménez, 2015).

In contrast to the Russian approach, the Latin American approach to multipolarity is based on the idea of prioritizing regional level development rather than global processes. Such dynamics generate centrifugal forces in different parts of the world, given that the emergence of new global actors causes changes in the ratio of costs and benefits of peripheral countries (Brun, 2015). Multipolarity implies a configuration of complex and continuous processes and transformations, which are a reflection of the desire of LAC governments to achieve greater political autonomy. In particular, Mariano Turzi (2011) explains multipolarity through the concept of multilateralism: there is multilateralism based on the idea of unipolarity as the liberal modality promoted by the US; and there is multipolar multilateralism, characterized by the complex interdependence of new actors in the international arena, primarily interstate associations. Turzi concludes that modern multipolarity is not identified with global multilateralism, but with regional multilateralism: from the point of view of practical applicability, multipolarity implies an even greater increase in competition between different regions. This approach is based on the idea of "complex multipolarity", which appeals to the multilateral distribution of power between various entities, regardless of whether they are states, in the context of their interdependence, interconnectedness, and correlativity in a globalized world. This line is continued by Amado Luiz Cervo (2010), who argues that the construction of a multipolar world is interpreted through the prism of "reciprocal multilateralism". As part of this approach, multipolarity is synonymous with shared responsibility, which implies the establishment of clear rules of the global order in all spheres of activity and international cooperation (in particular, economy, trade, security, environmental protection, health, and human rights). Concordant and universal compliance with these requirements will benefit all countries and their socio-political and economic systems, regardless of their level of development. The Left Turn of LAC at the beginning of the 21st century is considered as a new political experience of a radical transformation of economic structures and the paradigms on which both state power and public relations are built, which has made a significant contribution to consolidating the changes of the global system of international relations (Stoessel, 2014).

In the early 2010s, the Latin American approach to multipolarity changed markedly. Researchers admitted that the creation of a multipolar world, characterized by multi-actorism at the state and supranational levels, implies the coexistence of cooperation and conflict, which was a departure from the idea of building a multipolar world as an exclusively conflict-free process (Tokatlian, 2012). The prerequisites for the emergence of such conflicts are the irreconcilable class contradictions in the Centers and the Periphery, which emerged as a result of the growth of inequality between the North and South. This approach was subsequently followed by other authors who noted that "multipolarity means competition and open conflict between major state powers to shape a new world order, especially between the US, China, and Russia" (Rocha, 2019: 155). The idea began to come to the fore that in the context of confrontation, the LAC region should strive to derive maximum practical benefit from the turbulent context of global multipolarity.

Latin American researchers, when describing the process of building a multipolar world, focus not on reducing the influence of the US, but on the growth of new players, which noticeably distinguishes this approach from the

Russian one. The process of creating a multipolar world order for LAC is not proportional, but asymmetric, as this region historically includes politically and ideologically heterogeneous countries (Llenderrozas, 2015).

In the mid-2010s the opinion that the process of building multipolarity is inherently decentralized began to prevail, which would lead to most regional economic and political ties being concentrated beyond the region. This thesis was substantiated by the essential features of multipolarity, characterized by the simultaneous emergence of new poles of power in different regions and the tendency of small states to minimize the cost of access to the external resources they need (Giacalone, 2016). In the context of building a multipolar world, LAC plays the role of a geographic space subject to competition for power between traditional actors and new forces (Portillo, 2013). New emerging powers, such as Brazil, China, and India, have already gained international status, already playing the role of developers of the global agenda, mediators, and coalition builders, being able to influence the balance of power in the system of international relations (Pastrana, 2014).

The key factor in achieving multipolarity is integration, which is traditionally considered by Latin American authors as an "additional dimension" of autonomy. In particular, due to the integration processes developing in LAC, some of these countries were able to position themselves on the world stage as important protagonists of building multipolarity, which means gaining greater autonomy in relation to US hegemony (Lo Brutto, 2014). The important role of third countries in this process is noted, primarily China, which made a positive contribution to the economic development of the entire LAC region (Acuña Ortigoza, 2018; Vadell, 2018). An approach is singled out according to which multipolarity should be viewed exclusively through the prism of regional economic and financial integration. In this context, some authors emphasize that peripheral regions are able to successfully fit into the new multipolar world precisely through the launch of alternative regional projects, which are a manifestation of the diversity of types and forms of regionalism (Quiliconi, 2017). Other authors emphasize that forming a new multipolarity involves not only the main developing states representing different continents, but also the creation of regional economic groupings with their own financial institutions and currencies (Ugarte, 2015). Multipolarity is possible only through the construction of three geo-economic spaces—Latin American, Eurasian, and African—the creation of which can put an end to the dependence of each individual country on a developed center, and endow each of them with growing autonomous power, gradually replacing the system of center-periphery relations. Thanks to this, a new multipolarity will be created, in which the US and the EU become important poles among equal poles. The transformation of the world political system can entail a change in the model of economic development, enabling new global players to become more active and visible at the international level, thanks to which they are more effectively coordinated by political authorities, and also become more inclusive at the social level (Aguinaga Morínigo, 2016).

In the Latin American academic discourse, an approach has also formed, according to which the building of a multipolar world is directly related to the development of regionalism, covering cooperation in economics and other fields. Merino (2016) introduces the term "relative multipolarity" based on the strategy of autonomous regionalism. Relative multipolarity is twofold: the confrontation of new powers, which manifest themselves in a new international institutional structure; and interaction, which is expressed in the formation of a new system of economic, political, and strategic agreements. He argues that the process of building a relative multipolarity entails a situation where the central bloc, led by the US, faces the challenge of new powers. As a result, the old world order is questioned given the growing problems and disagreements in different regions of the world and a "new order" of global governance is built according to the priorities of the dominant actors of the old world order. All this gives LAC countries a difficult choice of the most preferable form of regionalism: regionalism with an Anglo-American pole or autonomous regionalism with new alternative power blocs.

Adherents of the approach according to which the rise of emerging powers (primarily Brazil, India, and China) opens up space for revising the goals and role of regionalism and its institutions note that in the 21st century three different kinds of regionalism emerged in LAC: neo-liberal "reset" regionalism, post-liberal regionalism, and multilateral regionalism. The last resulted from the shifting agenda of Latin American economic regionalism and the attempts of regional powers to demonstrate their leadership in the economic and political spheres (Quiliconi, 2017). The transition to multipolarity is associated primarily with the strengthening of regional organizations, thereby further strengthening the trend towards building a more regional international order. The strategy of promoting multipolarity, being considered compatible with building cohesive regional poles, is viewed in line with the principle of multilateralism and the concept of multipolar regionalism in the foreign policy of certain LAC nations (Fonseca, 2022). In this context, the cohesion between the countries of South America, as well as between them and other countries of the entire LAC region, is considered as the most productive movement towards the formation of a multipolar world (Fonseca, 2022). The decline of regional integration organizations, manifested primarily in the division of its members into supporters of one or another leading world power, has doomed all previous steps towards building multipolarity.

Sharing this point in many respects, Serbin (2019) links the emergence of a multipolar system to fragmented economic, political, and social developments, which together have a marked impact on the global integration and interdependence which globalization initially generated. He appeals to the emergence of new "powerful gravitational poles" in the international system: at the regional level, the emergence of new poles is associated with the creation of an effective institutional and regulatory framework, formed as a result of the compatibility and complementarity of interests and goals; and at the global level by reinforcing the common principles they share in their foreign policy. Examples of such new poles are Latin America and Greater Eurasia.

A popular approach is where the new multipolar order is seen as the result of building new geopolitics, setting guidelines for new forms of relations at the regional and global levels, which is in dire need of multipolar international institutions representing the interests of all parties involved—peoples, nations, states, and the private sector (Martín-Carrillo, 2019). The unacceptability of any aggressive ideology and policy in building a new world is emphasized, which is equated with the manifestation of imperialist ambitions (Landa Reyes, 2022). In this context, dialogue is vital for building a multipolar world, the task of which is to think about the present and future of all human life on the planet (Rodríguez Hernández, 2014). Respect for international law of the main actors of the multipolar system ensures its functionality, while shaping responsible international behavior (Rodríguez Hernández, 2022).

LAC is a region divided by different, sometimes conflicting principles and positions, which is a tangible obstacle to the formation of a common approach to multipolarity. As shown in the Latin American academic discourse, multipolarity is seen as a natural transition of the system of international relations to a new stage of development, in which the processes of colonial, neocolonial, and dependent domination are in decline, and where the power schemes of military, territorial, and usurper control are losing their power, significance, and ability to legitimize. For LAC, multipolarity implies the development of new forms of foreign policy relations, based on the idea of equality, and a focus on eliminating "underdevelopment", expanding production processes and regional integration, where the protection of national and regional sovereignty is of particular importance.

∙ ∙ ∙

The conflict between Russia and Ukraine causes serious concern among the world community. This crisis is gradually involving other states representing different regions, which openly support one of the parties to the conflict. Most Latin American countries have adopted a position of neutrality regarding this crisis, which raises the question of the relative proximity of the theoretical content of the concept of "multipolarity".

As shown by the theoretical content, the term "multipolar world" is important for LAC and is assigned to a collective Latin American identity built around the coordinated participation of the countries of the region in the system of international relations, and regional integration in a traditionally extremely fragmented region. This common identity is directly related to the complex history of colonialism and imperialism which the countries of this region have gone through and their traditional desire for economic and political autonomy from stronger powers.

In this regard, the feeling of commonality and unity of interests leads to a relative convergence of positions among LAC, which manifested itself in upholding a policy of neutrality in relation to the Russia-Ukraine conflict. LAC's non-intervention in this crisis is a manifestation of a pragmatic approach to foreign policy and of a convergence of positions reflecting a common desire to maintain stability, avoid the risks of being involved in an ideological struggle, and protect the economic interests of the region. At the level of researchers, the construction of a multipolar world is considered primarily from the point of view of the strategic rivalry between China and the US, rather than the confrontation between Russia and the West.

It should also be emphasized that not all Latin American nations are singularly concerned with such economic and strategic factors in terms of interpreting the concept of multipolarity: the governments of Cuba, Venezuela, Nicaragua, and Bolivia attach more importance to geopolitical considerations than those of the rest of the continent. A multipolar world is viewed by leftist LAC nations primarily as a necessary condition for breaking out of international isolation, ensuring greater autonomy and diversifying foreign policy, severely limited by US sanctions and embargoes. In this context, multipolarity is considered primarily on a geopolitical plane, where particular importance is given to creating the conditions for the gradual introduction of the necessary changes in updating the global system of international relations, in general, and in relations with the US, in particular. Unlike the rest of the LAC, such an approach links the emergence of a multipolar world to the idea of creating a more favorable international environment, which is characterized by all the necessary conditions for diversifying foreign policy and foreign economic activities at minimal socio-political costs.

CHAPTER 2

Inter-American Relations at the Beginning of the 21st Century

1   US Foreign Policy in LAC at the Beginning of the 21st Century: Innovation and Continuity

By the early 21st century, relations between the US and Latin America were characterized by four trends. *The first trend* is US hegemony over the region, which is especially noticeable in relations with Mexico and the states of Central America and the Caribbean. The model of relations between the "master state and subordinates" has become an established rule of interstate interaction between the US and LAC. *The second trend* is that the US foreign policy towards its southern neighbors has traditionally been subject to sharp fluctuations: from increased interest to a sharp drop into absolute neglect. *Third*, long periods of "forced" hegemony were replaced by rare moments characterized by a mood of good neighborliness, consensus, and unanimity. The *fourth trend is* cooperation in the field of security and defense, which has become an important tool for implementing Washington's strategy in Latin America, the characteristics of which are full-scale and multidimensional. The US national security strategy was an integral part of the socio-economic development strategy and was built into Washington's foreign policy strategy in the Latin American direction.

After gaining independence in 1776, the US began to successfully develop a national project aimed at gradually transforming the state, first into a regional and then into a world power. US foreign policy on its continent was initially based on the Monroe Doctrine, proclaimed in 1823, which stated that all attempts by European countries to interfere in the affairs of the newly independent American states would be considered acts of aggression against the United States. After a quarter century of struggle and military intervention with its southern neighbor, Mexico, by 1848 the US had successfully completed its Pacific territorial expansion. Since then, Washington has carried out hundreds of diplomatic, economic, and military interventions in various countries such as Cuba, Haiti, Honduras, Nicaragua, and Mexico.

The interventionist measures were partially weakened during the presidency of Franklin D. Roosevelt (1933–1945), who decisively changed course to pursue a "good neighbor policy" towards Latin America. During the Cold War

(1946–1991), Latin America emerged as a boundary of the global containment of the Soviet Union. Almost any political movement that advocated a progressive agenda was perceived by Washington as a pro-Soviet force and, therefore, a threat to US national security. A military coup organized by American intelligence services in 1954 led to the overthrow of the progressive government of Jacobo Arbenz in Guatemala. The US also tried unsuccessfully to stop the 1959 Cuban Revolution. In 1965, the US military invasion of the Dominican Republic took place, aimed at overthrowing the leftist government that had come to power. As a means of avoiding further leftist revolutions following Cuba's example, in 1961, President John F. Kennedy (1961–1963) established the Alliance for Progress, aimed at securing better social and economic conditions in Latin America through loans and donations from the US. This program was based on the American strategy of good neighborliness towards its southern neighbors, which characterized the mid-20th century. However, in less than a decade, it had become absolutely clear that the Alliance for Progress had completely exhausted itself, despite the fact that the project sent $22.3 billion to the LAC region.

The 1970s witnessed a new stage in the unfolding US presence in Latin America, which was characterized by Washington's active support for military and anti-communist regimes in Central and South America. 1979 marked the victory of the Sandinista Revolution in Nicaragua, which became a new challenge for the US. Initially, President Jimmy Carter (1977–1981) sought to take a pragmatic approach to Sandinism in terms of obtaining results that were practically useful for Washington. However, his successor Ronald Reagan (1981–1989) chose a much tougher strategy. The Reagan administration began an ongoing siege of the new government of Nicaragua, while providing economic and military support to the Washington-allied governments of El Salvador, Guatemala, and Honduras. This gradually led to the US becoming the main donor of economic and military aid to Central American countries as part of a strategy to contain the "communist threat" in the Caribbean.

As a result, the US was able to repel the "leftist blow" that was dealt to the LAC region as a result of the Sandinista revolution, and prevented the triumph of leftist guerrilla movements in El Salvador and Guatemala. Although Washington avoided overt military intervention, the US-led "low-intensity war" against Nicaragua and its support for counterinsurgent forces in the rest of Central America resulted in hundreds of thousands of deaths. As Abraham F. Lowenthal noted, such a foreign policy strategy actually pointed to US vulnerabilities rather than reflecting concerns about its own national security (Lowenthal, 1987).

Under the administrations of George H. W. Bush (1989–1993) and Bill Clinton (1993–2001), a consensus of "indisputable unipolarity" took hold in the Western Hemisphere. Effective economic and political decisions of Washington helped strengthen and confirm the dominant position the US occupied in the world after the end of the Cold War. In the 1990s, Washington relied on the internal development of the country, where huge financial resources were directed. Some of the positive results of the new policies launched by the Clinton administration were the reduction of the trade deficit, increased investment in infrastructure and the development of several sectors of "the new economy", which emphasizes services rather than manufacturing and is based on technology and innovation. This strategy allowed the US to resume economic growth and strengthen its hegemony more from the economic and ideological sides than from the military, as well as ensure the development of sectors of the new economy.

Clinton promoted the foreign policy concept of "liberal internationalism," which included five main directions. Firstly, in global politics, the signing of the Kyoto Protocol, the Illicit Traffic in Small Arms Convention, and the Chemical Weapons Convention. Secondly, on the European front, the US focused on reviving NATO and supporting the construction of the EU. Third, in the Middle East, Clinton forced Israel to enter into negotiations with the Palestine Liberation Organization (PLO), resulting in significant progress on agreements. Fourth, in Asia, Washington sought to ensure China's greater involvement in the global international system by promoting its inclusion in integration organizations such as the World Trade Organization (WTO). With Japan, the US sought to reduce tensions that arose in the 1980s and make Tokyo its ally in Asia. Fifth, with regard to LAC, free trade became the "core" of Washington's policy, which replaced the policy of military containment implemented by previous administrations.

In the 1990s the US began to pursue a less interventionist foreign policy in Central America. A number of factors contributed to this: the end of the Cold War, the collapse of the USSR, and the defeat of the Sandinista National Liberation Front (FSLN) in the presidential and National Assembly elections in Nicaragua in 1990, when the National Opposition Union won. The emergence of a number of peace initiatives at the regional level, promoted by Latin American countries through the Contadora Group (created in 1983) and the Esquipulas Peace Process (initiated in 1986), also had an impact on Washington's strategy. Similar regional efforts to resolve existing differences nonviolently set the course for peace negotiations, the integration of guerrilla groups into civilian life in El Salvador and Guatemala, and the elimination of counter-revolutionary forces (Spanish: contras) in Nicaragua.

The pacification of conflicts in Central America in the 1990s were also significantly influenced by the change of the US administration. Despite the US invasion of Panama in December 1989, the Latin American policy of George H. W. Bush was much more utilitarian compared to the course pursued by his predecessor Reagan, which was characterized by a pronounced ideological component. With the transformation of the international system occurring at an accelerated pace in the early 1990s, the Bush administration sought to avoid new problems in Latin America by focusing its efforts on US foreign policy priorities. At that time, Washington's main attention was focused on closely monitoring the collapse of the USSR and the countries of Eastern Europe as a former zone of Soviet political and ideological influence, and also on restoring its presence in the Middle East.

After the disappearance of the "Soviet threat" in Latin America, Washington abandoned the strategy of open "repression and liquidation," which allowed it to establish negotiations with the leftist forces of Central America. This policy quickly led to positive results, facilitating the beginning of a peaceful dialogue between the governments of El Salvador and Guatemala, on the one hand, and the Farabundo Martí National Liberation Front (FMLN) and the Guatemalan National Revolutionary Unity (URNG), on the other. Over time, these political forces took part in democratic elections.

In fact, softened versions of these radical movements won presidential elections in Central America: in 2008, Álvaro Colom Caballeros (2008–2012) became President of Guatemala with the support of a heterogeneous coalition that included former URNG members; and the 2009 presidential election in El Salvador was won by the FMLN candidate, Mauricio Funes (2009–2014). In 2007, the Sandinista National Liberation Front returned to power in Nicaragua, which in the 1980s caused the greatest concern for the US throughout Latin America.

With the gradual development of processes to achieve peace, stability, and development in the Central American states, the main emphasis in US policy towards the LAC in the 1990s. shifted from geopolitics to geoeconomics. Issues of trade and investment began to prevail over the geopolitical and military objectives that traditionally underlay all Washington's actions across the Western Hemisphere. The new US policy was reflected, among other things, in the launch of the Enterprise for the Americas Initiative (EAI), announced by President George H. W. Bush in 1990. The three strategic pillars of this initiative were negotiating the creation of an extensive free trade area that included the US and LAC countries; the creation of a $1.5 billion loan program and investment fund administered by the Inter-American Development Bank (IDB); and the launch of programs to ease the conditions for repaying the external debt of

Latin American countries. The ultimate goal of this project was the creation of a free trade zone from Alaska to the Tierra del Fuego archipelago, and a radical change in the entire system of Washington's priorities in Latin America. It was trade that acquired primary importance, relegating economic assistance to the background. "Trade, not aid" became the new leitmotif of the US strategy in the LAC.

In the 1990s US diplomacy in LAC had three key goals: protecting free enterprise, and free trade agreements, and promoting democracy. The central idea of Washington's strategy was that market mechanisms should act as a reliable basis for the transformation of Latin American economies and societies, which had previously suffered from protracted statism, inflation, rising external debt, and protectionism. All these concepts and ideas later became known as the Washington Consensus. Many Latin American countries enthusiastically joined the process. They wanted to consolidate their still fragile democracies and sought to leave behind the "lost decade" of the 1980s, marked by economic instability and debt crises (Hellinger, 2021). At this historical moment, regimes sympathetic to Washington came to power throughout LAC.

It was the Washington Consensus, based on the rules of economic liberalism, that became the main instrument for transforming the geoeconomic space of LAC. Its most striking manifestation, along with the confirmation of the reorientation of the US strategy in the LAC towards building a free market, was the creation of the North American Free Trade Agreement (NAFTA) in 1994. It is symptomatic that the signing of NAFTA took place with the support of both leading US political parties. For Washington, the NAFTA agreement was supposed to create new business opportunities for American companies and accelerate the development of neighboring Mexico, and as a result, reduce migration. After the launch of this ambitious agreement, Washington hoped that the rest of Latin America would follow Mexico's example and join the project of building continental free trade, at that time actively promoted by the US.

In addition to promoting the principles of economic liberalism as the foundations of the "Washington Consensus," the second pillar of US cooperation with LAC countries in the 1990s was the idea of promoting democracy. Unlike the Cold War, when, in the name of the fight against communism, Washington supported bloody dictatorships in the region, by the end of the 20th century the US adhered to a strategy that was based on the fact, that the preservation of democracy is not only a domestic political issue for an individual country, but also a matter of collective responsibility. In this context, the Organization of American States (OAS) acquired a new status as an institution dedicated to the defense of common values such as democracy and human rights. In 1994, in

Miami, Clinton held the First Summit of the Americas, where the heads of the countries of North and South America met under the slogan "Democracy, free trade, and sustainable development in America," which became a real leitmotif of the time. In 2001, already under the government of George W. Bush and after the negative experience of the authoritarian regime of Alberto Fujimori (1990–2000) in Peru, the Inter-American Democratic Charter was signed. This document formalized all OAS resolutions and protocols on the collective defense of democracy, including sanctions for countries that return to authoritarianism.

During the last decade of the 20th century the US and almost all Latin American countries shared a common vision of the balance of power in the international arena. The prevailing idea was that after the end of the bipolar conflict, the post-Cold War world eventually became unipolar. With the exception of Brazil, which had already embarked on the path of its "rise," and Cuba, as a bastion of socialism in Latin America, all countries in the region accepted the fact that no other country had sufficient economic, political, diplomatic, or military power to become a real counterweight of the US in world politics.

This concept was reflected in the practical foreign policies of most Latin American governments of the time. For example, Mexico radically changed its traditional mistrust of the US and began to actively demonstrate its readiness for large-format cooperation, which was called the "Spirit of Houston." In a clear articulation of his acceptance of Washington's hegemony in the Western Hemisphere at the 1991 IDB summit, Argentine Foreign Minister Guido di Tella said his country was not interested in a "platonic relationship" with the US, but in "carnal relationship". Washington's vision of its undeniable dominance in the Western Hemisphere was also manifested in the positions of extra-regional powers: after the collapse of the USSR, neither Russia, nor the EU, nor Japan, nor China played any noticeable role in LAC. In the context of the policy adopted after the collapse of the USSR, which was to promote liberal democracy and free markets, US policy towards the only rebellious state in the region, Cuba, was a policy of isolation and pressure in the hope that the Castro regime would fall without Soviet support. In 1996, with the consent of Clinton and with the active support of the Cuban community in Florida, the US Congress, through the adoption of the Helms-Burton Act, which provided for additional sanctions against foreign companies trading with Cuba, further strengthened the trade embargo against the island. Thus, in the 1990s the US effectively created a "hegemony by default" in Latin America.

The White House's confidence in the benefits of free trade was so great that after the signing of NAFTA, Clinton revived Bush's idea of creating the Free Trade Area of the Americas (FTAA), the central task of which was to unite all American economies as part of a unified regional integration initiative. At the first Summit of the Americas (1994, Miami), the heads of state and government of the 34 participating countries agreed to follow a common course towards the creation of FTAA and conclude negotiations in 2005. However, after several meetings at the level of presidents and ministers in 2005 as part of the IV Summit of the Americas, which took place in the Argentine city of Mar del Plata, this project was closed. The IV Summit of the Americas ended on the same note as the first Pan-American Conference, held in Washington in 1889: the idea of building an economically united Americas was not successful. 133 years ago, the then US Secretary of State Republican James Gillespie Blaine proposed the creation of a continental customs union. At the end of the 19th century, Washington's initiative clearly showed its hegemonic sentiments and desire to build an asymmetrical system of relations with the LAC, which was in unison with the slogan of the Monroe Doctrine: "America for the Americans" (Weeks, 2024).

In this regard, Argentina, having secured the support of Chile, categorically rejected this initiative. The Argentine delegate Roque Saenz Peña emphasized the importance of creating a new paradigm of "America for Humanity" in the Western Hemisphere, which was supported by other Latin American countries. Although the Pan-American Conference laid the foundations for what would become the Inter-American system, the idea of building a trade alliance between the two Americas failed. The 19th century ended in the complete absence of inter-American economic alliances. The beginning of the 21st century, characterized by the emergence of new political coalitions, demonstrated similarities with the processes of 1889: most Latin American countries rejected the idea of creating an inter-American free trade area with the US playing a leading role in it. The lack of success of the IV Summit of the Americas in 2005 was explained by a number of new factors: the growing global crisis of multilateralism and the individualistic approach of Latin American countries, characterized by aspirations for isolation and based on the logic of "everyone defends their own interests." On the other hand, during the negotiations held at the Summit, the US failed to present clear and precise proposals for the project. All this deprived the FTAA project of any chance of being created. This initiative failed precisely because of the harsh criticism leveled at it by the most radical Latin American leaders, who gained popularity amid the region's leftist turn. The only champion of the FTAA project was the then President of Mexico, Vicente Fox (2000–2006). This was explained by the fact that the US vector of Mexico's foreign policy under the administration of a representative from the National Action Party acquired the status of an unshakable priority. The principle of equidistance, as a traditional principle of the Institutional

Revolutionary Party, which monopolized power in the country from 1929 to 2000, was temporarily forgotten by Mexico City.

An important factor that negated active US attempts to completely reorient the region towards the Washington Consensus and move towards hemispheric trade integration was the emergence of a powerful leftist wave in LAC in the 2000s. The ideology and political practice of the newly emerged Latin American regimes, the number of which has sharply increased in South America, maneuvered between social democracy and populism, on occasion turning into hard-line nationalism. While the governments of Argentina, Bolivia, Ecuador, and Venezuela embraced varying levels of statism in their policies with anti-imperialist rhetoric, other countries, such as Brazil and Chile, maintained a policy of non-intervention by the state in the activities of private companies (Ellner, 2008). At the beginning of the 21st century, leftist parties of varying levels of reactionary and revolutionary nature began to win presidential and parliamentary elections throughout LAC. Beyond their political practices and varying levels of respect for representative democracy, the left-wing regimes shared a need to distance themselves from the neoliberal policies pursued by the centrist and right-wing governments that came to power in Latin America in the 1990s. The rise to power in the region of leftist leaders who sought to shape a more autonomous and diversified foreign policy further widened the distance between the US and Latin America.

The first months of the George W. Bush administration confirmed the high level of continuity of the Latin American policy shaped by his father and supported by Clinton. George W. Bush, in particular, announced that Mexico would be a priority in his administration's foreign policy, and real actions confirmed this statement. The first international trip of the newly elected US President was to Mexico. Then, in February 2001, he visited Fox's ranch. This was the only time in the history of US foreign policy when a head of state made his first foreign visit to Mexico. As a rule, Canada or Great Britain take precedence. However, the terrorist attacks of September 11 changed this reality, causing Mexico to cease being a "priority" for the US and become merely a diplomatically "important" country. Washington put forward security issues, especially the fight against international terrorism, as its central tasks, making the topics of migration and expanding the integration process in North America secondary. Since September 11, 2001, the US key interest in its relations with Mexico has been to keep its common border as trouble-free as possible; in US relations with the rest of Latin America, it has been to persuade the LAC countries to support Washington in the emerging fight against terrorism.

By then, the neoliberal reforms promoted by the US in the LAC had shown their limits and inefficiency, and rising poverty and inequality in many Latin

American countries emphasized the importance of the "social question." The leftist governments that came to power in South America at that time (some moderate, others more radical) were able to successfully respond to the new social demands of the population, helped by a boom in commodities caused by increased demand from China.

The most famous of LAC's anti-American leftist leaders was Venezuelan President Hugo Chavez (1999–2013). With an increasing flow of petrodollars, Chavez sought to create a "polis of power" consisting of countries that opposed Washington. Over time, it was joined by Cuba, Bolivia, Ecuador, and some Caribbean countries. The Bush administration, having supported a failed coup d'état against the Chavez government in 2002, began to lose support within LAC, which at that moment was clearly looking "to the left." A number of LAC countries maintained demonstrably good relations with Washington. For example, during the Bush administration, several free trade agreements were signed with LAC countries and Colombian President Alvaro Uribe (2002–2010) openly supported Bush's war on terrorism.

Since the turn of the millennium, the importance of combating drug trafficking has risen again on the US agenda toward Latin America. In 2000, Clinton launched Plan Colombia, under which the US would provide Colombia with extensive financial assistance over the coming years to combat drug trafficking. The example of Colombia revealed the weaknesses of the "war on drugs" unleashed by Washington in Latin America. Financial support from the US has allowed the Colombian state to weaken drug cartels and armed groups. This did not help reduce the flow of drugs into the US, since drug cartels were able to effectively adapt to new conditions, shifting their activities to Mexico and Central American countries.

Since 2003, South American exports of oil, soybeans, copper, iron, and other commodities have increased sharply in quantity and price, fueling the economic growth of LAC countries. This has further increased skepticism about the formation of free trade zones based on the tenets of neoliberalism. After more than 20 years of weak economic performance, the Latin American region entered the new millennium with accelerating economic growth that showed signs of stability. Although this economic recovery was still lower than in the 1970s, and countries such as Argentina, Brazil, Peru, and Venezuela experienced only five years of sustained economic growth, Latin America as a whole managed to recover quickly from the Great Recession of 2008–2010. Taking into account the lessons of the crises of the 1980s and 1990s Latin American governments noticeably improved social policies and attempted to eliminate the obvious "abuses" of the Washington Consensus. The economic growth of LAC countries has been largely driven by China's demand for raw materials.

The economic recovery returned the region to the map of global economics and politics. The long-awaited period of economic recovery in Latin America, which occurred in 2003–2013, was marked by a number of positive consequences for the region: first, the prices of soybeans, copper, oil, and precious minerals increased significantly; secondly, the terms of trade improved markedly. As a result, the total revenues of states increased: Argentina—by 120%, Chile—by 156%, Brazil—by 131%, and Venezuela—by 274% (Kosevich, 2020). The share of people living in poverty and in dire need across the region decreased significantly: from 48.4% in 1990 to 43.9% in 2002 and 28.8% in 2012.

Another significant event occurred in global politics: the American-led invasion of Afghanistan (2001) and Iraq (2003) challenged US hegemony and complicated Washington's relations with key international players such as the EU, China, and Russia. Given the complex history of US interventions in LAC during the 20th century, many of them in the name of democracy, it is not surprising that the Bush administration's unilateral approach was particularly resented in this region.

As noted above, Washington's main initiative in Latin America, the FTAA, had been stymied by the silent Brazilian diplomacy and the outright resistance of radical leftist governments such as Venezuela. The US and Brazil, two key players in the FTAA project, had different views on the goals, methods, and development of Western Hemisphere integration. In other international forums, Brazil also actively opposed the signing of a US-sponsored global trade agreement within the WTO and openly criticized the use of Colombian military facilities by US troops (León-Manríquez, 2016). Rather than promoting a continental free trade system, Brasília focused on further strengthening its leadership in South America, primarily through the MERCOSUR agreement. This was confirmed by the words spoken at the III Summit of the Americas, held in Quebec in 2001, by the then President of Brazil Fernando Henrique Cardoso (1995–2003): "For Brazil, FTAA is just an option, and MERCOSUR is our destiny".[1]

As a reaction to Brazil's skepticism of the FTAA initiative, other Southern Cone countries gradually began to move away from the political and economic influence of the US. Although the US accounted for an average of 23% of FDI flows into Latin America between 2007 and 2012, countries such as the Netherlands, Canada, and China managed to significantly increase their investment presence in the region (CEPAL, 2013). This caused a positive response in

---

1 https://www.lanacion.com.ar/politica/para-brasil-el-alca-es-una-alternativa-nid56019/.

South American countries, which saw these new capital flows as an important tool for diversifying their foreign economic relations.

Against the backdrop of the failure of the FTAA project, the US foreign policy strategy in Latin America prioritized the conclusion of new bilateral treaties in its "comfort zone." The result of this minimalist approach was the signing of a number of trade agreements: Chile (2004), Central America and the Dominican Republic (CAFTA, 2006–2009), Peru (2009), Colombia (2012) and Panama (2012). Most of these trade agreements have been concluded since the mid-2000s—just when it became absolutely clear that Washington's bet on the FTAA did not work. With the exception of the free trade agreement with Chile, the remaining agreements were signed with countries that belonged to the traditional sphere of US trade influence—Central America, the Caribbean, and the Andean countries.

Free trade agreements became special tactical steps by the US aimed at saving face by forming free trade zones. Washington was left without a thoughtful foreign policy towards those Latin American countries that were not included in the bilateral trade network formed by the US. After the events of September 11, US political disinterest in Latin America deepened, and Washington's foreign policy priorities shifted to the Middle East. From the beginning of Barack Obama's (2009–2017) presidency, the US tried to strengthen its presence in the Asia-Pacific region, and Latin America has once again remained out of focus of the White House's priorities. The resulting vacuum of influence contributed to the gradual transformation of a number of extra-regional powers, primarily China, into noticeable players in the Latin American region, especially in the economic sphere.

Obama tried to restore relations with Latin America to the stable and positive tone lost under his predecessor. Obama's course, characterized by a policy of soft power regarding LAC and the development of cooperation in a number of targeted areas, generally caused a positive reaction in the region. In particular, initiatives were launched such as expanding access to education in the US for Latino students, establishing closer ties with the governors of a number of federal states, developing joint measures with the Mexican government to prevent violence at the border, as well as restoring diplomatic relations with Cuba. On the other hand, it was Obama who began reforming the system of immigration legislation in the US, developing an amnesty mechanism, and a noticeable strengthening of border controls as a measure to curb the growth of illegal entry into the country.

Under Obama, Washington's strong concerns about Southern migration have remained strong, although their focus has changed. By 2010, the percentage of Mexicans among new undocumented migrants to the US had declined.

The number of citizens from the Northern Triangle (Guatemala, El Salvador, and Honduras) attempting to enter the United States increased sharply. Many of these migrants were fleeing violence and economic crisis in their countries. Domestically, Obama accelerated the deportation of undocumented immigrants, but also through the DACA program sought to protect those who immigrated to the US at a young age. It is noteworthy that, despite the positive note of the migration discourse, about 2 million people were deported from the US during the presidency of Barack Obama, which is more than during the entire presidency of George W. Bush. Obama also launched the Alliance for Prosperity in the Northern Triangle, a project to address the root causes of migration from Northern Triangle countries. Coordinated by then-Vice President Joe Biden, the initiative's main goal was to help countries achieve economic development and the rule of law. However, the project quickly stalled due to lack of support from Latin American governments. Years later, for the same reason, Biden's attempts, now as President, to revive the Alliance would again reach a dead end.

Perhaps the most important decision of the Obama administration regarding Latin America was the normalization of diplomatic relations with Cuba. Already during his second presidential term, Obama admitted that the policy of isolation and "economic strangulation", in force since 1962, had failed. In this context, the long-term goal of the Obama administration was to expand economic, social, and cultural contacts between the US and Cuba, which would help strengthen the middle class of Cuban society. Additionally, under Obama, the US supported the peace process between the Colombian state and the Revolutionary Armed Forces of Colombia (FARC). In 2015, Plan Colombia was replaced by a program to help implement the "Peace Colombia" agreement. However, despite the fact that the Obama administration recognized the ineffectiveness of the punitive approach to the problem of drug trafficking, in reality, Washington's anti-drug policy in Latin America was never revised.

Although the Obama administration had a number of initiatives towards the LAC countries that were well received by Latin American governments and populations, they failed to significantly change inter-American relations. After the end of Barack Obama's first presidential term, strategic competition with China became the main factor in US foreign policy. In his second term, Obama launched a policy of containing China called the "Pivot to East Asia", which included diplomatic, economic, and military gradients of US foreign policy oriented at guaranteeing American dominance in the Asia-Pacific region. Following this logic, the United States participated in negotiations for the Trans-Pacific Partnership (TPP), which aimed to bring together 12 countries from four regions that accounted for 37% of global GDP.

With the advent of Donald Trump (2017–2021) as president, the US strategy regarding mega-regional agreements changed dramatically. On his first working day as president, he signed a decree on the US withdrawal from the TPP. The "Pivot to East Asia" policy began to imply, first of all, the active containment of China. The Trump administration had a more explicit geopolitical orientation, which contrasted with the pattern of the Obama administration. Trump, through his policies, brought LAC back into the Cold War atmosphere with a tough and aggressive approach, supported by an increase in the military budget and provocative rhetoric against those countries considered "hostile" to US interests. In Latin America, President Trump used Mexico as a scapegoat on two issues critical to his base: immigration and trade. To solve the migration problem that had worsened on the border with Mexico, Trump promised to stop migration from Mexico by building a border wall. However, in reality this was never achieved: during his presidency, the border barriers built by his predecessors were only strengthened.

Trump left behind Obama's relationship model, which focused on multilateralism and diplomacy, returning to a geopolitical model reminiscent of US international engagement under George W. Bush. In world politics, Trump again turned to a bipolar geopolitical approach, that is, to the model of "friend-enemy" relations, which he applied to both traditional and new enemies and dangers that surrounded the US in the system of international relationships. Now it was no longer about communism or international terrorism, but about new revisionist powers identified with perceived enemies such as China, North Korea, Iran, and Russia.

LAC countries have been seen as some of the Trump administration's top issues, from building a wall with Mexico and migration challenges to the "communist threat" from Venezuela, Nicaragua, and Cuba.

The president's racist rhetoric, which called Mexican migrants "criminals and rapists," was complemented by a sharp tightening of immigration policies that exacerbated human rights violations along the US-Mexico border. At the height of the COVID pandemic in the US, and just days after launching the "Framework for a Peaceful Democratic Transition in Venezuela," Trump announced the launch of a large-scale counter-narcotics operation in the Caribbean and the Pacific. He explained the new initiative by saying that drug cartels are taking advantage of the unstable situation during the pandemic to endanger the lives of Americans. Just weeks earlier, the head of the Southern Command had warned that the US military presence in LAC would increase. Thus, the Trump administration gave new impetus to the next wave of US expansionism in the region, increasing economic, political, military, and diplomatic pressure on Venezuela, including the economic strangulation of Cuba, and support for coups. An example of the latter is the political crisis in Bolivia in 2019.

Under Trump, the term "dependence" began to be heard again in US-LAC relations, which affected not only economic aspects, but also the political, technological, cultural, and ideological spheres of interaction. For example, the landmark sale of the Brazilian multinational aerospace corporation Embraer to Boeing took place, which had a significant impact on the military-industrial and civil aviation complex not only in Brazil, but also in the entire LAC region.

In unison with the logic of this geopolitical approach, an agreement was signed that allowed the presence of a US humanitarian aid base in Neuquen (Argentina), in the area of key regional hydrocarbon fields such as Vaca Muerta. This was a direct demonstration of US intentions to increase its military presence in Patagonia, expanding the already wide "span of control" along the triple border between Argentina, Paraguay, and Brazil.

It was during the Trump presidency that the peak of American investment in the LAC countries and some of the largest investment projects occurred. For example, in Panama in 2017, logistics companies FedEx (US) and Kuehne + Nagel (Switzerland) announced the expansion of their logistics operations, investing $84 billion.[2] In Chile, in 2018, Bordeaux Holdings, a subsidiary of US-headquartered UnitedHealth Group, acquired healthcare services company Banmédica for $3.4 billion.[3] US FDI into Guyana increased from $58 million in 2016 to $212 million in 2017. In 2019, ExxonMobil began the first phase of development of the Liza field, investing US$4.4 billion.[4] And in 2022, Guyana received $2 billion in FDI.[5]

The competition between the US and China began to have an increasingly noticeable influence on Washington's policy towards Latin America. Under Trump, the US began to strive to achieve increased aid to Latin America (as well as to Africa) in order to counteract China's trade and investment influence. One of the key initiatives of the Trump administration was to strengthen the role of the US International Development Finance Corporation (DFC) in order to counter the influx of Chinese investment in the region through the China Development Bank (CDB). The Trump administration also launched a program

---

2 https://newsroom.fedex.com/newsroom/latin-america-english/fedex-express-inaugura tes-logistics-center-panama-strengthen-supply-chain-services-latin-america-caribbean.
3 https://www.diarioestrategia.cl/texto-diario/mostrar/996034/grupo-estadounidense-adqui ere-968-banmedica.
4 https://www.nsenergybusiness.com/news/exxonmobil-liza-phase-1-guyana/.
5 https://www.state.gov/reports/2023-investment-climate-statements/guyana/#:~:text=Guy ana's%20foreign%20direct%20investments%20

called "Grow in the Americas", which was designed to consolidate investments from the American private sector and government agencies.[6] The project was initially focused on energy infrastructure, and then expanded to cover broader infrastructure facilities, including telecommunications, ports, roads, and airports (those areas where China primarily invests). As part of the initiative, the US signed formal memorandums of understanding with Argentina, Brazil, Colombia, Panama, El Salvador, Chile, Ecuador, and Jamaica.[7] Under Biden the program was canceled and replaced by a similar Build Back Better World (B3W) with an emphasis on other areas and with the involvement of G7 partners. B3W funding has not yet been announced, but intended to use DFC, USAID, and EXIM Bank to stimulate larger private investment from G7 countries. The trade war between the US and China, which escalated under Trump, has benefited exports from some Latin American countries in the short term.

By blaming Mexico for the deindustrialization of the US, Trump managed to revise the NAFTA agreement. A new trade agreement, called USMCA, was signed in 2018 and entered into force in 2020, replacing NAFTA. USMCA contained few practical changes, but still allowed Trump to secure the realization of his campaign promise that was important to his base. Trump also managed to establish dialogue with a number of governments of the LAC countries. For example, Mexico's leftist President Andrés Manuel López Obrador (2018–2024) accepted a number of concessions imposed by the US renegotiation of NAFTA, and also significantly strengthened Mexico's border security with Guatemala in order to prevent migrants from Central America from passing through Mexico to the US.

In exchange for concessions on issues central to Trump, several Central American presidents who are openly sympathetic to Washington secured White House silence on issues such as human rights, corruption, and attacks on the independent press and civil society. In dealing with the regimes in Cuba, Nicaragua, and Venezuela, Trump returned to a hard-line approach, due, among other things, to his close contacts with the Florida Republican lobby.

Trump reinstated many of the sanctions against Cuba that Obama had lifted and also introduced some 243 additional restrictive measures, aggravating the economic, commercial, and financial embargo imposed against Cuba more than 60 years ago.[8] All this has worsened the standard of living of the ordinary

---

6   https://www.thecentralamericangroup.com/america-crece-initiative/#The_America_Crece_Initiative_as_a_Counterweight_to_China.
7   https://2017-2021.state.gov/wp-content/uploads/2020/04/FAQs-English-April-2020-508.pdf.
8   https://misiones.cubaminrex.cu/es/articulo/conozca-las-243-sanciones-de-trump-contra-cuba-adicionales-al-asfixiante-bloqueo.

population in Cuba, which had already experienced all the benefits of the period of "normalization" of US relations with Cuba under the presidency of Barack Obama. Trump also banned the purchase of Venezuelan oil, and even threatened an invasion in Venezuela to overthrow the government of Nicolas Maduro. Despite Washington's open support for Venezuelan opposition leader Juan Guaido, the "maximum pressure" strategy on Caracas failed to topple Maduro, who was backed by Russia and China. The assistance provided by the White House to more than 4 million people who immigrated from Venezuela between 2015 and 2020, fleeing the economic and social crisis in the country, was minimal.

Joe Biden took office as president in January 2021 in very difficult conditions: American democracy had just barely overcome a domestic political crisis that culminated in the seizure of the Capitol, the COVID-19 pandemic continued to rage, and the global economy plunged into another crisis. The arrival of the Biden administration in the White House was accompanied by a diplomatic offensive under the slogan "America is back", the main goal of which was to restore confidence in the US government in terms of international relations.

From the outset, his administration's priorities were to fight the pandemic and restore the economy with an ambitious reform program. Rather than abandoning geopolitical competition with China, Biden has made the issue a central axis of his foreign policy, emphasizing the need to respond more forcefully to China's military, economic, and technological growth. Biden assembled a team of competent experts on Latin America and promised that his agenda in the region would be based on promoting democracy and combating climate change. However, the LAC region continued to occupy a very secondary place in US foreign policy. Within LAC, Washington was unable to find new reliable partners.

From the early days of his presidency, Biden sought to restore the positive image of the US among LAC after its sharp decline under the Trump administration, primarily by addressing the practical problems of countries in the region. The lack of leadership in the fight against COVID-19 in the Western Hemisphere only fueled doubts about the US role in Latin America, something Biden sought to change. Despite the massive production of COVID-19 vaccines in the US, the Biden administration took months to donate vaccines to LAC countries. As a result, by the end of 2021, the US had donated 53 million doses of COVID-19 vaccines to LAC, which was noticeably more than the amount of assistance from the EU (11.5 million doses), and China (5 million doses). In contrast to Trump's international isolationism, Biden launched the Americas Partnership for Economic Prosperity (APEP), aimed at promoting regional cooperation to achieve more inclusive and equitable economic growth in America. APEP, along with the US, includes Barbados, Canada, Chile, Colombia, Costa Rica, Dominican Republic, Ecuador, Mexico, Panama, Peru, and Uruguay. This group of countries represents about 90% of the Western Hemisphere's GDP and almost two-thirds of its population. With the exception of Ecuador, Barbados, and Uruguay, the US already has free trade agreements with most of these countries.

Biden's goal early in his presidency was to reverse the Trump government's harsh immigration policies toward Mexico by halting construction of the border wall and increasing the annual refugee quota. However, in 2023, under pressure from the migrant crisis on the US-Mexico border, Biden abruptly changed his position. The Biden administration announced in the fall that it was adding a new section of wall on the border with Mexico in an attempt to limit the arrival of migrants, echoing a key measure of former President Trump.

The flaring confrontation between the US and China has significantly transformed trade relations between Washington and Mexico City. Mexico's rise to prominence in the US economy began before the COVID-19 pandemic, when Trump imposed the first tariffs on some Chinese goods and signed the updated trade agreement between the US, Canada, and Mexico. In 2023, imports of Chinese products were at their lowest level in 20 years, giving neighboring Mexico an advantage over other countries seeking to fill vacated niches in the US trade system. This led to the fact that by the beginning of 2024, Mexico had become the main trading partner of the US, ahead of Canada and China. During the first quarter of 2023 the trade of US with Mexico amounted to 15.4% of total US trade with the world, which is ahead of the total US trade with Canada (15%) and China (12%). Cars, electronics, and furniture became the main imports from Mexico to the US. Although the global economy is gradually recovering from the crisis resulting from the COVID-19 pandemic, the ability of Mexico to wrest the position of the US's top trading partner from China, which has held that status for the past two decades, is a clear sign that the state of instability and uncertainty is a determinant of the global economy. This also confirmed that the degree of US influence on its Latin American partners is forming in direct proportion to their geographic proximity.

Washington has sought to maximally support Colombia, as the US's main Latin American ally under the Biden administration, in its peace program. Biden has demonstrated a willingness to promote the "Total Peace" policy of negotiating with the guerrillas and illegal armed groups.

To summarize, the Biden administration's LAC strategy has taken a liberal-internationalist approach, with human rights and democracy as a priority and diplomacy as its primary tool. This is confirmed by measures to ease some sanctions against Venezuela, adopted by the White House in May 2022.

Anti-Russian sanctions, which began in February 2022, may eventually affect Russian-Venezuelan cooperation: they are so strong that over time they will also affect the governments to which Russia provided economic support under the "special period" scenario in Cuba. This will gradually push countries economically dependent on Russia to search for new partners or return to traditional partners.

In this regard, one can predict a repetition of the situation of the 2000s, when economic and, above all, energy cooperation between the US and Venezuela was characterized by a partnership based on national interests, uniquely coexisting with rivalry in the political and strategic sphere (Bonfili, 2010). In the new environment, for Washington, interaction with the Venezuelan regime is critical to protecting core US interests in Latin America, as well as containing the Chinese and Russian influence in the Western Hemisphere. The reversal of the White House's course towards continued cooperation with the Maduro regime is also confirmed by the fact that in mid-May 2022, 18 House Democrats from the left wing of the party insisted on completely lifting sanctions against Venezuela. At the end of November 2022, Washington eased sanctions against Venezuela: the US oil and gas company Chevron was allowed to resume oil production in the country, which will make it possible to legally supply it to the US and the EU, as well as restoring partial control over Venezuelan fields. The easing of sanctions came after the Venezuelan government and the opposition signed an agreement to create a fund under a UN mandate. The fact that the US, despite everything, continued to interact with the "striking" South American country will provide Washington with every chance of quickly returning to the country and rapidly ousting extra-regional actors such as China and Russia.

Thus, Biden's policy is aimed at ensuring openness and creating a system of connections with other regions of the world, such as LAC, where extra-regional influence becomes important. Despite the difference in approaches to their Latin American policy, during the beginning of the 21 century different US administrations are creating and using soft and hard power tools in the LAC, with the goal of strengthening Washington's hegemony in this part of the world.

Like its predecessors, the Biden administration's LAC policy has been limited to responding to crises with domestic implications within the US itself. For example, a plan to address the root causes of immigration from Northern Triangle countries, namely the restoration of Obama's Alliance for Prosperity, quickly failed. The initiative did not find support from the presidents of Honduras, Guatemala, or El Salvador. Although Biden has banned some practices that openly violate human rights at the US southern border, the White House's migrant policy has remained fairly aggressive in curbing the flow of migration. However, such repressive immigration policies are doomed to fail, given the desperate situation of many people in Central America and Mexico, as well as the growing demand for low-skilled workers in the US. The lack of coordination of steps taken by the US in the Latin American direction confirms the extreme passivity of the White House in the face of the political crisis in Haiti, completely destroyed by violence and chaos.

As it did under Obama and Trump, under Biden the US appears resigned to imposing economic sanctions on Latin American politicians accused of drug trafficking, corruption, and human rights abuses, even though, without a consistent strategy, such sanctions are almost symbolic in nature. Economic restrictions imposed by the Trump administration continued to apply in Cuba, and the US reacted very cautiously to the outbreak of protests that swept across the island in July 2021. In January 2021, the US designated Cuba as a "State Sponsor of Terrorism." This decision came nine days after Trump left the White House and was due, according to Secretary of State, Mike Pompeo, to the fact that Havana "repeatedly provides support for acts of terrorism". This decision was a colossal blow for the entire commercial sector of Cuba, but Biden did not cancel it.

The IX Summit of the Americas held in Los Angeles, in 2022, one of the key topics of which was migration management, was also practically unsuccessful. For Biden, the event was especially important because the US was hosting the Summit of the Americas for the first time since the first Summit was held in Miami in 1994. In addition, the forum represented a unique opportunity to restore its relations with LAC, which had noticeably deteriorated during the Trump administration. The US, ignoring threats from other LAC countries, did not invite Cuba, Venezuela, or Nicaragua to participate in this Summit, arguing that they are autocratic governments that imprison the opposition and rig elections. This decision provoked fierce criticism from the Mexican President, who began to actively campaign for other countries "to fight against the policy of dividing the region." Biden's intransigence led to other leaders such as Xiomara Castro (2022–present), the president of Honduras, and Luis Arce (2020–present), the president of Bolivia, did not attend the summit, supporting the Mexican president.

The merger of the US unilateral approach; the rise of the Latin American left; and economic growth of LAC countries—which took place in the 2010s—sharply strained relations within the inter-American system, a trend that continued in the subsequent decade. For the US, other regions of the world, such as the Middle East and Asia, have become priorities. Washington looked towards its southern neighbors only when an acute crisis broke out that affected the internal stability of the US itself, for example, such as migration on the border with Mexico.

At first glance, by the beginning of the 2020s trade relations between the US and Latin America seemed stronger and more resilient than ever before. US exports to the region increased from $52 billion in 1990 to $395 billion in 2012; and in the first half of 2023, the LAC accounted for $258 billion of total US exports ($1005.2 million). In relative terms, Latin America has also become important to US foreign trade: in 1990, the region accounted for 13.3% of US exports, and in 2012 this figure increased to 25.6%, which also remained in 2023 (Table 1).

However, a closer look reveals a different picture. The increase in US foreign trade was ensured only by an increase in trade operations with a few Central American countries, as well as with its closest neighbor, Mexico. Mexico accounted for almost 55% of US imports to Latin America in 2012. By 2022, US trade with Mexico accounted for 68% of total trade with Latin America and the Caribbean.

By the 2020s, the US continued to be the largest trading partner in terms of imports and exports for most Latin American countries. In this sense, the economic presence of the US acquired its greatest scope in Mexico, Central America, and the Caribbean. In bilateral relations with these countries, the

TABLE 1 Volume of US trade turnover with Latin American countries (US dollars, billions)

Country	2000	2011	2022
Argentina	7,794	14,62	20,14
Brazil	29,17	75,85	94,94
Bolivia	0,438	1,583	1,182
Venezuela	24,17	56,25	2,715
Colombia	10,63	38,05	39,97
Mexico	247, 21	463,42	783,37
Suriname	0,269	0,781	0,615
Guyana	0,299	0,795	4,066
Ecuador	3,271	16,09	18,94
Peru	3,655	15,24	23,01
Uruguay	0,851	1,562	3,845
Chile	6,729	25,72	40,13

SOURCE: UN COMTRADE DATABASE

key role was given to the areas of trade and investment. In terms of export and import volumes, the US continued to maintain its status as the main trading partner of Mexico, Central America, Colombia, and Ecuador (Table 2). Although Latin American trade with the US has shown a gradual decline in relative terms, it still accounts for between 30% and 80% of the total.

The regionalization trend in LAC has taken hold not only in trade and investment, but also in issues such as migration and drug trafficking, which have long been central to the agenda of US-Latin American relations. The rise of China and its growing diplomatic and economic presence in Latin America

TABLE 2 Data on US exports and imports to Latin American countries (US dollars, billions) and place among all trading partners of the country in terms of export and import volumes

Country	Exports to the US in $ billion + place among all trading partners in terms of export volume for 2023	Exports from the US in $ billion + place among all trading partners in terms of import volume for 2023
Argentina	6,701 (3rd)	11,44 (3rd)
Brazil	38,14 (2nd)	54,33 (2nd)
Bolivia	0,372 (The US is not in the top ten)	1,127 (4th)
Venezuela	0,438 (4th)	2,211 (2nd)
Colombia	15,38 (1st)	18,99 (1st)
Mexico	452,29 (1st)	265,42 (1st)
Suriname	0,057 (1st)	0,439 (1st)
Guyana	2,083 (4th)	0,914 (1st)
Ecuador	9,803 (1st)	8,568 (1st)
Peru	8,431 (2nd)	14,27 (2nd)
Paraguay	0,256 (4th)	1,472 (3rd)
Uruguay	0,696 (5th)	2,049 (3rd)
Chile	13,59 (2nd)	21,79 (2nd)
Guatemala	5,297 (1st)	9,739 (1st)
Honduras	5,838 (1st)	6,794 (1st)
El Salvador	2,574 (1st)	4,261 (1st)
Costa Rica	10,83 (1st)	9,144 (1st)

SOURCES OF DATA: UN COMTRADE DATABASE, SANTANDER TRADE, TRENDECONOMY

marked a change in the established paradigm of the Western Hemisphere. For the first time in a century, the US was no longer the sole power in the region. From the beginning of the 21st century all LAC countries, regardless of their size and geographical location, as well as history of relations with the US, have actively sought to formulate diversified policies.

The concept of diversification was closely connected to achieving the goals of socio-economic development, which is impossible without increasing the autonomy of states. LAC countries realized that with the increasing redistribution of influence, the possibilities for internal prosperity and security increase noticeably precisely with the country's active involvement in the global economy. Even Latin American leaders, who were characterized by pro-American sentiments, also tried to build a partnership dialogue with China, which was dictated by their own economic interests and the political line of "turning towards Beijing", adopted by their closest neighbors.

For example, Argentine President Carlos Menem became the first Latin American president to visit China (November 1990) after the tragic incidents in Tiananmen Square, occurred in the summer of 1989. After Venezuelan President Hugo Chavez visited China for the third time in January 2005, Colombian President Alvaro Uribe paid an official visit to Beijing in April of the same year. Uribe's delegation included 144 businessmen and 32 university rectors. Borota's main task was to attract Chinese investment in the Colombian energy sector. The activities of LAC states within the UN were also quite symptomatic, when several countries, which were not marked by anti-American sentiments, took a position of open "detachment" from Washington. For example, Chile and Mexico did not support the US attempt to legitimize the attack on Iraq in 2003 in the UN Security Council. An illustrative example of successful diversification of foreign policy, which was largely determined by internal factors, was Chile. By the beginning of the 2000s this South American country managed to sign a Free Trade Agreement with the US, turn East Asia into its main trading destination, and also significantly expanded military-technical cooperation with European countries, especially Germany, Spain, France, the Netherlands and the UK.

∙ ∙ ∙

It was the end of the first decade of the 21st century, which was characterized by the emergence of a hybrid world order (a world order with elements of unipolar and multipolar systems), that became a relatively favorable environment for Latin America for intensifying foreign policy diversification. One result of this trend is that Washington's influence, which still remains significant, especially in Mexico and Central America, rapidly declined across the entire region. The boom in inter-American cooperation occurred at the end of the Cold War, after which stagnation began in the 2000s, which continued in 2024.

At the end of the 20th century, Lars Schoultz identified three aspects on the basis of which US policy toward Latin America was formed for almost two hundred years. The strong pressure of US domestic politics; promoting the economic welfare of the US; protecting US security (Schoultz, 1999). Although Latin America has changed dramatically since the beginning of the 2000s, thanks to leftist turns, progressive governments, social movements, and integration initiatives, US policy in this part of the world is still characterized by a high degree of continuity. The next section of the book will show how important the provision of a "security perimeter" is for the US, within which Washington seeks to strengthen its dominance at the continental level.

2 US Security and Defense Policy toward Latin America: Ensuring an Enduring Influence

The end of the Cold War was marked by another rise in the concept of imperialism, which again became central to understanding and studying the configuration of the international system (Borón, 2013). The superiority of the US was provided by a unique combination of military and economic power, together guaranteeing a stable and unquestioned world influence (Long, 2017). However, in the late 1990s, Washington was forced to change its approaches to Latin America, which clearly indicated its rejection of the "unipolar" US hegemony in the Western Hemisphere (Buzan, 2009; Arenal, 2015; Zapata, 2020). A new geopolitical challenge for the US was the beginning of the region's left turn, characterized by the coming to power in several LAC countries of regimes that sharply criticized the neoliberal model of development and aimed at forming a multipolar world.

The 9/11 attacks forced the US to reconsider its approaches to confronting new security threats, which led to the development of a new strategy for global leadership. It was from that moment, and for the first time since the beginning of the Cold War, that Washington formed a new geopolitical strategy, which was characterized by a comprehensive and multi-scale scope of policies and actions through which the US was able to shape and maintain a new world order. The updated paradigm was that from now on the US would become less dependent on its international partners and would play a more independent role in the system of global governance (Ikenberry, 2002; Calle, 2003). Such a strategy replaced the strategy of "deterrence", which was the basis of US foreign policy during the Cold War.

The gradual "withdrawal" of the US from LAC, which began under George W. Bush, who, after 9/11, reoriented the country's foreign policy towards the Middle East and other regions. This led to LAC countries, for the first time in many decades, getting a taste for a more autonomous foreign policy, which was built primarily based on their own national interests. US attempts to return to the model of "hegemonic-subordinate communities" were rejected by LAC states, which over time were further aggravated (Sanahuja, 2016). This predetermined the need to develop new foreign policy mechanisms, most of which were based on a new understanding of the region, interaction with which was built according to the "double asymmetry" hierarchy (Manwaring, 2001; Sánchez, 2011; Loveman, 2004).

This section of the book looks at the degree of continuity and change in US security policy and defense towards LAC at the beginning of the 21st century.

2.1 Tracing the Evolution of the US Security and Defense Policy toward Latin America

2.1.1 1991–2001

When the collapse of the USSR was already evident, resulting in the formation of a unipolar system of international relations, the US began to promote a strategy focused on its leadership in two central areas of the international system: military superiority and alliance building.

The discussion about "expanding the concept of security" had reached the countries of Latin America by 1991, when this approach was first enshrined in the "Commitment of Santiago" ("Compromiso de Santiago"), adopted as part of the third plenary meeting of OAS.[9] It was with the adoption of this document that the transformation of the approach to security began, culminating in the second Summit of the Americas in 1998, when the Hemispheric Security Committee was instructed to analyze the meaning, scope, and projection of the concept of security in the hemisphere. The issue of security has become one of the central problems of democracy.[10]

In this context, the Andean Trade Preference Act (ATPA) was adopted in 1991—a bilateral program under which the US allowed the duty-free entry of goods from Bolivia, Colombia, Ecuador, and Peru. Spreading primarily in the economic sphere, the main task of ATPA was to combat drug production and

---

9 Compromiso de Santiago con la Democracia y la Renovación del Sistema Interamericano (Santiago, 1991).
10 Conceptos para la Seguridad Hemisférica. OEA/Ser.G. CP/CSH-301/00. 8 mayo 2000.

drug trafficking by providing commercial incentives that helped countries to diversify and strengthen the legal economy, thereby reducing the shadow economy.[11]

Washington's new policy towards LAC during the 1990s began to focus on the common threat facing fragile Latin American democracies and the difficult transition from authoritarian or totalitarian regimes. This approach was continued by the Clinton administration. His doctrine of "democratic expansion" became a key strategy for the Western Hemisphere, the main directions of which were strengthening democracy (the US recognizes that all LAC countries, except Cuba, are democratic); the promotion of free trade; and combating "regional problems", which included drug trafficking, organized crime, money laundering, illegal migration, environmental degradation, and political instability.

Clinton's policy towards LAC was characterized, as in previous administrations, by maintaining his leadership and dominance over the region. Only the tone and the tools used changed, with the emphasis shifting towards economics. The Clinton administration placed great importance on combating the proliferation of small arms and light weapons, both domestically and at the level of the Western Hemisphere. Washington played a prominent role in the adoption of the Inter-American Convention Against Illicit Firearms Trafficking in the Americas (CIFTA), which was adopted in 1997 as part of OAS and became the first regional instrument of its kind.

In formulating US foreign policy towards the region, the geo-economic aspects of US national security were considered in addition to the strategic and political dimensions that continued to predominate. In this context, there were three main areas of security in relation to LAC, to which Washington paid the most attention: Colombia, Mexico, and Central America.

Plan Colombia (PC) was a unique initiative in the Western Hemisphere, agreed between the governments of Colombia and the US in 1999 (Rochlin, 2011; Nieto, 2007). PC became the institutional basis for bilateral cooperation in enhancing the capacity of Colombian forces in the fight against the drug production chain and armed criminal groups; promoting disarmament, demobilization and judicial reform processes; and improving the economic and social conditions of the Colombian population (Vaicius, 2003). On the other hand, for Colombia, PC became an apparatus of submission in economic, political, and military matters to the US (Ramírez, 2017). The Clinton administration tried

---

11   http://www.sice.oas.org/tpd/usa_atpa/usa_atpa_s.asp#:~:text=La%20Ley%20de%20P referencias%20Arancelarias,diversificar%20y%20fortalecer%20industrias%20 leg%C3%ADtimas.

to influence the "downward asymmetrical" relationship between Colombia and neighboring Peru, which also developed at the level of drug trafficking. In this context, in 1995, when Peru's relations with the US received a particularly positive momentum, Washington launched the "Air Bridge Denial" program to "interrupt air transfers" between Peru and Colombia, which operated until early 2000 (Zevallos, 2014).

In Mexico, Washington's attention was focused on two issues: the fight against drug trafficking, given that in the 1990s, almost all Mexican organized crime was associated with drug trafficking, and illegal migration. In February 1995, the High-Level Contact Group on Drug Control was created. The US fight against the Mexican cartels, which intensified in the 1990s, was carried out with the same methods and tactics as against the Colombian drug cartels—to try to capture drug lords and eliminate key members of the cartels. In this context, in 1999, the Kingpin Act was adopted, which froze the assets in the US of internationally recognized drug traffickers including members of the Mexican and Colombian cartels.

The search for a solution to the problem of illegal migration of Mexicans to the US also gained momentum. In September 1993, the Joint communication mechanism at the federal level on border incidents was launched. The next winter the US government announced a plan to tighten immigration controls, where the US-Mexican border came under special control. Washington began building a border wall with a sophisticated level of security and surveillance on the border with Mexico, where every year hundreds of Mexicans risked their lives trying to get into the US.

Regarding Central America, through which the drug trade flowed from South America to the US, Washington paid special attention to the fight against drug trafficking. In 1994, the Joint Interagency Task Force South (JIATF-South) began its activities. Its mission was to improve the US ability to stop drug dealers and other criminal organizations. In 1997, the area of responsibility of the US Southern Command was expanded to include the entire Caribbean and the waters bordering South America, and control of the entire JIATF structure was transferred. In 1995, at the initiative of Bill Clinton, the International Law Enforcement Academy (ILEA) was created—a network of international academies created to combat transnational crime, such as international drug trafficking, crime, and terrorism. To maintain multifaceted coverage of US security policy since 1996, at the initiative of Washington, meetings of the ministers of defense of the region began to be held every two years, where questions on defense and security were discussed.

The Clinton administration advocated the promotion of free trade as a central theme of its Latin American policy, which resulted in security issues often being combined with Washington's economic and trade policy. It is in this context that in 1998, Argentina became the first Latin American country to receive the Major Non-NATO Ally (MNNA) status. Such status provided Buenos Aires with priority access to cooperation programs with NATO in the military and other fields, and the absence of strict obligations to take part in military operations. Washington hoped to enlist the political support of Argentina in negotiations on the creation of the Free Trade Area of the Americas (FTAA), thereby trying to take advantage of the double asymmetry that Buenos Aires already occupied in South America. It was assumed that Argentina would promote Washington's initiatives at the level of its "downward asymmetrical" relations with partners in MERCOSUR. However, these plans never materialized.

Under Clinton, the US tried to further increase its influence in the field of security in LAC on an institutional level. The network of US military bases was expanded. In December 2000, School of the Americas (SOA)—Washington's special political leverage—was formally liquidated, but only a few months later it was re-established under a different name, as the Western Hemisphere Institute for Security Cooperation (WHINSEC). WHINSEC became a key instrument to maintain friendly military-military ties to Latin America, since it was seen by the militaries in the region as a prestigious place to go.

2.1.2   2001–2009

As part of its security policy, the Bush administration had given increased attention to potential threats directed at its closest neighbors in North America. In this context, the US Northern Command (USNORTHCOM) was created in 2002 as a military innovation primarily aimed at combating terrorism after the 9/11 attacks. The scope of USNORTHCOM covers all of North America, including Canada, Mexico, and part of the Caribbean. The 2005 signing of the agreement on the Security and Prosperity Partnership of North America (SPP) between the US, Mexico, and Canada became a new instrument of institutional cooperation that expanded the interaction of the three countries in various fields, with special attention to security (LeoGrande, 2007).

The left turn in LAC in the 2000s, which was mainly a rejection of the Washington Consensus model, led to the fact that most LAC states set themselves the goal of playing a more prominent and independent role in world politics. The absence of the Cold War factor allowed the countries of the region to develop military-technical cooperation more freely, which gradually acquired geopolitical significance for Beijing and Moscow. In the speeches of Chavez, as one of the most prominent representatives of the "Socialism of the 21st century", anti-American ideology manifested itself most clearly. The renewed foreign policy pursued by the administrations of Hugo Chavez and then of Nicolás Maduro was based on the desire to reduce the US influence, first in Venezuela, by "omnibalancing" with other non-regional actors, to then include the rest of LAC in this process. In this context, the military-technical and political-diplomatic components of Venezuela's rapidly developing relations with China, Russia, and Iran merged into a single mechanism to counter US ambitions in the context of Caracas's unconditional rejection of the model of relations with Washington that was characteristic of the end of the 20th century (Mijares, 2017). Gradually, this led to Caracas being elevated to the rank of a threat to US security.

LAC's left turn made its own adjustments to the map of WHINSEC's presence in the region (Katz, 2006), while the presence of US military bases in the region did not diminish at all.

Chávez's pragmatic "omnibalancing" policy resulted in a very slow decline in bilateral interaction between the US and Venezuela in military-technical cooperation and in the field of combating drug trafficking, which was influenced by a long history of successful interaction (Figure 1). The suspension of cooperation with the DEA in 2005 did not prevent Venezuela from continuing to cooperate with the US in the fight against illegal drug trafficking, which is considered separately from the issues of "big politics".

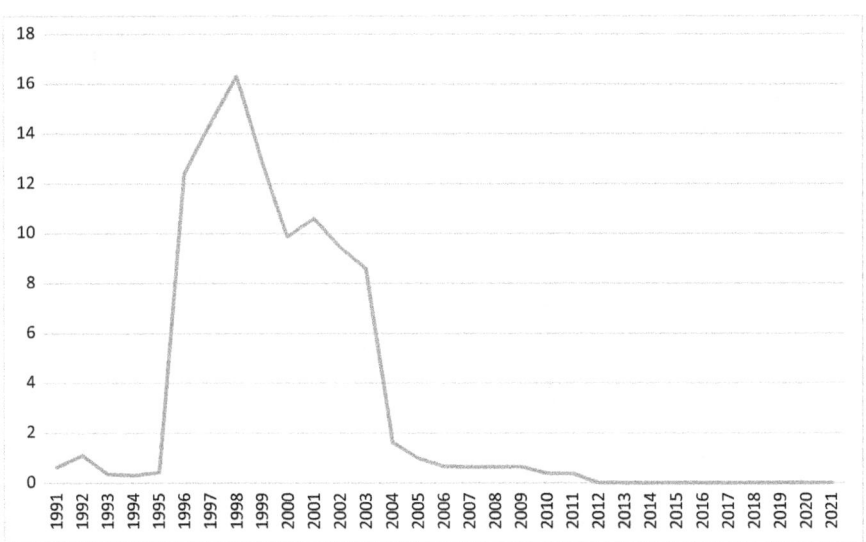

FIGURE 1   US foreign military financing to Venezuela 1991–2021, US dollars
SOURCE: COMPILED BY THE AUTHOR BASED ON DATA FROM HTTPS://CATA LOG.DATA.GOV/DATASET/U-S-OVERSEAS-LOANS-AND-GRANTS-GREENBOOK

By 2000, the US Department of State the central security objectives in LAC were combating drug trafficking and organized crime, and confronting domestic security challenges. In this context, the Department of State's attention was focused on relations with Colombia and the Andean region as a whole, which was dictated by Washington's focus on forming a stable system to counter internal threats to national security; and on bilateral dialogue with Mexico for the purpose of securing the border. It was these two countries that received the most attention in the US national security strategy (NSS) 2000.[12] This led to the need to form new programs for US-LAC security cooperation (Prevost, 2014).

The pressure of anti-drug programs launched in Bolivia and Peru in the 1990s resulted in the large-scale migration of coca crops from these countries to Colombia, giving it all the resources it needed to be the world's leading producer of cocaine—a process known as the "balloon effect". This prompted the George W. Bush administration in 2001 to launch the Andean Counterdrug Program (ACP), designed as a complement to Plan Colombia and aimed at limiting the flow of drugs from the Andean region.

In the US NSS 2002, LAC took a secondary place.[13] However, in terms of the primary security threats to the US, which included drug trafficking, Colombia received the most attention as a country with severe security issues due to the violence caused by the illegal activities of drug cartels. This predetermined the emergence of the second lever strengthening Washington's security policy in relation to Colombia: the Andean Regional Initiative (ARI) (Bonilla, 2006). As part of ARI agreements, Washington sought to support the governments of the Andean countries, primarily in their fight against the production and trafficking of illicit drugs.

ACP and ARI, which covered the entire Andean sub-region, focused on Colombia, whose government was to intensify its efforts to prevent the spread of the drug problem throughout the Americas. More than half of the entire budget of the ACP was allocated to Colombia. As part of the ACP and ARI initiatives, it was assumed that Colombia would be able to use it as efficiently as possible due to its "double asymmetry" position: Bogota has played a leading role in expanding regional security cooperation with its neighbors while simultaneously experiencing an "ascending asymmetry" towards the US.

---

12   The White House (2000). "A National Security Strategy for a Global Age": https://hist ory.defense.gov/Portals/70/Documents/nss/nss2000.pdf?ver=vuu1vGIkFVV1HusDPL2 1Aw%3d%3d.

13   The White House (2002). "The National Security Strategy of the United States of America": https://history.defense.gov/Portals/70/Documents/nss/nss2002.pdf?ver=oyV N99aEnrAWijAc_O5eiQ%3d%3.

Since 2000, one of the main military tasks of the US in LAC was the suppression of drug trafficking from Mexico, for which Washington was ready to provide large-scale funding (Auchter, 2013). For Mexican President Felipe Calderon, the main content of the policy was the fight against drug trafficking. This involved the army, and the extension of US participation in the "war on drug cartels" which had become a really serious problem for Mexico due to the rampant violence it caused, was of greatest interest. In this context, Calderon proposed to George W. Bush, during his visit to Mexico in March 2007, his own scheme of cooperation in this area. The meeting resulted in a cooperation program called The Mérida Initiative (MI). The main goal of MI was to improve the effectiveness of Mexican security and justice institutions and personnel at the nation and local levels in combating transnational criminal organizations. As a result of MI, a new architecture of US-Mexico bilateral security cooperation was built.

Tangible financial support was provided to Mexican security services and the judiciary, and US efforts were intensified to reduce the trafficking of weapons, drugs, and money. The agreements on MI were distinguished by relative stability and continuity. Created under Presidents George W. Bush and Calderone, it was continued by the next administrations. However, MI failed to grow into a new paradigm as announced by the two administrations, and ultimately did not lead to a decrease in the level of violence in Mexico, which had been the main objective of the project (Romero, 2016).

The turbulent internal situation in the countries of Central America led the US to support the creation in 2007 of the Central American Security Strategy (CASS), which became a tool for improving the coordination of actions in order to counter the main threats to their security and institutional strengthening of justice. CASS had four main components, the main one being the fight against crime, in which Mexico, Colombia, and the US played the role of co-chairs. CASS became for Mexico, already in a "double asymmetry" position, one of the main directions of the "downward asymmetrical" relationship with its closest neighbors from Central America, within which Mexico sought to form partnerships that contributed to the creation of an atmosphere of peace and security on its southern borders.

All security programs, which were launched jointly by LAC and US governments in the first decade of the 21st century, were characterized by regional and subregional coverage, focusing on the involvement of several countries of Central and South America at once. The implementation of these programs led to a significant increase in the US military presence in the region, an increase in the number of civilian casualties and the number of abuses by the special services. At the Latin American level, the implementation of these programs led to a noticeable growth in the presence of the armed forces in the system of internal security and order, which merged with the police (Cruz, 2011) (Table 3).

The result was that the level of conflict increased sharply, primarily between Colombia and its neighbors, Venezuela and Ecuador, and on the US-Mexico and Guatemala-Mexico borders (Kosevich, 2021; Delgado and Romano, 2011). All this happened against the backdrop of the development of integration processes in the Western Hemisphere, which were, for the most part, beyond the control of Washington. This was a confirmation of the transformation of interstate relations in the Western Hemisphere towards an increase in the level of LAC autonomy and a focus on reducing the US influence on the politics and economics of LAC countries. During the presidency of George W. Bush, the level of military-technical cooperation between the US and the LAC countries temporarily decreased in 2003 and 2004, after which figures returned to the same levels as at the beginning of the Bush presidency (Figure 2).

NSS 2006 US NSS featured Venezuela for the first time, whose government, led by Chávez, was seen as a threat capable of "destabilizing the region." Cuba was also included among Washington's security challenges in LAC.[14] All this required new steps from Washington towards deepening cooperation in the field of defense and security in LAC, one of which was the re-establishment in 2008 of the US Fourth Fleet, which was under the jurisdiction of USSOUTHCOM and was responsible for all operations in the Caribbean, and Central and South America.[15] The restoration of the Fourth Fleet came at the height of the left turn, when the eleven largest LAC states were led by center-left or left-wing presidents.

By the beginning of the 2010s, Washington had obtained two important military security tools in LAC: USSOUTHCOM and the Fourth Fleet. At the turn of the millennium, the broader concept of security, known as multidimensional security, was put forward by Washington within OAS and became the basis of the US strategic guidelines in LAC (Celi, 2015; Ramos, 2015). In the Declaration on Security in the Americas, adopted in 2003, the concept of multidimensional security was enshrined as a guiding principle for cooperation

---

14   The White House (2006). "The National Security Strategy of the United States of America": https://history.defense.gov/Portals/70/Documents/nss/nss2006.pdf?ver=Hfo1-Y5B6CMl8yHpX4x6IA%3d%3d.

15   US Fourth Fleet was created in 1943 during the Second World War, having existed until 1950.

TABLE 3 US foreign military sales to Latin America and the Caribbean, US dollars

1991		2001		2010		2011		2021	
El Salvador	71,308,000	Venezuela	35,426,000	Mexico	342,784,000	Colombia	220,607,000	Chile	585,584,473
Colombia	52,751,000	Mexico	19,362,000	Brazil	142,244,000	Brazil	176,415,000	Brazil	101,744,476
Bolivia	31,167,000	Colombia	17,197,000	Colombia	119,477,000	Chile	55,887,000	Mexico	78,789,219
Brazil	19,108,000	Argentina	8,967,000	Chile	82,677,000	Argentina	17,493,000	Colombia	71,639,158
Venezuela	23,980,000	Uruguay	3,527,000	Argentina	30,111,000	Mexico	17,249,000	Peru	14,793,456
Mexico	9,585,000	Chile	2,489,000	El Salvador	9,198,000	El Salvador	9,414,000	Dominican Republic	14,673,068
Honduras	9,171,000	Bolivia	2,092,000	Belize	3,742,000	Peru	4,530,000	Belize	6,970,422
Ecuador	6,148,000	El Salvador	1,780,000	Costa Rica	3,195,000	Haiti	2,758,000	Argentina	6,159,446
Chile	4,744,000	Honduras	754,000	Haiti	2,604,000	Panama	2,667,000	Panama	2,216,038
Peru	3,649,000	Dominican Republic	515,000	Peru	1,789,000	Honduras	2,322,000	Honduras	1,280,000

SOURCES: FOREIGN MILITARY SALES, FOREIGN MILITARY CONSTRUCTION SALES AND MILITARY ASSISTANCE

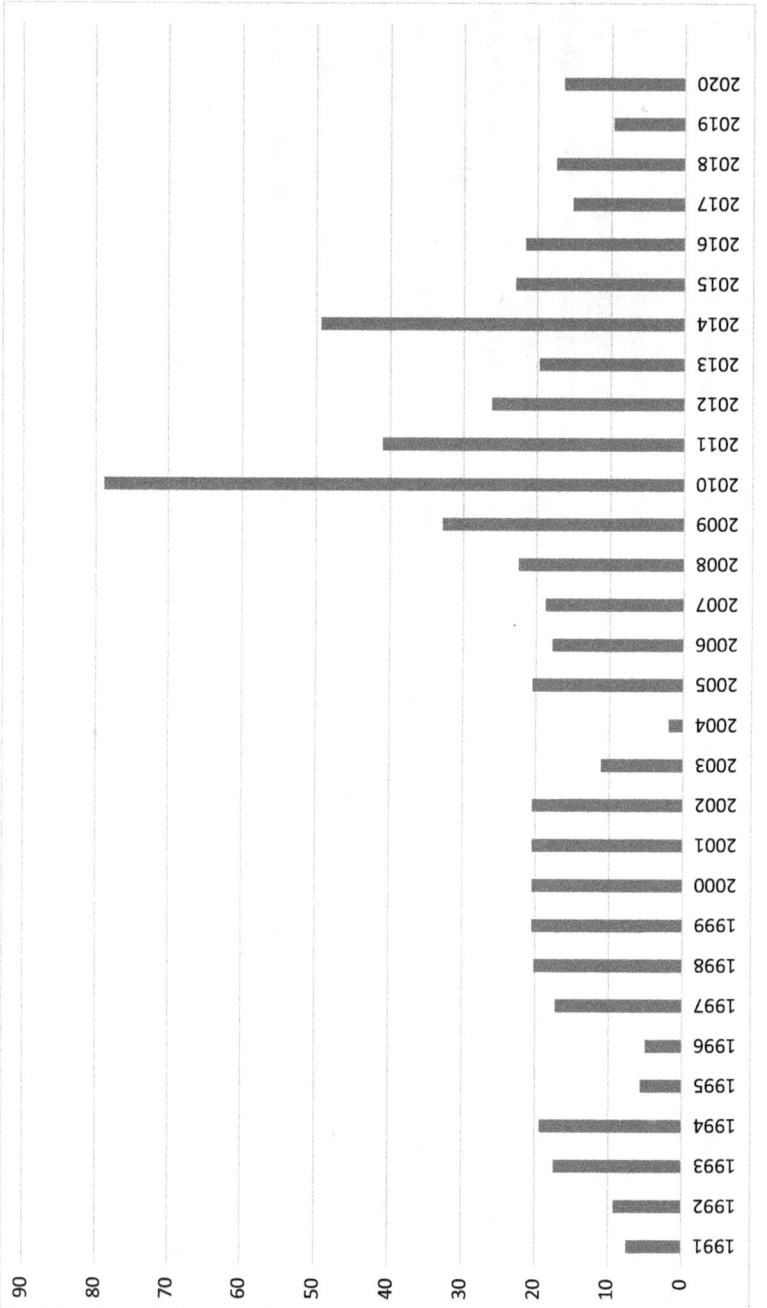

FIGURE 2   US arms sales to Latin America and the Caribbean, US dollars, thousands
SOURCE: UNCTAD, CRS REPORT

between the countries of the Western Hemisphere in this area.[16] It was based on the commitment of member countries to confront all the challenges that could adversely affect development at regional and subregional levels. Several LAC countries also developed cooperation with the US Indo-Pacific Command (USINDOPACOM).

The region's left turn, which took place simultaneously with the successful diversification of international relations, and the lack of a consistent policy of Washington towards its closest neighbors, together led to the necessary conditions for strengthening the "omnibalancing" foreign policy of LAC countries. The updated foreign policy, and new options for "alternative development" in various areas (economy, ecology, and indigenous peoples) adopted by individual countries, clearly showed that the LAC began to condemn the imposition of decisions that meet only the interests of the US A confirmation of this was the transformation of the system of interaction within OAS, the prerequisites for which were laid in the 1990s: at the beginning of the 21st century it became clear that the US could no longer continue to use it as a foreign policy tool. The positions of Washington and OAS openly diverged regarding the 2002 putsch in Venezuela. It was also significant that in 2005, the Chilean José Mª Insulza, the first candidate in the history of this organization, who was not supported by Washington, was appointed to the post of Secretary General of OAS. The US proposal to create a monitoring system to assess the democratic states of the hemisphere failed to reach a consensus within the OAS: it faced uncompromising criticism from a LAC group of countries led by Venezuela, which was also joined by Brazil and Argentina.

The rapid strengthening of the positions of new non-regional actors in Latin America has become one of the results of the "omnibalancing" policy of the LAC countries, which intensified under the pressure of the general regional trend of the first decade of the 21st century: public demand for rapid changes in LAC, capable of providing a higher level of independence in relation to the centers of world economic and political influence, primarily the US This guaranteed China, which previously had extremely modest ties with the LAC countries, an unprecedented rapid rapprochement with this region: China established strategic partnerships with Brazil (1993), Venezuela (2001), Mexico (2003), Argentina (2004), Peru (2008), and Chile (2012).

Since the early years of the 21st century, cybersecurity cooperation has become a new instrument of US security in LAC. In matters of the cooperation

---

16 Organization of American States (2003). Declaration on Security in the Americas: http://www.oas.org/en/sms/docs/declaration%20security%20americas%20rev%201%20-%2028%20oct%202003%20ce00339.pdf.

and consolidation of regional efforts in this area, a special role was assigned to OAS. In 2004, the Comité Interamericano contra el Terrorismo (CICTE) became responsible for the overall control and development of guidelines for cybersecurity; in 2005, a regional network of computer emergency response teams (CERTs), copied from US policy, began to form in LAC. The general control of the state of cybersecurity in LAC countries was carried out by OAS and Washington. Since 2006, under the auspices of OAS and jointly with the US Secret Service, joint seminars on cybersecurity and cybercrime have begun to be held, aimed at strengthening the capacity of countries and private organizations in preventing cyber-attacks, and exchange of knowledge and information. In addition, the OAS Working Group on Cybercrime was established, whose task was the development of a special training program for Member States on cybersecurity issues.[17] This led to the fact that LAC's cybersecurity policy was formed under the strong influence of the US approach (Kosevich, 2024).

2.1.3   2009–2017

The beginning of Obama's presidency was characterized by his administration's lack of attention towards LAC, despite the relative amount of activity at the ministerial level. Here, the activities of the US Department of State stood out, within which a special team was formed for negotiations with the countries of the region. Due to the financial crisis of 2008, and a number of US domestic problems, such as economic recession and growing social inequality, the importance of security cooperation dropped markedly on Washington's priority list in LAC policy. The volume of US financial assistance for the military in LAC countries for the period 2010–2014 almost halved: from $503 million (2010) to $236 million (2014) (Figure 3). Unlike Bush, Obama gave clear priority to other international affairs and domestic crises.

It was under Obama that American foreign policy toward LAC shifted from a regional approach to a national approach, which had lost its significance under the previous administrations. The new approach was based on the readiness of the US government to engage in dialogue with its neighbors where the interests of individual countries were considered as far as possible. As a result of this policy, the US Department of Homeland Security achieved significant success in cooperation with several LAC countries: in 2010, Brazil and the US signed a landmark military cooperation agreement for the first time in 30 years, and through the Smart Ports programs, US military personnel were allowed to

---

17   Comité Interamericano contra el é Interamericano contra el Terrorismo. Organización de los Estados Americanos (OEA). Informe Noviembre-Diciembre (2007): https://www.oas.org/es/sms/cicte/Boletin/Informe_51_spa.pdf.

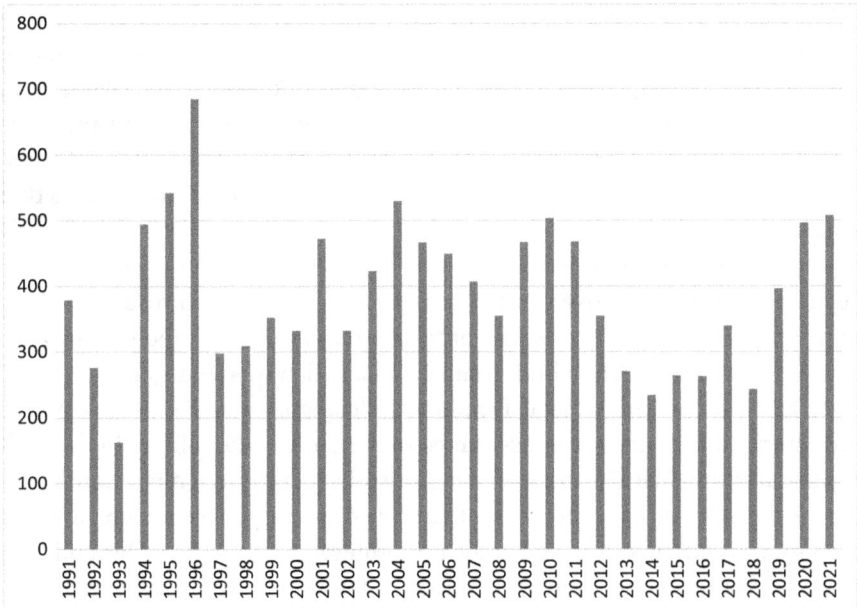

FIGURE 3   US foreign military assistance to Latin America and the Caribbean, US dollars, millions
SOURCE: US OVERSEAS LOANS AND GRANTS, US FOREIGN ASSISTANCE TO LATIN AMERICA AND THE CARIBBEAN: FY2021

conduct search and seizure operations in several LAC countries. The Obama administration also expanded and strengthened the network of US military bases in LAC: since December 2015, various attempts were made to deploy the US military in Argentina, by the end of the term of Christina Kirchner, who denied such initiatives; in April 2016, Palmerola base in Honduras was reinforced. Negotiations in 2009 on the possible establishment of a US military base in Colombia were prompted by the desire of Bogotá to use its position of "double asymmetry" as pragmatically as possible, allowing them to enlist new instruments of force against their ideologically distant neighbors, such as Ecuador and Venezuela, also fitting into the omnibalancing logic.

The US opening to Cuba under Obama, which was a major change in US policy, especially since the Castro regime had been a major security concern during the Cold War.[18]

---

18   The White House (2014). "Charting a New Course on Cuba": https://obamawhitehouse.archives.gov/issues/foreign-policy/cuba.

The focus of US military cooperation under the Obama administration shifted to the Caribbean Basin, as the most frequent drug trafficking route to the US, and Central America, as a macro-region traditionally problematic in terms of security and migration. In 2010, the Caribbean Basin Security Initiative (CBSI) was launched, under which the US and the Caribbean increased cooperation in combating drug trafficking, as well as other cross-border crimes that threaten regional security.

Key US security initiatives in Central America were the Central America Regional Security Initiative (CARSI) and the Alliance for the Prosperity of the Northern Triangle (APNT). As part of the CARSI agreements, the US Congress has allocated more than $1 billion since 2009, which was sent to Belize, Costa Rica, El Salvador, Guatemala, Honduras, Nicaragua, and Panama. Funding was intended for three areas: assistance to the police and military in the fight against drug and illegal arms trafficking, organized crime and migration; building the capacity of law enforcement and the criminal justice system; and the formation of an effective system for the protection of public order and programs for young people from at-risk groups. However, since 2012, after the election of Obama for a second term, the volume of US financial assistance under CARSI gradually began to decline. The situation was further exacerbated by the 2016 murder of the famous indigenous rights activist Berta Cáceres, whose killers included WHINSEC-trained Honduran officers. To achieve a higher level of cooperation between the LAC countries and other international partners to combat threats to regional security, several programs of the US Agency for International Development (USAID) were launched. CARSI became not a consolidated security strategy but a set of separate initiatives, which affected its effectiveness.

In 2014, a new initiative, APNT, appeared, in the development of which, then-US Vice President Joe Biden was actively involved. As a result of the agreements with Honduras, El Salvador, and Guatemala, APNT was aimed at addressing the increasing flow of migration from Central America to the US, through the provision of financial assistance for improved security and development.[19]

As part of the security cooperation at the regional level, CBSI, CARSI, and APNT successfully complemented Washington's other LAC security instruments. Meanwhile, the launch of these programs did not lead to any noticeable positive results in Central American and Caribbean security issues. This

---

19   https://www.whitehouse.gov/briefing-room/statements-releases/2021/07/29/fact-sheet-strategy-to-address-the-root-causes-of-migration-in-central-america/.

was primarily due to the structural disproportion that formed in the system of cooperation between the US armed forces and LAC civilian governments due to the policies of previous American administrations (Tulchin, 2010). The lack of full-scale multilateral cooperation in the fight against organized crime, drug trafficking, and natural disasters led to the Pentagon becoming the only US security policy outpost in LAC, causing the even greater disproportion in US-LAC dialogue.

This situation was further exacerbated by two factors. First, there was no LAC regional institution that was responsible for a timely response to emergencies. This led to the fact that USSOUTHCOM, endowed with the authority and resources to tackle such problems, cooperated exclusively with LAC military structures, and only at the bilateral level, that is, with each country separately (Tokatlian, 2015). Second, there was no unified and well-thought-out collective regional policy in security and defense, and special civilian institutions aimed at combating the main LAC security problems. This led to the Pentagon being forced to cooperate in countering potential threats or challenges only through the armed forces.

Understanding the need to develop a collective and multilateral approach to solving common regional problems led the Obama administration to develop country-level strategies that were built taking into account the interests and needs of individual LAC countries. Brazil became a US strategic outpost in LAC security. This was explained, first, by the fact that Brazil had already become a US strategic partner in the training of the Latin American military for the entire region. It was Brazil that received the most attention in the 2010 US security strategy. It was recognized as the leader of the entire LAC region in terms of new threats such as climate change and energy security.[20] Subsequently, this approach was adopted by Donald Trump, who, in the absence of a clear LAC strategy, recognized the special important role of Brazil in US security policy in the region.

Brazil itself only partially shared Washington's opinion regarding its mission as Washington's outpost in the LAC security system. This was because, from the late 2000s, Brazil had begun to pursue a more active security policy characterized by its ambitions as the "single LAC superpower". In 2008, as part of the UNASUR, the Council of South American Defense, which was initiated by the then Brazilian President Lula da Silva, was created. Brazil also signed a bilateral agreement with France on the construction of submarines (2011), and military

---

20   The White House (2010). "National Security Strategy of the United States of America": https://history.defense.gov/Portals/70/Documents/nss/NSS2010.pdf?ver=Zt7IeSPX2uNQtoo_7wq6Hg%3d%3d.

aircraft were purchased from Sweden (2013). All these steps confirmed Brazil's growing intention to gradually withdraw from the US security umbrella.

Comprehensive migration reform was one of the main campaign promises in both Obama's election campaigns, which predetermined the important role of Washington's cooperation with Mexico and the countries of the Northern Triangle as the main sources of LAC migration to the US The approach to LAC on security issues, which was dominated by "soft power" tools, led to the fact that Mexico and the US achieved certain successes regarding the migration issue during the Obama presidency.[21]

Obama's presidency was characterized by two important events that confirmed that a narrow group of LAC countries were in the sphere of Washington's heightened interest in security issues. As part of Edward Snowden's revelations published in 2013, it became known that the US National Security Agency received classified data belonging to several LAC governments, with a particular focus on Brazil, Venezuela, Mexico, and Colombia, using two programs: "Prisma" and "Boundless Informant". It is noteworthy that these countries were given the most attention in the 2015 US security strategy.[22] The main task of this program was to obtain classified information on military, trade, and energy issues. Information also appeared, showing that the US was spying on LAC countries through a communication channel, the optical fiber of which passed through their territory.These cases, which were violations of state security and espionage, caused discontent throughout LAC, which is extremely sensitive to issues of sovereignty, including digital sovereignty. These revelations led to the stepping-up of the development of LAC's cybersecurity policy.

The key stages in the deterioration of US-Venezuela relations at the political level occurred during the Obama administration. In 2010, in retaliation for the Chavez government's refusal to accept Larry Palmer as ambassador-designate, Washington canceled the visa of Venezuela's ambassador to the US Since 2010, relations between Caracas and Washington have been headed not by ambassadors, but by ministers-advisers on economic issues. After the protests that took place in Venezuela in 2014 against the government of Maduro, Obama for the first-time imposed sanctions against high-ranking Venezuelan officials

---

21 Unidad de Política Migratoria (2016). "Boletín Mensual de Estadísticas Migratorias 2016". México, Instituto Nacional de Migración.
22 The White House (2015). "The National Security Strategy of the United States of America":https://history.defense.gov/Portals/70/Documents/nss/NSS2015.pdf?ver=TJJ2Qf MoMcCqL-pNtKHtVQ%3d%3d.

accused of corruption and human rights violations. The policy of tough sanctions was subsequently continued by the Trump administration.

The crisis of 2008 and the economic rise of China markedly undermined US influence in LAC, which was not the focus of Washington's attention. It was the feeling of "closeness" that was an important factor in China's rapid expansion into LAC: for example, if any Latin American country was in dire need of funding or investment, it knew that China would help quickly. It was the speed of development of relations that characterized Beijing's dialogue, while contrasting with the dialogue with the US and the EU. The result has been that China has begun to be present in strategic sectors of the Latin American economy where it had not previously been present, gradually turning into a "threat to US security". Under the Obama administration, Washington decided to gradually move away from increasing the role of the military in civil-military relations in the region. However, the growing competition from other extra-regional powers dramatically changed this trend. US security services became more willing to help and cooperate with the region's military to prevent China and, to a lesser extent, Russia, Iran, and other international rivals, from gaining influence in LAC. This is also confirmed by the fact that during the Obama presidency two peaks in arms sales to the region occurred: a massive peak in 2010 and a further peak in 2014 (Figure 2).

2.1.4   2017–2021

In a relatively short period, Washington began to perceive China as a significant threat to US national security. As a result of the policy of expansion China launched in 2004, when it announced plans to invest $100 billion in Latin America over the following ten years, Beijing became a real competitor to Washington in LAC, something that no other extra-regional power has been able to do in the 21st century. In 2004, US concern about China's inroads into LAC appeared more clearly,[23] although the US had been concerned about this well before then. As early as 1993, Washington recognized the importance of containing or balancing China's entry onto the world stage—a process already considered from the standpoint of protecting the national interests of the US;[24] starting in 1994, Washington recognized that China was becoming an

---

23   US Southern Command (2004). "China Focuses on Latin America": www.southcom.mil.
24   The White House (1993). "National Security Strategy of the United States": https://nssarchive.us/wp-content/uploads/2020/04/1993.pdf.

increasingly prominent actor in world affairs, while the future of Russia after the collapse of the USSR was regarded as very uncertain.[25]

Russia also appeared on Washington's list of issues on the Western Hemisphere's security agenda, primarily in the context of expanding military-technical cooperation with Venezuela, Nicaragua, and Cuba. However, the "priority of the political over the economic", which characterizes Moscow's strategy in this region, together with low economic growth rates, did not make Russia a real competitor to the US in defense and security in LAC, unlike China (Kosevich, 2022).

The tension between China and the US began to be most noticeable after 2015, influenced by a number of factors, such as the growing authoritarianism of the Xi Jinping government, allegations of large-scale cyber-attacks, the crackdown on Hong Kong protests, the aggressive policy in against Taiwan, and the outbreak of COVID-19 in Wuhan, China. The US NSS 2017[26] and the 2018 US National Defense Strategy[27] made it clear that the priority of security threats had shifted from the fight against terrorism to competition with other powers, where Beijing had a special place.

Although LAC continued to play a marginal role in the intensifying US-China rivalry, reports from US regional security officials confirmed Washington's growing concerns about "the extra-regional influence" on its southern neighbors (Faller, 2021).

Starting in 2017, the term "preventing the arrival" of competing extra-regional players began to be heard more often in US public discourse in hemispheric security and defense, which emphasized the importance of expanding interaction with LAC governments, above all with their national security forces, in order to remain the "preferred military partner". This created fertile ground for the revival of the principles of the Monroe Doctrine.

Trump's arrival in the White House did not bring significant changes to the US security strategy toward LAC, which continued to be a low priority compared to Asia and the Middle East. Unlike Obama, Trump was characterized by aggressive and racist rhetoric against a number of LAC countries, which he recognized as a source of serious problems affecting the security of Americans. Under the Trump administration, anti-immigration policies became a key

---

25   The White House (1994). "A National Security Strategy of Engagement and Enlargement": https://nssarchive.us/wp-content/uploads/2020/04/1994.pdf.
26   National Security Strategy of the United States of America. December, 2017. https://trumpwhitehouse.archives.gov/wp-content/uploads/2017/12/NSS-Final-12-18-2017-0905.pdf.
27   US Department of Defense (2018). National Defense Strategy: https://www.defense.gov/Spotlights/National-Defense-Strategy/.

focus of the US security strategy in LAC, which was in keeping with the 2017 NSS. The focus of Washington's attention again shifted to Mexico, cooperation with which was built on the basis of two White House foreign policy priorities: a revision of US-Mexican trade relations and the transformation of Mexico into a "stopper" of migration flows from Central America.

In December 2018, the Trump administration announced a new program called the "Migrant Protection Protocols" that required migrants to remain in Mexico until their hearing in US immigration courts.[28] The program began operating in January 2019 and has been used to send almost 70,000 migrants back to Mexico. Another key issue of US national security was the fight against transnational organized crime. In January 2018, the US allocated more than $98 million for the purchase of military weapons for the Mexican authorities to fight international crime and strengthen the country's defense. The volume of US aid provided for LAC military needs became lower than the level recorded during the administrations of Bush and Obama.

Cooperation between the US and Mexico as part of the Merida Initiative continued, taking into account the importance of Mexico, which Trump attached to his election campaign. In particular, in 2019, the US Congress allocated $149 million to Mexico as part of this project, and another $133 million in 2020. The main objective of the budget was to curb the flow of heroin and fentanyl through Mexico. On the other hand, Trump was never able to expand the capabilities of US security forces in Mexico with the announced goal of eliminating drug cartels, which have noticeably intensified in the context of the Mexican government's inability to build an effective national security strategy.

US arms sales to LAC under the Trump administration continued the downward trend that began in 2015. In 2019, the lowest value of arms sales since 2005, amounting to less than $10 million, were registered. This confirmed the high level of continuity of each US administration's policy of detachment in security in relation to LAC. Trump's announcement in the spring of 2020 of the need to deploy a large navy to intercept narcotics in the Caribbean and the Eastern Pacific was the only exception to this course of detachment. Washington did not refuse to comply with previously reached security agreements; joint exercises, training and contacts between the US and LAC armed forces continued. For example, large-scale military exercises were held in 2017 on the triple border between Brazil, Colombia, and Peru, with the participation of USSOUTHCOM and these three LAC countries (Senra, 2017).

---

28 American Immigration Council. https://www.americanimmigrationcouncil.org/research/migrant-protection-protocols.

In 2019–2020, the Pentagon announced a decision to cut 20% of USSOUTHCOM's budget for programs in Latin America. The head of SOUTHCOM announced plans to increase the US military presence in the Western Hemisphere, despite cuts in funding for partner security programs that help Latin American partners fight drug cartels. Intentions to expand the US military presence in LAC countries included an increase in the number of ships, aircraft, and military personnel, which could compensate for losses in funding for security cooperation programs.[29]

Military and security relations between Brazil and the US also deepened. During this period, the volume of trade related to the defense industry increased markedly, several new agreements were signed in this area,[30] such as the agreement on joint military projects,[31] and the Technology Assurance Agreement for the use of the launch center in Alcantara, which allowed US companies to launch their missiles and warheads from Brazil (Milani, 2021; Vitelli, 2016).[32] In 2019, Brazil received Major Non-NATO Ally Status.[33] In matters of security cooperation, Colombia continued to be one of the main US allies in the region, which was explained by its military presence in several Central American countries, and its strategically important geographic position in terms of resolving the political crisis in Venezuela. Since 2019, US security funding to Colombia has markedly increased. The Trump administration continued the policy of imposing harsh economic sanctions on high-ranking officials in the government of Nicolás Maduro, begun by its predecessor.

2.2 *The Biden Presidency*

The new Biden cabinet made adjustments to the US security policy in LAC, in which two main directions can be identified. The first direction is confronting illegal migration from the three main donor countries of migration—Guatemala, El Salvador, and Honduras. Unlike its predecessor, the main mechanism was to build diplomatic bridges with Mexico and the Northern Triangle countries. In this context, Biden, even before taking office as the US President, proposed a four-year strategy with $4 billion in financial support for Central

---

29 https://www.vozdeamerica.com/a/jefe-comandosur-lamenta-recorte-fondos-america-latina/5324995.html.
30 https://www.gov.br/aeb/pt-br/centrais-de-conteudo/publicacoes/acordo-de-salvaguardas-tecnologicas/ast.pdf.
31 https://www.reuters.com/article/us-usa-brazil-defense-idUSKBN20V0X7.
32 http://latamsatelital.com/entro-en-vigencia-el-acuerdo-por-alcantara/.
33 US Department of State (2021). "Major Non-NATO Ally Status": https://www.state.gov/major-non-nato-ally-status/.

America. This initiative was a continuation of APNT, agreed by himself in order to solve migration problems in 2014. The main tasks of the Biden administration's security policy in LAC were addressing the problem of increasing migration from Central America; increasing the effectiveness of bilateral cooperation at the level of the Prosecutor General's Office; and enhancing dialogue between civil society organizations. In an open letter to Biden, dozens of LAC civil society organizations expressed concern that the plan replicated the ineffective US policies of the 2010s, which had already led to increased poverty, inequality, and violence in Central America.

The Los Angeles Declaration, adopted at the Summit of the Americas 2022, confirmed that migration continues to be one of the main threats to US security posed by LAC. The main goal of the Declaration was to create incentives and mechanisms for countries that receive the largest number of migrants, and to distribute responsibility throughout the region.[34] This underscored the transition from Trump's "America First" strategy to cooperating with the LAC states on an equal footing.

At the 2022 Americas Summit, Biden emphasized a prosperous and inclusive future for all of America.[35] However, Cuba, Venezuela and Nicaragua, which account for a significant number of undocumented migrants crossing the continent, were not invited to the Summit, which led to a boycott by several LAC countries, in particular Mexico.[36] The absence from the summit of the leaders of the countries of the Northern Triangle, the source of most of the migrants, called into question the effectiveness of the proposed Biden plan to manage LAC migration. The sharp cooling of relations with El Salvador, which began after the publication of the report of the US Department of the Treasury at the end of December 2021,[37] also creates additional obstacles for building an effective strategy to counter the main threats to the US emanating from the LAC—drug trafficking and migration.[38]

---

34 The White House (2022). "Fact Sheet: The Los Angeles Declaration on Migration and Protection US Government and Foreign Partner Deliverables": https://www.whitehouse.gov/briefing-room/statements-releases/2022/06/10/fact-sheet-the-los-angeles-declaration-on-migration-and-protection-u-s-government-and-foreign-partner-deliverables/.
35 https://www.washingtonpost.com/world/2022/06/10/biden-summit-of-americas-south-dud/.
36 https://elpais.com/argentina/2022-05-27/cumbre-de-las-americas-estados-unidos-desconectado.html.
37 https://home.treasury.gov/news/press-releases/jy0519.
38 The White House (2021). "Interim National Security Strategic Guidance": https://www.whitehouse.gov/wp-content/uploads/2021/03/NSC-1v2.pdf.

The second key direction of the Biden administration's policy in the LAC was the increase in US influence in security in South America. Here, a special role was assigned to Colombia and Brazil. For Colombia, relations are truly special for Biden himself, given that, while still a senator, he personally participated in the negotiations on Plan Colombia in 2000. Colombia was elevated to the status of a regional priority for the Biden government, taking into account the fact that, due to its geographical location, this country could counterbalance the Venezuelan government and the extra-regional powers that are most actively increasing their presence in the Western hemisphere.[39] In May 2022, Colombia was designated as a Major Non-NATO Ally of the US, which was another confirmation of the long-term common strategic interests of the countries.[40]

Russia's military actions in Ukraine, which began on February 24, 2022, unexpectedly led to rapid positive changes in US-Venezuela relations, once again reminding everyone that these countries have historically been large trade and economic partners. Just two weeks after the start of the Russo-Ukrainian conflict, Venezuela received an US delegation presumably with a purely practical task—to find new suppliers of oil to compensate for the shortage caused by anti-Russian sanctions. With this step, Washington pursued the geopolitical goal of getting Caracas out of the influence of Vladimir Putin and regaining the ability to influence Venezuela's foreign policy. This correlated with repeated calls from Maduro himself to Washington to establish dialogue and normalize relations. In the new environment, for Washington, engaging with the breakaway regimes of Venezuela and Cuba was critical to protecting core US interests in LAC, and containing Russian and Chinese influence in the Western Hemisphere. The latter is confirmed by the fact that the decision to ease sanctions against Venezuela was made the day after Washington lifted several restrictions on Cuba.[41, 42]

Brazil once again became another US priority in LAC, whose government has focused on inclusion into NATO and the OECD. Although Jair Bolsonaro

---

39 US Department of Defense (2022). Fact Sheet: 2022 National Defense Strategy. https://media.defense.gov/2022/Mar/28/2002964702/-1/-1/1/NDS-FACT-SHEET.PDF.
40 The White House (2022). "Memorandum on the Desigantation of Colombia as a Major Non-NATO Ally": https://www.whitehouse.gov/briefing-room/presidential-actions/2022/05/23/memorandum-on-the-designation-of-colombia-as-a-major-non-nato-ally/#:~:text=2321k)%20(the%20%E2%80%9CAct%E2%80%9D),determination%20in%20the%20Federal%20Register.
41 https://www.washingtonpost.com/world/2022/05/17/venezuela-oil-sanctions-chevron/.
42 https://www.washingtonpost.com/national-security/2022/05/16/biden-cuba-travel-remittances-visas/.

had close ties to Trump, but a very difficult relationship with Biden, at the beginning of 2021, a five-year plan was agreed upon to develop partnerships and intensify interaction of joint military training.[43]

Biden's move to a less aggressive security policy towards LAC is confirmed in The Mexico-US Bicentennial Framework for Security, Public Health, and Safe Communities, designed to replace the Mérida Initiative, which had become a source of new bloodshed for Mexico. This bilateral action plan reinforces new "humanistic" forms of cooperation, focusing on the solving of the Mexico's social problems, which were given little attention in the Merida Initiative, meeting the interests of Mexico to a much greater extent, implementing the shift in the previously existing paradigm of bilateral cooperation between Mexico and the US in the field of security towards a more social orientation. Washington was able to return the level of interaction between security agencies to its previous level. For example, the US Congress approved assistance to Mexico in the amount of $159 million for distribution in 2022, of which $100 million was aimed at improving drug control and law enforcement, and the ongoing fight against drug trafficking continued to be carried out primarily by force.

In general, the tone between Presidents Biden and Obrador has gradually become friendlier, in contrast to the tense dialogue with Trump. This was confirmed by several bilateral agreements, establishing new forms of cooperation in various fields. In addition, in 2023, Biden became the first US president in the past decade to visit the country. The Mexican president is clearly resorting to a foreign policy of omnibalancing regarding the Russia-Ukraine conflict: openly calling Washington's support for Ukraine a "big mistake" and avoiding criticism of the Kremlin's actions, which earns him the sympathy of the Putin administration, Obrador on occasion denounces the US for providing Kiev with military funding faster than economic assistance to the countries of Central America.

The escalation of the Russia-Ukraine conflict led to the fact that confronting new extra-regional threats has become a priority of US security policy in LAC. As part of the XV Conference of Defense Ministers of the Americas (CDMA), held in the summer of 2022, the US presented a new concept of Western Hemisphere cooperation aimed at combating the increasing influence of China and Russia. This concept was called "complex deterrence", which meant a new form of struggle, using all fronts, means, and resources. "Comprehensive containment" has become a new whole-government approach, where in a full-scale struggle against nations considered by Washington as enemies, LAC countries, considered as "natural allies," have acquired new significance.

---

43   http://br.usembassy.gov/brazilian-u-s-military-leaders-emphasize-partnerships-at-joint-training-exercise/.

The US NSS 2022 also confirmed Washington's shift in priorities towards geopolitical competition with China and Russia, cooperation on transnational issues such as climate change and food security and strengthening international law.[44] In LAC, a region far from new global conflicts, the US will focus on promoting democracy, economic prosperity, and citizen security through hemispheric cooperation based on common ties. It emphasizes that greater prosperity for LAC means greater national security for the US. Multilateral initiatives will be the means to achieve this regional prosperity, and the Alliance for Promoting Democracy and Prosperity in the Americas is Biden's main regional commitment. It was launched in July 2022 and should become an alternative source of development financing to Chinese investments. The section on LAC also draws attention to migration crises, climate change, organized crime, and threats to democratic governance, including interference from China, Russia, and Iran. Although the document is a regional analysis, Mexico is mentioned as an outstanding economic partner. It is noteworthy that transnational drug cartels are hardly mentioned in a regional context, which is perhaps the biggest threat to the national security of several LAC countries.

Unlike Trump, Biden's strategy towards LAC took a liberal-internationalist approach, where the protection of democracy, human rights, and minorities became a priority. Biden almost immediately made it clear that he was not ready to acquiesce to blatant violations in this area by some LAC regimes. Immediately after coming to power, Biden took several measures that ran counter to the interests of several LAC governments, some of which were in the category of US traditional and stable partners.

The change in approach did not affect the level of cooperation in security: USSOUTHCOM did not reduce its presence at the Soto Cano air base in Honduras, and Colombia and Brazil, as part of a joint training program, sent generals to the headquarters of USSOUTHCOM for advanced training in Miami. It is symptomatic that Biden announced his intention to close the notorious Guantanamo prison in Cuba, which Obama proposed to liquidate but which did not receive approval from Congress. At the IX Hemispheric Security Conference (HSC), held in May 2024 in Miami, Florida, the head of USSOUTHCOM, General Laura Richardson, said that Beijing is pursuing military goals by expanding its presence in the LAC region, primarily by obtaining more

---

44 NATIONAL SECURITY STRATEGY OCTOBER 2022. https://www.whitehouse.gov/wp-content/uploads/2022/10/Biden-Harris-Administrations-National-Security-Strategy-10.2022.pdf.

TABLE 4   The top 10 recipients of US foreign military assistance

1991	2001	2011	2021
Israel	Philippines	Israel	Colombia
Egypt	Hungary	Egypt	Tunisia
Turkey	Morocco	Jordan	Libya
Greece	El Salvador	Colombia	Philippines
Philippines	Tunisia	Morocco	Vietnam
Portugal	Venezuela	Mexico	Ukraine
El Salvador	Bolivia	Poland	Georgia
Colombia	Nigeria	Tunisia	Estonia
Morocco	Bahamas	Greece	Latvia
Bolivia	Thailand	Philippines	Lithuania

SOURCE: US OVERSEAS LOANS AND GRANTS (GREENBOOK)

influence in terms of critical infrastructure. In the context of growing strategic competition in the field of telecommunications, Richardson emphasized the importance of expanding US cooperation with LAC countries in the areas of cybersecurity and data protection.[45] Despite the reduction of the SOUTHCOM budget for the security programs of partners from the LAC countries that began under Trump, the actual presence and influence of SOUTHCOM in this region of the planet has not decreased in any way.

Biden's policy towards LAC is in many ways similar to Trump's strategy: a course has been taken to restore US leadership in this region, including by maintaining its influence on security and defense issues amid falling funding in this area. For example, in 2021, only 0.4% of the total US military assistance to the world went to LAC, denoting a significant reduction compared to 2011 (2.2%) and 2005 (8%). Colombia became the main recipient of US military assistance in 2021, which since the beginning of the 2010s has been one of the main recipients of US military assistance (Table 4).

According to the 2023 USAID Report on Top US Funding Areas, among other regions such as Asia, Africa, Europe and Eurasia, Middle East, LAC leads in the categories of "RD–Democracy, Derechos Humanos y Gobernanza" and "Peace

---

45   https://www.telesurtv.net/news/comando-sur-eeuu-critica-presencia-china-latinoamerica-20240512-0022.html.

and Security". LAC, compared to other regions, recorded low rates of financial support in categories such as Private Sector Productivity, Higher Education, and Malaria.[46]

Dealing with the increase in the presence of extra-regional actors occupies a special place as China is boosting trade and investment with LAC, considered it from the standpoint of "strategic competition" and the need for geopolitical confrontation. Unlike his predecessor, Biden's liberal-internationalist approach recognizes that most of the problems that negatively affect LAC are caused by the lack of an effective institutional structure, which leads to situations in which the US can help the countries of the region while they maintain their autonomy.[47] The aim of LAC countries to maintain an equidistant position in relation to the US and China—two opposing powers on which it's sustainable development depend—means applying "omnibalancing" foreign policy, which contributes to the creation of a "regional balance" through the development of pragmatic relations with two rival forces.

∴

Even though since the end of the Cold War, Washington-LAC dialogue has undergone significant transformations under the influence of several external and internal factors, all the changes that have occurred have not derailed the overall continuity in the US security policy toward LAC. Washington's approach has always been based on the concept of aid and the predominance of US geostrategic interests. The author asserts that there is both continuity and change inthe US security policy toward Latin America. The continuity is manifested in the policy of detachment in security in relation to LAC, which has manifested in a divergence between the rhetoric, reflected in the low incidence of the region in government documents, and reality, reflected in the constancy of military cooperation. Changes appear in the intensity of certain areas of cooperation within the US security policy toward Latin America. The intensity of cooperation varies in a systematic way in certain US administrations when looking at cooperation in traditional security and defense matters (such as, the initiatives in the fight against organized crime, drug trafficking, security personnel collaboration programs, and joint military exercises) in

---

46   USAID. Agency Financial Report. Fiscal year 2023.
47   US Department of State (2022). "Bureau of Western Hemisphere Affairs": https://www.state.gov/bureaus-offices/under-secretary-for-political-affairs/bureau-of-western-hemisphere-affairs/.

comparison to cooperation on non-traditional issues (migration, development and institutional strengthening programs, the defense of democracy, and trade relations). The empirical evidence presented suggests that by the beginning of the 2020s, the trend towards a weakening of Washington's hegemony in Latin America is becoming more evident, which is the result of such factors as the hostile posture of many LAC governments towards the US, the decrease in the Washington's influence within the OAS, and the increase of China's influence in the region.

CHAPTER 3

China and LAC in the New Global Context

1 "Fast and Furious" Strategy: Chinese Foreign Policy in LAC

China's strategy in LAC – was initially based on the concept of the "Third World", which arose under the pressure of changes in the international political landscape after the end of World War II. The concept of the "Third World," later revised by China, garnered a strong positive response and fostered a desire to develop relations among countries in the region during the mid-20th century. The emergence of new independent states in the 1950s, the development of the Non-Aligned Movement in the 1960s and the creation in 1964 of the "Group of 77," whose goal was to strengthen the role of developing countries in the international arena, led to the formation of new independent political forces on the world stage. This changed the pre-existing balance in the international system, significantly softening the pattern of the post-war bipolar confrontation between the US and the USSR and contributing to the transition of international politics to a multipolar format.[1]

The concept of the "Third World" was intended to reflect the changes taking place in the system of international relations of that time. The concept was first proposed by Mao Zedong in 1974 during a meeting with Zambian President Kenneth Kaunda. According to this concept, the superpowers—the US and the USSR—represented the "First World", the developed countries of Europe, Japan, Australia, and Canada constituted the "Second World", and most countries in Asia, Africa, and Latin America were the "Third World".[2] The countries of the Third World were united by a colonial past and opposition to imperialism, colonialism, and hegemony. China was considered a Third World country. Before it was formally formulated in 1974, the theory of the "Three Worlds" was based on the idea of "one intermediate zone", proposed in the second half of the 1940s, then modified under the pressure of the new idea of "two intermediate zones" that arose in the 1960s. The concept of "one intermediate zone" assumed three actors—the USSR, the US, and an intermediate zone between the two powers, which included the capitalist countries of Europe, colonial and semi-colonial countries of Asia and Africa. The US was a stronghold of

1 https://baijiahao.baidu.com/s?id=1779891267857357973&wfr=spider&for=pc.
2 https://www.fmprc.gov.cn/eng/ziliao_665539/3602_665543/3604_665547/200011/t20001117_697799.html.

reactionary force, the USSR was a stronghold of democracy, and between are an independent political force in the form of an "intermediate zone".[3] However, this "intermediate zone" did not include LAC. The struggle for control over the "intermediate zone" lay at the heart of the system of international relations. The US sought to subjugate the countries of the "intermediate zone" in order to provoke a conflict with the USSR (An, 2013). Thus, the main threat to China's security was the US, which would lay claim to Chinese sovereignty.

In the mid-1950s, two events occurred that forced Mao to reconsider the concept of "one intermediate zone": the Bandung Conference (1955) and the Suez Crisis (1956). The Bandung Conference showed the world that the newly independent countries of Asia, Africa, and LAC acted as an autonomous political force in the international arena. However, the Suez crisis drew attention to the fact that there was already a rift between the UK, and the US and France. Thus, the intermediate zone was divided into two intermediate zones. The first zone included Asia (except Japan), Africa, and LAC, the second zone included the countries of Europe, Japan, and Canada. The division of countries coincided with the later theory of the "three worlds" and was based on economic indicators (developed, developing, and undeveloped countries). Both zones had conflicts with the USSR and the US and tried to act independently on the world stage. The transition to two intermediate zones reflected the weakening positions of the US and the USSR among their allies in the 1950s and 1960s and the increasing share of "intermediate zones" in a system that resisted pressure from the superpowers.

The theory of "three worlds" became an attempt by the Chinese leadership to "explain" the existing balance of power, and to analyze its own place in the system of international relations.

The concept of the "Five Principles of Peaceful Coexistence" proposed in 1953 by Zhou Enlai formulated the key axioms for all Chinese foreign policy (1) non-aggression; (2) non-interference in each other's internal affairs; (3) respect for sovereignty and territorial integrity; (4) equality and mutual benefit; (5) and peaceful coexistence. The five principles became fundamental in the international strategy of China and were the only constant in all Chinese foreign policy concepts starting from the 1950s. In 1982, the Five Principles of Peaceful Coexistence were incorporated into the Constitution of the People's Republic of China.

The concept of the "Third World" began to take on new meaning after Beijing's policy of opening up and reform in the late 1970s. China became

---

3 https://bit.ly/4bYqtXd.

actively involved in the affairs of developing countries and sought to strengthen its diplomatic and economic relations with the rest of the Third World. From the 1980s, Beijing constantly emphasized the "increasing weight of Third World countries" in international political life, which no one could ignore. The Chinese leadership were aware that the "Third World" as a single community, united by one goal and a common past, existed only in the ideological guidelines of the 20th century.

This theoretical concept for China gradually turned into a practical desire to create a just and equitable world where developing countries can achieve sustainable economic growth and prosperity and where LAC countries gradually began to play an increasingly significant role.

1.1 History of the China–LAC Relationship

The origins of China–LAC interaction date back to the 19th century and were largely associated with the mass migration of Chinese to the LAC region. In total, at the beginning of the 20th century, there were more than Chinese immigrants in LAC, occupying positions as "labor hands", who were difficult to integrate into local societies. By 1900, the Chinese government had established diplomatic relations with Peru, Brazil, Mexico, Cuba, and Panama to promote the rights of Chinese workers in these countries and boost trade. During this period, interaction with LAC countries was not considered a priority by Beijing.

With the proclamation of the People's Republic of China on October 1, 1949, Cuba became the first country in the Western Hemisphere to establish diplomatic relations with Beijing. On September 2, 1960, Fidel Castro officially announced that his country would sever ties with Taiwan and establish diplomatic relations with Beijing. Less than a month later, on September 28, a joint statement was published establishing diplomatic relations between them. Subsequently, China reaffirmed its strong support for the Cuban people's struggle against imperialism. In the 1960s trade and economic interaction between Cuba and China began to develop. In 1965, bilateral trade turnover reached a record figure of more than $350 million. However, the instability of China's economy, exacerbated by the Cultural Revolution, led Beijing to abandon its role as a sponsor of Cuba's rice supply. This ultimately influenced the fact that Havana was inclined to cooperate with the USSR.

In the 1960s, China repeatedly and openly demonstrated interest in activating relations with Latin American countries. But Beijing's ability to develop relations with the region before the end of the 1960s were limited by hostile relations with the US and by the difficulties of competing with the USSR in the struggle for influence on leftist forces in the region. It is because of pressure from the US that most of Beijing's initiatives in this direction encountered obstacles. A clear example was Ecuador, which planned to recognize China, but was forced to abandon these plans due to pressure from Washington. While not achieving success in developing practical and diplomatic relations with LAC, China was nevertheless able to exert a significant influence on local politics through the export of ideology and support for Maoist parties and movements (Kashin, 2023).

At that moment, Beijing was able to influence a number of Maoist groups, which launched a long and bloody armed struggle with local authorities. In the 1970s, China collaborated with the Revolutionary Party of the Mexican Proletariat of Florencio Medrano operating in Mexico, and the "Sendero Luminoso" organization founded in 1969 by Abimael Guzmán in Peru. Both leaders were ideological followers of Maoism who were trained in China in the 1960s.

There were steps to strengthen relations at the party level. The first example of a rapprochement between a Latin American political force and the Chinese Communist Party (CCP) was the Communist Party of Brazil, which sent a delegation to China in July 1953. In September 1956, 12 leaders representing communist forces in LAC were invited to the 8th CCP Congress, which was held in Beijing. By 1960, 22 Latin American communist parties had established working relations with the CCP. The parties gradually established connections through the exchange of delegations, the organization of seminars and meetings on topics of mutual interest, and participation in congresses and events. On several occasions, political leaders from LAC countries were invited to visit China.

In December 1970, a turning point in the LAC direction for China finally arrived. Chile, under the leadership of Salvador Allende, became the first South American country to establish official relations with China. After the military coup in Chile on September 11, 1973, which overthrew the Allende government, Chilean—Chinese relations were formally maintained, but actual contacts and trade exchanges were very limited.

In the early 1970s, two major events changed China's international status: the restoration of China's rights in the UN and the visit of US President Richard Nixon (1969–1974) to Beijing, which confirmed the long-awaited normalization of bilateral relations. The "rules of conduct" at the UN, at that moment imposed by the US on most countries in the region, were rejected by LAC countries, which recognized the difficult context of the Cold War. During the regular session of the UN General Assembly, held in 1971, Guyana, Cuba, Mexico, Peru, Trinidad and Tobago, Chile, and Ecuador voted for the admission of China to the UN and the exclusion of Taiwan. All this led to LAC governments beginning to see China in a new and promising light. During the period 1971–1980, 12 LAC countries established diplomatic relations with Beijing. As a result, by the 1980s Beijing had finally abandoned the course of supporting foreign Maoist movements, focusing on increasing the number of diplomatic partners of China and the isolation of Taiwan.

Beijing and Taipei have at times fought for the loyalty of LAC countries, even the smallest ones, and Beijing has lost more than once. Seven of the 13 countries that still maintain diplomatic relations with Taiwan are in LAC: Belize, Guatemala, Haiti, Paraguay, Saint Kitts and Nevis, Saint Lucia. The reluctance of LAC countries to sever ties with Taiwan is due to the LAC tradition of broad foreign policy autonomy, Washington's position condemning Chinese pressure on Taiwan's diplomatic ties, and Taiwan's effective economic diplomacy.

However, the continuous struggle for diplomatic recognition of the countries of the region, which Beijing was not yet interested in, still allowed China, even in the absence of significant trade and economic cooperation, to establish effective channels of diplomatic communication with even the smallest LAC countries, which played a role in China's future successful policy in LAC. In the 1970s, an active exchange of visits at the highest state level began between China and LAC countries, which became more interested in building diplomatic bridges with a permanent member of the UN Security Council and in the doctrinal patterns of the Chinese government, in particular, the concept of the "Third World".

By the 1970s, China had already formed the main principle of its LAC policy, which was the "priority of economic relations over political ones" and was accompanied by a clearly defined pragmatism. For example, like Romania, China, being socialist, did not break off diplomatic relations with the Pinochet regime in Chile and China's purchases of Chilean copper continued. The years of Somoza's dictatorship in Nicaragua also had no effect on China's interest in purchasing Nicaraguan goods.

Beijing has always tried to ignore the continuation of diplomatic relations with Taiwan by a number of LAC countries, while maintaining intensive trade and economic exchanges with them. China took a demonstrably wait-and-see attitude when, following the opening of Chinese diplomatic missions in LAC countries, the latter were in no hurry to open embassies in Beijing. Such a policy, characterized by both patience and a desire to wait for better times, showed respect for LAC's leisurely temperament, thanks to which China's approval in LAC gradually increased.

In the 1980s, there were virtually no serious economic ties between China and LAC. During this period, interaction between China and LAC countries developed mainly on individual scientific and technical projects of mutual interest. One example of such cooperation was a landmark space project with Brazil. It was the first international space exploration project where both the participants were developing countries. This project took China–Brazil relations to a new level. In 1988, a bilateral agreement on cooperation in the field of space exploration was concluded. The result of this partnership was the launch of the CBERS program (China-Brazil Earth Resources Satellites). Both sides demonstrated continued interest in the development of this program. The first satellite was successfully launched in 1999, and the last satellite of this series was launched in 2019. Brazil actively expanded its technical capabilities from the 1980s, seeking to gain experience in designing spacecraft and using space infrastructure to launch satellites into orbit and use Chinese launch vehicles, something it did not have at that time. Thanks to participation in this program, China gained access to both Brazilian and Western technologies, which gave impetus to the development of Chinese technologies for military and civilian satellites.

Another important area of cooperation was the partnership with Argentina, which played a significant role in the establishment of the Chinese Antarctic research program. In 1988, China and Argentina signed an intergovernmental agreement on cooperation in Antarctic exploration, which was the result of Argentina's technical assistance in organizing China's first year-round Antarctic research station, established in 1984. The agreement coordinated a wide range of areas of cooperation in Antarctic research, which has survived to this day. China later entered into similar agreements on cooperation in Antarctic exploration with Peru and Chile.

In the 1990s, Beijing's clear desire to establish interaction with interstate associations that had begun earlier in the LAC emerged. An impetus for this new direction was given by the establishment of official relations with the Rio Group, which gradually resulted in a dialogue at the level of foreign ministers. An important factor in the rapprochement of the parties during this period was the interest that formed among a number of LAC states in the countries of the Pacific basin, as they have unique experience in economic expansion. In the 1990s, in LAC countries, special committees for cooperation with the countries of the Pacific basin appeared en masse. In Colombia, at the highest level, an initiative was voiced to create a "dry canal" that would connect the country's Atlantic coast with the Pacific coast, but the project remained unrealized. The increase in the mutual interest of LAC and Asian countries included in the Pacific region was due to the large number of FTAs between both regions concluded in the early 2000s. In 2004, there were only two free trade agreements between LAC and Asia: one between Korea and Chile, and the other between Taiwan and Peru (both countries have access to the Pacific Ocean), and by 2007 the number of FTAs between these regions was nine, and by 2013 it was 22.

At the beginning of the 21st century, the diversification of the diplomatic policies of LAC countries demonstrated a clear orientation towards the Asia-Pacific region, which attached increasing importance to China. The Pacific Alliance (PA) was created in 2011 between Mexico, Chile, Peru, and Colombia, which demonstrated a clear focus on cooperation with the Asia-Pacific region, where China occupied a prominent position. In May 2013, China became an observer country of PA. Following this, the importance of negotiating a FTA between China and PA based on the China-ASEAN negotiation model, was actively discussed in Chinese business and academic circles.

Taking advantage of this positive environment, China gradually began to form its own network of official ties with LAC integration associations—MERCOSUR and the Andean Community. China became an observer of OAS. In addition, it received observer status in the UN Economic Commission for Latin America and the Caribbean and the Latin American Integration Association.

Although, LAC was not a priority in Chinese foreign policy during this period, China strived to maximally expand the platform for communication with LAC countries. In 1990 Beijing ratified Protocol II of the Treaty of Tlatelolco, which enshrined a ban on the transit and deployment of nuclear weapons in LAC. 1999 marked the beginning of a new stage in Chinese policy in LAC, the impetus for which was Beijing's implementation of a strategy of global expansion of state and private Chinese businesses abroad. This strategy, called "Going Outward" (走出去战略), was approved by the CCP Central Committee and envisaged a sharp increase in the investment activity of Chinese businesses abroad. The new road map, which was aimed primarily at solving the problems of the country's internal development by intensifying international economic cooperation, pursued three main goals: the acquisition of raw materials and technological assets, the expansion of presence in previously unknown markets, and increasing the recognition of Chinese brands.

In the new strategy, great importance was given to the diversification of China's economic cooperation with other countries of the "global South". This successfully resonated with the emerging trend towards the formation of a new foreign policy guideline in a number of LAC countries, namely the development of relations along the "South-South" line, which became an important stage in the creation of a "new world economic order." It was this factor that became one of the key reasons for the intensification of China's relations with Brazil, which eventually materialized into the formation of BRIC in 2006.

It was in the context of mutual interest that the 2001 tour of the LAC countries by Chinese President Jiang Zemin (1993–2003), who was the first Chinese leader to make such a trip to this region, took place. He visited Chile, Argentina, Uruguay, Brazil, Cuba, and Venezuela, and in 2002 visited Mexico.

The main goal of this tour was the accelerated development of economic cooperation, an important place in which should have been the achievement of "joint development"—a term that occupied a central place in the discourse of the president of China. Despite the fact that the discussion of trade issues occupied a central place in Jiang's speeches, the thesis of ensuring "common development" found a positive response in LAC, for which the possibility of transition to sustainable development has traditionally been a priority. All this created the necessary ground for the intensification of Chinese diplomacy in LAC in subsequent years.

New Chinese President Hu Jintao (2003–2013) showed particular interest in LAC, also organizing a Latin American tour in 2004, during which he paid visits to Brazil, Argentina, Chile, and Cuba. He also attended the APEC summit in Santiago, Chile, that year. The visit, joined by about 300 Chinese businessmen and a number of ministers, focused on strengthening economic and trade cooperation between China and the four largest LAC economies, with which Beijing recorded a trade deficit of $7 billion in the previous year. The Chinese delegation first visited Brazil, then Argentina, still reeling from the 2001 default, followed by Chile and Cuba. In 2005, Hu made a separate visit to Mexico, which resulted in the parties announcing a "strategic alliance" (Kosevich, 2019). Negative factors in Chinese–Mexican relations emerged. These countries had a similar range of export goods, which made them not only partners, but also rivals, especially for the US market. In addition, mutual trade revealed a significant trade imbalance in favor of China.

In 2008, the Chinese leader visited Costa Rica, Cuba, and Peru, and Brazil in 2010. In September 2011, a special meeting on investment was held in Beijing, in which more than 500 businessmen took part. The main purpose of this event was to explore new opportunities for Chinese investment in LAC.

In the 2000s, a multi-level legal framework was created to promote the development of relations between China and LAC. The first free trade agreement was signed with Chile (2006), and a second with Peru (2009).

The first legal document that confirmed the importance of LAC in China's foreign policy framework was the White Paper on LAC Policy, first published by China in 2008.[4] The document set out the priority areas of cooperation, especially emphasizing the importance of direct contacts both at the level of top leadership of countries and at the level of legislative bodies and political parties. China was interested in developing political consultations and interaction

---

4 China's Policy Paper on Latin America and the Caribbean. URL: https://www.chinadaily.com.cn/china/2008-11/06/content_7179488.htm.

at the UN and other international organizations, as well as expanding trade, including through concluding trade agreements with individual countries and with integration structures. China clearly stated its intention to build an effective system of interaction, capable of ensuring the growth of trade. For example, the document discussed the importance of establishing a direct channel of communication between customs authorities and chambers of commerce representing China and LAC countries. In the White Paper, China reaffirmed its commitment to ensuring investment in a range of economic sectors in LAC: agriculture, industry, mining, and infrastructure. Beijing's intention to establish direct contacts through the armed forces and law enforcement agencies was also confirmed. However, there was no general response from the LAC region to this White Paper. The only exception was Chile, which published its own White Paper on this issue. This confirms that the development of relations between China and LAC lies in the plane of bilateral strategy, and not regional politics: each individual LAC country is looking for opportunities, markets, and investments with China, leaving aside the development of large-scale joint regional policies.

In 2016, the second White Paper on Chinese policy in LAC was published. In the updated document, Beijing emphasized the advent of a "new stage" in its partnership with the region. Unlike the 2008 White Paper, the 2016 version included a significantly expanded and specific section on economic cooperation, which included: the creation of an extensive system of agreements on FTAs between China and LAC, increasing investments, expanding the supply of Chinese technologies and modern equipment to LAC, and the export of technologies in agriculture. In the new section "International Cooperation", which touches on the topic of partnership between China and LAC countries in global governance, China's intention to expand interaction with the LAC countries within various international platforms (APEC, IMF, World Bank, WTO and G20) was enshrined, along with increasing cooperation on climate change, cybersecurity, and achieving greater representation of developing countries in global governance.

China's diplomatic activity in LAC continued after Xi Jinping became Chinese president in 2013. Just a few months after taking office, Xi visited Trinidad and Tobago, Costa Rica, and Mexico, and the following year, as part of the BRICS summit in Brazil, visits were made to Brazil, Argentina, Venezuela, and Cuba. In 2016, Xi visited Ecuador, Peru, and Chile, and also took part in the APEC summit in Lima. The publication of a new White Paper on China's policy towards LAC countries was timed to coincide with the visit to Peru.

2013 marked the beginning of a new wave of Chinese diplomatic activity in LAC, which was accompanied by new mechanisms of rapprochement at the political level. Before 2013, there was virtually no institutionalized cooperation or dialogue between China and LAC, and interaction between the parties was limited to the areas of trade and finance. In addition, China had not yet become an influential player in the international arena. In this regard, the creation of a system of institutions for cooperation with LAC states had not yet been an important area of Beijing's foreign policy activities in the Western Hemisphere. Xi's visit to Latin America in 2014 marked the beginning of large-scale institutionalization not only at the state and government level, but also at the international level. When building a system of institutions for China–LAC cooperation, Beijing paid attention primarily to the areas of economics and trade, which had noticeably intensified since the beginning of 2000s. However, the trade war with the US, problems in Taiwan, the outbreak of the COVID-19 pandemic, to which was added the Russia–Ukraine and Israel–Hamas wars became important factors in the transformation of the system of priorities of China's cooperation institutions with LAC. All this led to issues of political partnership in science, technology, and innovation acquiring importance.

In July 2014, Xi successfully held a historic meeting with leaders of LAC countries, which announced the creation of a comprehensive mutually beneficial partnership between China and LAC. As a result of the event, the China–LAC (China–CELAC) Forum was officially established, and the parties also announced their intention to hold the first ministerial meeting of the forum as soon as possible, marking a consensus on promoting cooperation at the highest level. The central objectives of the China–CELAC forum were to promote integration and rapprochement, and provide policy recommendations that would contribute to the development of partnership between the parties.[5]

As a result of the reduction of agricultural land, China's food problem by the end of the 2000s became significantly more complicated. That forced China to pay special attention to developing ties with Brazil and Argentina, the leading countries in the region but with which Beijing did not yet have FTAs. In addition to gaining access to the agricultural output of these countries, China also wanted to supply their markets with more affordable household appliances.

An important factor in China's rapid advance in this LAC subregion is the fact that since 2000, LAC had experienced a fundamental restructuring of its trade patterns, characterized by the redirection of trade flows previously directed towards the US and the EU towards Asia, where China has occupied a special place. The booming Chinese economy began to actively import soybeans, iron ore, sugar, coffee, and oil from Brazil, which in turn began to purchase

---

5 http://www.chinacelacforum.org/eng/.

various goods from China, such as electronics, textiles, cars, and mechanical products. From the Brazilian and Argentine perspectives, the reorientation towards China was marked by the commodity boom of the 2000s, when high world prices for raw materials led to the fact that their markets increasingly gravitated towards China, which had established itself as the world's main industrial power and which had already become a major buyer of this product categories. From the Chinese point of view, the "conquest" of Brazil and Argentina was dictated by the "Going Outward" policy that China began to develop and through which the Chinese government began to encourage its companies to internationalize.

US dominance in trade with LAC was undermined by the 2008 financial crisis and this contributed to the formation of complementarity between the economies of Brazil and China, ultimately leading to deepening of relations. In 2009, China overtook the US as Brazil's main trading partner and in 2024 it accounted for 31% of Brazilian exports and 21% of imports.[6] In 2023, the total value of Brazilian exports to China was $104 billion, while imports were a record $53 billion.[7] China has emerged as the main destination for Brazil's three most exported products: soybeans (73.1%), oil (46.6%) and iron ore (64.2%).

China's relations with Argentina followed a similar scenario. The Argentine economy, like Brazil's, is dependent on the sale of goods, especially soybeans and beef, which paved the way for increased interaction with China precisely when it had already become the world's largest consumer of commodities. By 2023, China had become the second largest destination for Argentine exports, second only to Brazil, and an important Argentine supplier (21.5% of all Argentine imports).

Brazil and Argentina became China's main trading partners in the region and cooperation in the investment sphere gradually began to develop. In the early 2000s, bilateral projects with Brazil worth more than $1 billion were launched. Since 2010, China has begun investing heavily in the Brazilian economy, reversing Beijing's trade focus which characterized the previous decade. It is estimated that China invested more than $66 billion in Brazil between 2007 and 2020, with 48% of this amount invested in the electricity sector and 28% in the oil and gas sector.[8]

---

6   https://portal.fgv.br/en/think-tank/trade-and-investment-bilateral-brazil-china-agenda.
7   https://comexdobrasil.com/brasil-e-china-batem-em-2023-recordes-da-serie-historica-no-comercio-bilateral/#:~:text=Maior%20parceiro%20comercial%20do%20Brasil%2C%20a%20China%20foi%20o%20destino,%2C8%25%20registrados%20em%202022.
8   https://oglobo.globo.com/economia/noticia/2023/08/28/investimento-chines-no-brasil-muda-de-perfil-atinge-recorde-de-projetos-e-tomba-78percent-em-valor-diz-cebc.ghtml.

Most of these investment projects are long-term, with the purchase of companies (for example, seven concessions from the energy companies Cobra, Elecnor and Isolux in 2010) or the large-scale financing of comprehensive projects (such as the participation of state-owned China National Offshore Oil Corporation (CNOOC) and China National Oil and Gas Exploration and Development Company) in partnership with Petrobrás to explore for oil and gas beneath salt deposits on the ocean floor. In the 2020s, Chinese investment has increased in Brazil's services and telecommunications sectors.

A similar trend was observed in Argentina. The 2010s were marked by an explosion of Chinese investment. 2010 was marked by the conclusion of a bilateral deal worth more than $10 billion covering the use of railways in Argentina. China also made progress in purchasing some of Argentina's strategic assets, acquiring the Argentine operations of Occidental Petroleum through China Petroleum & Chemical for $2.5 billion and 60% of Pan-American Energy through CNOOC for $7.1 billion. CNOOC also acquired 50% of Argentine oil company Bridas for $3.1 billion. As in Brazil, China has paid increased attention to investment in infrastructure in Argentina, with a strong emphasis on the energy sector. Notably, Argentina received more Chinese investment than Brazil in 2022 ($1.34 billion vs. $1.30 billion), which was the result of cooling relations between Brazilian President Jair Bolsonaro (2019–2022) and the Chinese government.[9]

Brazil is a priority for China in the LAC region because of the vast Brazilian market and joint membership in BRICS. By 2004, the partnership between China and Brazil had reached a new level. During the first presidency of Lula da Silva (2003–2011), the foreign policy concept of "uniting the giant countries" into a single strategic partnership increased in importance, which was aimed at restoring the balance of power that had been disrupted after the Cold War. As a result, BRIC was founded in 2006 with the participation of Brazil, Russia, India, and China. Later, initiated by Brazil, South Africa joined the bloc. The heads of Brazil and China, the heads of its foreign affairs departments, and a number of government agencies constantly communicate, making visits and organizing meetings. Interaction is actively developing at the BRICS, G-20 summits, and other international forums.

However, Brazil and Argentina do not have direct access to the Pacific Ocean, which prompted China to implement a project to create large-scale transoceanic transport corridors in LAC, where Chile and Peru were to play

---

9 https://automotivebusiness.com.br/pt/posts/noticias/china-expande-investimentos-na-argentina/.

the role of Pacific platforms that would provide stable transport links between China and the two South American giants.

Relations between China and Chile, which built its Pacific foreign policy strategy in the 1960s, developed differently from its Latin American neighbors. Chile pursued a policy of trade openness through the conclusion of FTAs with countries in other regions, forming a whole system of similar agreements, of which there were four dozen. By 2011, China had become the main importer of copper and iron ore from Chile, which managed to build trade with Beijing in such a way as to ensure a positive trade balance. Chile also supplies China with coal, molybdenum, cellulose, fishmeal, and lumber. China is the largest consumer of coal, and Chile is its main supplier. A similar situation was observed in Peru, which also supplied China with its copper and iron ore, in addition to fishmeal, which accounted for 70% of Peruvian exports to China. By 2010, Peru had become the leading destination for Chinese investment on the continent. Peru–China trade turnover exceeded $13 billion by 2012, which was the result of an increase in the number of Peruvian export-oriented enterprises.

Using a new transoceanic canal through Nicaragua, the Chinese planned to further consolidate their presence in the Western Hemisphere. During the presidency of Chavez, Venezuela also became a strategic partner of China. Beijing's relations with Mexico, which became the fourth country in LAC to establish official diplomatic relations with China, went much less smoothly. The first difficulties in establishing a bilateral dialogue emerged during the 1980s and 1990s. While China was laying the groundwork for its leapfrog development, dubbed the "Third Chinese Revolution," Mexico entered another phase of economic and social problems. In the 1980s, Mexican–Chinese trade turnover was characterized by a small surplus in favor of Mexico. From the first years of the 1990s there was an increasing surplus in favor of China, increasing exponentially every year (Kosevich, 2020).

The first tensions between Mexico and China were caused by the fact that the two countries became competitors in the production of low-cost, low-tech, low-wage, hand-made goods such as textiles and clothing, plastics and toys, leather and shoes, along with electronics. The level of wages for similar production in China was from three to seven times less than the payment of equivalent labor in Mexico. In 1993, Mexico introduced countervailing import duties and customs duties of more than 1000% on various products from China, which had already begun to crowd out Mexican production. Despite the different rates of economic growth of both countries, their bilateral trade has increased sharply since the 2000s. By 2010, the difference in the volumes of exports and imports had become enormous. Chinese imports to Mexico are 5.5 times greater than Mexican exports to China. It was precisely thanks to the growth in the volume of imported Chinese goods that by the end of the 2010s they accounted for more than 10% of all world trade. Economic cooperation was achieved by an agreement on a bilateral treaty for the protection and mutual promotion of investments, signed in July 2008 and ratified by the Mexican Senate in March 2009. That gave bilateral economic relations between Mexico and China a special dynamism and led to the creation in 2013 of the Integral Strategic Partnership agreed upon by Heads of State Enrique Peña Nieto and Xi Jinping. Although there is still no bilateral FTA agreed upon between Mexico and China, since 2003, China has become its second largest trading partner. China has also become an important market for some of the largest and most prominent Mexican companies, such as Bimbo (bakery products), Maseca (corn and wheat products), Nemak (auto parts), Softek (information technology), Grupo Kuo (chemical sector) and ICC (finishing materials), who worked through representative offices in China. Despite the zigzag relationship, China has already become Mexico's second-largest source of imports and the third destination for Mexican exports. Mexico continued to remain China's second largest trading partner among all Latin American countries, after Brazil. The main negative aspect of this relationship was that for every $1 that Mexico exported to China, China exported an average of $12 to Mexico.

This contrasted with the development of relations with Cuba. Since the 1990s, China has become Cuba's second most important trading partner. Cuba has become a supplier of traditional export goods to China: sugar, rum, and biotechnology. China sells cars, buses, electronics, televisions, and refrigerators to Cuba. Trade turnover in 2010 was a record $1.8 billion. In 2022, China exported goods worth $404 million to Cuba and imported $426 million, which was the first place among all Cuban partners.[10]

In 2011, China National Petroleum Corporation announced its intention to invest $6 billion to expand the Cienfuegos refinery, which was the largest deal in Cuban history. Even during the most difficult "special period" for the Cuban population, which came after the collapse of the USSR and the abrupt end of Soviet funding for Cuba, China demonstrated that it was not going to become a sponsor of Cuba. The situation that developed created the conditions for China to become one of the main creditors of Cuba, but the ideological component of the relationship did not affect it in any way. It is noteworthy that Cuba was inferior in terms of Chinese interest even when compared to Panama, which did not maintain diplomatic relations with China. Beijing's reluctance to become a donor to even ideologically similar regimes was manifested later with the

---

10   https://oec.world/en/profile/bilateral-country/chn/partner/cub.

President of Venezuela, Nicolas Maduro, to whom China refused to provide funding to plug holes in the budget at a critical moment for the country.

Since the beginning of the 21st century, LAC's relations with China have been developing dynamically in a variety of areas, pushing more and more LAC countries to be included in the orbit of global Chinese politics. A striking example is the visit on June 12, 2023, to Beijing by Xiomara Castro (2022–present), the President of Honduras, who severed relations with Taiwan in spring 2023. This was a truly significant event, since the issue of Taiwan remains extremely sensitive for China. Receiving the guest, the Chinese leader said that relations with Honduras were taking on an unprecedented meaning.

1.2 The Institutionalization of Cooperation

In 2008, China published the first White Paper on LAC Policy, which indicated the growing status of this region for Chinese diplomacy. This document defines the discursive framework of China's strategy in the region, which has been periodically repeated in China's diplomatic rhetoric towards the LAC (Abdenur, 2013). The White Paper enshrined a strategy that involved multidisciplinary cooperation, avoiding restrictions on several areas of potential partnership, which were not specified. Four areas are listed as areas of comprehensive cooperation between China and LAC: politics; economy; cultural and social sphere; peace, security, and justice.

These areas became the framework of the Chinese strategy, which were reflected in the institutionalization of cooperation, based on three principles (Mosquera, 2018). Firstly, the principle of institutional flexibility, which refers to the need for constant adaptation of agreements and projects, which requires continuous institutionalized dialogue. Secondly, the principle of non-unconditionality, which is a refusal to perceive the system of agreements and understandings created by Beijing with LAC as a rigid mechanism of cooperation that does not accept modifications. Thirdly, the principle of plurality, which encourages a variety of forms of dialogue which manifests in the diversification of institutional spheres of interaction.

The China–CELAC summits, created in 2014, is China's most significant institutional platform for developing its political relations with the LAC countries. This platform successfully complemented the doctrine of the "global network of partnerships" created in the same year on the sidelines of the Central Conference of the Communist Party of China on foreign policy. Within the framework of this doctrine, Beijing formed a special approach to the already existing network of 80 strategic partnerships with countries representing different regions. At the center of these relations was the idea of the progressive development of economic cooperation and the achievement of joint development.

The main mechanisms of interaction within the Forum include several levels: (1) ministerial meetings; (2) regular meetings of foreign ministers, which have become a key mechanism for cooperation in the forum; (3) meetings of senior officials; (4) consultations at the level of department heads; (5) forums and conferences in various professional fields: including the Forum of Ministers of Agriculture, the Forum of Young Politicians, the Forum of Friendship between Nations, the Forum for the Exchange of Think Tanks, the Entrepreneurs Summit, the Forum on Scientific and Technological Innovation, the Forum on Infrastructure Cooperation, and the Forum of Political Parties. Within the framework of the China-CELAC Forum there are eight subcommittees that regulate interaction in various areas of cooperation.

The first "China–Latin America" forum, held at the ministerial level, took place in January 2015 in Beijing. Based on the results of the event, three final documents were adopted: the Beijing Declaration of the First Ministerial Conference of the China-CELAC Forum, the Cooperation Plan between China and LAC countries for the period 2015–2019, and the rules for the establishment and functioning of the China-CELAC Forum. China announced a $35 billion funding package for LAC countries. The Chinese government also announced an increase in the number of scholarships and training places for CELAC member countries, and the first "Bridge for the Future" training and exchange camp, designed to exchange experiences between young Chinese and LAC leaders. The second ministerial meeting of the China-CELAC Forum took place in 2018 in Santiago, Chile. The third Forum, held in 2021, put forward five key principles for cooperation and published a Joint Action Plan for Cooperation in Key Areas between China and CELAC Member States for the period 2022–2024. The parties agreed to further expand and deepen cooperation and adhere to the principle of multilateralism. Gradually, the China-CELAC Forum has become a key intergovernmental platform for the development of cooperation. It is thanks to this forum that China and LAC are promoting and implementing programs, taking the agreements reached as a basis. Cooperation between the two sides has become deeper and more multifaceted.

The second important institution for the development of political dialogue was the Chinese-Latin American Community of Common Destiny. This mechanism was formed at the initiative of China. In 2013, Xi Jinping proposed a new foreign policy concept called the "Community of of Common Destiny and Mankind" (人类命运共同体), which was focused on achieving five main goals: building lasting peace through dialogue; creating an environment of security through common efforts; building a world of shared prosperity based on mutually beneficial cooperation; creating an inclusive and open world; and the gradual transition to green and low-carbon development.[11] According to this concept, people all over the world are united by a common future, and therefore, each country must take part in ensuring this future is bright. In Xi's "community of common destiny," a special place was given to LAC countries. In July 2014, Xi delivered a keynote speech at a meeting between China and LAC leaders, proposing to develop a model of cooperation that would promote the creation of a "Community of Common Destiny and Mankind". The main task of this Community is the creation of a common value base between China and LAC, which will not accept any manifestation of hegemony and power politics. Thus, Xi said that China and LAC "will cooperate in improving global governance, maintaining international order and commitment to multilateralism, and promote the formation of a new model of global politics."[12] The Chinese-LAC Community of Common Destiny includes two main directions: providing financial support to LAC countries as part of the Belt and Road initiative put forward by Xi in 2013–2014 and the development of cooperation in science and technology.

In relation to this interaction, the results of a survey conducted in 2018 are indicative. The Center for Peruvian Studies at Hebei Normal University conducted a study in Peru entitled "China through Peruvian Eyes" To the question "what exactly is China associated with among the residents of Peru", where the Chinese presence is felt extremely strongly, respondents answered as follows: 50.0% with the economy, 25.9% with science and technology, 7.4% with culture, 3.7% with the social sphere, and only 1.9% with politics. This shows that science and technology are noticeably more significant for Peruvians than the political, cultural and social spheres, which is the result of the important place of these areas of cooperation initially occupied in the Belt and Road Initiative and the China-LAC Community of Common Destiny.

In 2012, at the initiative of China, the Forum of Young Politicians of China and LAC was created.[13] Formed jointly by the Central Committee of the Communist Youth League, youth organizations of major political parties, and the government departments of youth of LAC countries, this policy dialogue aimed to promote exchanges between young leaders of China and LAC in order

---

11 «A Global Community of Shared Future: China's Proposals and Actions», Ministry of Foreign Affairs of the People's Republic of China, September, 2023, https://www.mfa.gov.cn/eng/zxxx_662805/202309/t20230926_11150122.html.
12 https://baijiahao.baidu.com/s?id=1707871484012200185&wfr=spider&for=pc.
13 http://www.chinacelacforum.org/esp/zyjz_2/zylyflt/zlqnzzjlt/201507/t20150706_6803203.htm.

to lay the social foundations for the development of China-LAC relations. In May of the following year, the First Forum was held in Beijing, in which 50 young politicians took part. Since then, such an event has been held every year.

In December 2015, the first China-CELAC Political Parties Forum was held in Beijing, aimed at promoting dialogue between different political parties representing both sides. The forum, which is held every three years, has become an innovative form of communication between Chinese and LAC political parties to promote high-level multilateral and strategic dialogue, to enhance the exchange of experience at the party and government level, and to enhance mutual understanding and mutual trust.

The formats of cooperation between Chinese and LAC banks should be highlighted separately. In 2005, a network of Chinese banks began to form, which provided loans to LAC countries. Until that year, there had been no such cooperation. Between 2005 and 2011, Chinese banks lent $75 billion to LAC, of which the China Development Bank accounted for about 82%, the Export-Import Bank of China 12%, and the Industrial and Commercial Bank of China 6%.[14] In 2010 alone, China provided $37 billion in loans to LAC, which was more than the total amount of loans provided by the Inter-American Development Bank (IDB) and the World Bank (WB). Compared to Western countries, Chinese loans are mainly aimed at infrastructure construction and heavy industries such as energy, mining, transportation, and real estate.

The establishment of the China-LAC Business Summit was initiated by the China Council for the Promotion of International Trade in November 2007, which became China's first institutional platform for the development of economic and trade cooperation in the region. A year later, the Chinese government published the White Paper on LAC Policy, which outlines important channels for the development of trade and economic relations. In early 2015, a summit was included in the Cooperation Plan between China and LAC for the period 2015–2019 and became an institutional event in the trade and economic sphere within the China-CELAC Forum. The China-LAC Business Summit is held once a year alternately in China and LAC.

The China–LAC Development Financial Cooperation Mechanism, established in April 2019, has provided strong financial impetus to China–LAC economic and trade cooperation. The China Development Bank led the formation of this partnership, which became the first multilateral mechanism for financial cooperation between China and LAC. This mechanism was aimed at facilitating the signing of currency swap agreements between Argentina,

---

14   https://www.un.org/zh/node/137339.

Brazil, and other countries with China, facilitating the internationalization of the yuan.¹⁵

In 2015, the 1st China–LAC Infrastructure Cooperation Forum was held, which was the first professional sub-forum in the China-CELAC forum. It was organized by the Chinese Ministry of Commerce, the China International Contractors Association, and the Macau Trade and Investment Promotion Institute. This platform promoted new dialogue on infrastructure in LAC, where the participation of Chinese companies is increasing, and the scope of cooperation continues to expand. The 1st forum was attended by more than 700 people from government departments, financial institutions, industry associations, and businesses from China and LAC. The event was attended by the Costa Rican Vice President and Minister of Finance, the Bahaman Vice Prime Minister and Minister of Labor and Urban Development, and other high-level representatives from 12 LAC countries and the Inter-American Development Bank.¹⁶

China actively invites LAC countries to participate in the China International Import Expo (CIIE), the world's first national-level import exhibition, which has been held annually in the fall since 2018 in China. Several LAC countries are taking part in this event, hoping that it will become another trade link connecting them with China.¹⁷ For example, the first CIIE was attended by about 100 Brazilian companies and 60 Mexican companies operating in food and beverages, logistics, transportation, information technology, and other areas.

An important place in the structure of interethnic dialogue between China and LAC is occupied by a network of institutions in the educational and cultural sphere. In this regard, the creation in 2017 of the Dialogue between the Civilizations of China and LAC Forum, the formation of which was initiated by the Institute of Latin American Studies of the Chinese Academy of Social Sciences, stands out. This forum is focused on simplifying communications in the field of humanities in order to eliminate obstacles created as a result of existing civilizational differences between the parties. The specific objectives are to eliminate misconceptions and stereotypes about China, promote Chinese values, and promote the development of more diverse cooperation. Although by early 2024, 22 Latin American countries had signed a memorandum of understanding to cooperate with Beijing under the Belt and Road Initiative, ongoing changes in the political landscape of the LAC countries have had a negative impact on the overall trajectory of cooperation between China

---

15   https://www.gov.cn/xinwen/2019-04/22/content_5385158.htm.
16   2005 至 2020 年间，中国在拉美基建投资超 940 亿美元 (br-cn.com).
17   http://www.xinhuanet.com/world/2018-10/20/c_1123587952.htm.

and this region. As Yuan Chengdong from the Chinese Academy of Humanities emphasizes, it is to bridge the gaps in the complex Sino-Latin American interaction that the Dialogue between the Civilizations of China and LAC was created, an important aspect of which is the elimination of institutional restrictions.[18]

Following the goal of "bringing nations closer together," China is expanding the system of government scholarships and the network of Confucius Institutes. As of 2018, China has provided government scholarships to 31 LAC countries. The number of LAC students coming to China to study is also growing rapidly: in 2002 there were only 588 students; in 2018 it was estimated at 10,241. As of 2020, China has opened 43 Confucius Institutes and 7 Confucius Programs in 24 LAC countries, promoting Chinese culture in the Western Hemisphere.[19]

In 2021, the China–LAC Think Tank Forum was established as a new diplomatic tool to enhance the potential of cooperation.[20] The same year Shanghai hosted the China–LAC Youth Development Forum, organized by the All-China Youth Federation and Shanghai International Studies University. The objectives of the forum were to deepen mutual understanding among young people, promote cooperation in the field of education, and to promote dialogue at the level of civil society.[21]

In the post-pandemic period, China has revised its institutionalization strategy in LAC. The new version of Chinese policy was based on the need to quickly adapt to new changes that affected different levels of cooperation. From this point on, China's focus on the development of LAC countries, the expansion of the governance space to further promote greater development of infrastructural interconnectivity, and the formation of more competitive geo-economic advantages of China against developed countries, became increasingly clear.[22]

1.3 *Military-Technical Cooperation*

One of the areas in the overall Chinese foreign policy strategy in LAC has become military and military-technical cooperation, which currently plays a relatively modest role in the overall system of Beijing's priorities in the region. China's activities in developing military-technical cooperation with LAC countries are receiving unreasonably wide coverage, which is explained by the

---

18   iolaw.cssn.cn/xszl/gjfio/zglm/201910/t20191021_5017764.shtml.
19   中国和拉美教育交流与合作60年_进展、问题及策略—道客巴巴 (doc88.com)
20   https://baijiahao.baidu.com/s?id=1716677064676727058&wfr=spider&for=pc.
21   https://sghexport.shobserver.com/html/baijiahao/2021/10/24/568719.html.
22   ilas.cssn.cn/xschengguo/xslunwen/202111/t20211126_5377444.shtml.

growing fears of the US, which is seeking to maintain its primacy in this region (Kashin, 2024).

The key goals of the Chinese policy of gradually including LAC countries in military-technical cooperation are supporting Chinese economic interests, and strengthening China's negotiating power in its global agenda (Agramont, 2021). The main factors influencing the intensification of ties in this area can be divided into two groups: economic, which include China's desire to gain greater access to the resources of LAC countries and the progressive increase in Chinese investments in the region, which cover more and more areas; and geopolitical factors such as the technological war with Washington, and Beijing's intentions to gradually balance out US military power.

The emergence in the 1990s of China as a major naval power with a fleet with a global presence, led to Chinese naval ships regularly visiting LAC countries. The first visits to the region by Chinese warships occurred in 1997 and 2002, predating the overall expansion of China's presence in LAC. Since 2009, visits by Chinese warships have become regular, usually sailing to ports in Peru, Chile, Argentina, and Brazil.

In 2003, LAC countries began receiving regular visits from high-ranking Chinese military delegations. This year, the first Chinese delegation, including members of the Central Military Commission, visited nine LAC countries for the first time. In 2009, a regular practice of mutual visits by defense ministers and chiefs of staff began. Venezuela, Ecuador, Chile, Mexico, Brazil, Colombia, Peru, Bolivia, and Cuba are the most involved in such exchanges. The number of lower-level Chinese military visits to LAC countries has grown exponentially in recent years: from 2000 to 2022 more than 200 such visits were made to the region, during which issues of cooperation in training military personnel and the possibility of Chinese naval ships visiting the region were discussed.

Since the mid-2000s, China has been the host country for the programs to upgrade the training of the military and police from LAC countries. Nearly two dozen LAC countries have sent their officers to Chinese military institutions for training, and members of the Chinese People's Liberation Army (PLA) also visit countries in the region to undergo training and exchange experiences. Long-term cooperation agreements were concluded between military colleges in LAC and China. It is noteworthy that Chile and Colombia, which are traditional partners of the US in the field of security and defense, are participating in cooperation with China in this area.

In 2009, an agreement was reached between China and Brazil to train a group of Chinese officers on the only Brazilian aircraft carrier, the Sao Paolo. This cooperation helped China, which at that time was building its first aircraft carrier, Liaoning, gain direct experience in managing such ships. Russia had refused such cooperation with China. Although the number of LAC military personnel training in China has been very modest, even these limited contacts have raised concerns in the US, which views such partnerships as the Chinese government's intelligence-gathering practices about LAC.

In 2010, the first joint military medical exercises were held with the armed forces of China and Peru, which opened the door to the practice of conducting joint military exercises. The next year, joint anti-terrorism exercises of airborne troops were held with Venezuela, and in 2012, anti-terrorism exercises with Argentina. In 2013, joint naval exercises between China and Chile took place. In the summer of 2022, officially unconfirmed reports appeared about China preparing jointly with Iran and Russia for exercises in the territorial waters of Venezuela.

In the 2010s, attempts to institutionalize China's military ties with LAC countries began (Mantilla Baca, 2015). An important precedent in this direction was the China–LAC Forum in the field of military logistics, held in October 2015 in Beijing. Eleven Latin American countries took part in this event, which has become regular. The concept of bilateral dialogue has come to characterize conferences involving high-level delegations from China and LAC to discuss broader issues related to international security. The fifth forum with the participation of 24 LAC countries was held in December 2022.[23] The Chinese Minister of National Defense, Wei Fenghe, made a speech noting that the relations between China and LAC reaching a new level contributes to the construction of a "community of common destiny"—one of the ruling principles of Xi Jinping.

China has failed to take over as a supplier of military personnel for UN peacekeeping operations in LAC. The only example of such cooperation in the field of peacekeeping was the participation of Chinese civilian police officers in the multinational peacekeeping force in Haiti, 2004–2010.

It is significant that the military sphere is mentioned in the Chinese 2019 White Paper on National Defense as one of the important areas for the development of China–LAC relations.[24] The document emphasizes that China has experience in cooperation with this region in terms of providing assistance in the development of the armed forces and defense capabilities, partnership in the training of military personnel, and the development of contacts between officers.

---

23 http://www.chinacelacforum.org/esp/zgtlgtgx_2/202212/t20221215_10990788.htm.
24 China's National Defense in the New Era. 2019. http://english.scio.gov.cn/node_8013 506.html#:~:text=In%20the%20new%20era%2C%20China,RMA%20and%20the%20 demands%20of.

In LAC, only one Chinese facility has appeared that can be indirectly associated with the Chinese military—the Espacio Lejano deep space tracking station in Argentina, created in 2012—the official task of which is space exploration, including by the Chinese. This is the first Chinese ground station for the study of deep space built outside China. Legally, this ground station belongs to the National Space Administration of China and is part of the Chinese deep space network. However, virtually all infrastructure that supports China's national space program is typically managed by the Space Systems Bureau of the People's Liberation Army Strategic Support Force. This worries the US, which calls this station, and in particular the 450-ton antenna installed there, a Chinese spy structure.[25]

Since the beginning of the 2000s, what has stood out is China's desire to expand its presence in the arms market of LAC countries. In this policy direction, Beijing has used more advanced forms of cooperation, such as joint scientific development in dual-use technologies (with Brazil), and the transfer of defense technologies (with Argentina). China's willingness to share defense technology is being welcomed by Brazil and Argentina, which are seeking greater industrial self-sufficiency, including in security matters.

The main factor that has a negative impact on the flow of Chinese weapons into LAC was the regional policy of the countries which mutually avoid any territorial conflicts. With the exception of Brazil and Chile, all LAC countries have gradually reduced their expenditure on arms imports over the past decades,[26] and both of these arms markets are effectively closed to China. All this explains the general downward trend in the number of new Chinese arms export deals in LAC in recent years.

However, in 2015, China temporarily became the main supplier of weapons in LAC. There were four main partners which purchased Chinese weapons in significant quantities: Venezuela, where since 2015 China has become the main arms seller, displacing Russia, then Bolivia, Peru, and Ecuador. Venezuela acquired light armored vehicles, radar stations, transport and combat training aircraft, and anti-tank weapons from China. Bolivia purchased combat training aircraft, anti-tank missile systems, helicopters and light armored vehicles from China. Peru bought light and medium transport aircraft, and Ecuador bought trainers and light attack aircraft. All four countries have purchased artillery systems. Transactions with other countries in the region, in particular Argentina, Guyana, and Mexico, were inconsistent and ad hoc. For example,

---

25 https://dialogo-americas.com/es/articles/argentina-estacion-espacial-china-sigue-despertando-sospechas/.
26 Stockholm International Peace Research Institute (SIPRI) datas.

Mexico bought 2 batteries for 105 mm howitzers from China, the Bahamas received two armored vehicles as assistance, and Argentina purchased four Chinese-made armored personnel carriers for its UN peacekeepers.

The peak of Chinese arms sales in LAC, reached in 2015, has not been repeated. Since 2016, a gradual decline in Chinese arms exports to LAC began. The last known large shipment of Chinese weapons to the region occurred in 2018, when China donated ten armored vehicles to Bolivia. This was also caused by the ongoing economic crisis in Venezuela, once the main buyer of Chinese military products in LAC, the failure of several major deals with Argentina, and the lack of interest in Chinese weapons from other large countries in the region. US interference often hinders Chinese exporters in their quest to expand their presence in LAC. For example, the US essentially disrupted the deal for the supply of Chinese MVT-2000 tanks to Peru, previously agreed upon in 2009.

China's very limited presence in the LAC arms market is pushing Beijing towards the free supply of weapons systems in the form of military aid or selling them at discounts. China has donated military trucks and jeeps, uniforms, tents, engineering equipment, and field hospitals to Bolivia, Guyana, Colombia, and Peru. In 2018, the Argentine government received $18 million in military aid from China in the form of military vehicles. China is trying to use defense technology transfer to expand its presence in the Argentine market. In 2015, Argentine President Cristina Fernandez de Kirchner (2007–2015), during her visit to China, signed a memorandum of understanding on the joint production of VN1 armored personnel carriers and P18 corvettes to strengthen the potential of the Argentine armed forces. However, this project was never realized due to Argentina's economic instability. The deal to supply Argentina with a squadron of modern Chinese–Pakistani fourth-generation FC-1 fighters, which involved the purchase of ten single-seat and two double-seat fighters with a small number of air-to-air missiles from China for $665 million, was not implemented. The negotiations, which began in 2013, were frozen in December 2022 by the Argentine government for economic reasons. Unlike Africa and Asia, the presence of Chinese private security companies in Latin America is extremely limited.

China's cooperation with LAC in dual-use technologies is developing in a much more positive way. The successful and long-term Chinese–Brazilian satellite program to study the Earth's resources stands out. The CBERS project started in the late 1980s, and the practical result of the interaction between the parties was the launch of six satellites, which took place in the period 1999–2019. The program was co-financed equally by the two countries. The effectiveness of this program is confirmed by the evolution of the launched satellites: in the period 1999–2003 satellites model CBERS-1 and CBERS-2 were launched from Earth; in 2007, the improved CBERS-2B satellite was launched; in 2013–2019 parties launched second generation satellites (CBERS-3, CBERS-4 and CBERS-4a). All CBERS satellites were launched into orbit using Chinese CZ-4B launch vehicles from China's Taiyuan Satellite Launch Center. Participation in this program was important for both countries. For Brazil, the CBERS project was important in terms of its new global projection as a world power. While the West was unwilling to share dual-use technology, Brazil, at the expense of China, was expanding the list of its counterparties in the field of space exploration. In addition, satellite imagery of the Earth has been made available free of charge to developing countries to help solve practical problems, such as better methods of combating landslides. For China, participation in the satellite program has improved its domestic industrial base and has also provided incentives for the development of China's Ziyuan series of Earth observation satellites. This successful 30-year cooperation under the CBERS program, which is a civilian dual-use technology project, has become an important example for the entire LAC region in the implementation of complex technology projects with China.

The Brazilian transnational aerospace corporation Embraer S.A. and the Chinese state-owned aerospace and defense conglomerate, Aviation Industry Corporation of China, agreed to jointly produce passenger aircraft. However, this project was subsequently frozen.

In addition to Brazil, other LAC countries have also developed cooperation with China in the space sector. In 2008, a contract was signed between the Chinese company Great Wall Industries Corporation and Venezuela to design, build, and launch the Simon Bolivar telecommunications satellite. The project cost $406 million. A little later, a similar contract was concluded with Bolivia for the construction and launch of the Tupac Katari satellite. The $300 million project was 95% financed by a loan issued by the China Development Bank. In 2012, Venezuela purchased two Earth remote sensing satellites (VRSS-1, VRSS-2) from China. With Argentina, China implemented a project for the licensed production of Chinese Z-11 helicopters, which were unlicensed copies of the French AS350 Écureuil helicopters. In 2012, the first flight of Chinese helicopter models assembled in Argentina took place.

Of particular importance for China across LAC has been the export of smart-city and safe-city technologies, including new technical solutions for urban and border surveillance and security-related software and equipment. In 2007, Mexico began large-scale purchases of Chinese urban surveillance equipment. In 2012, Ecuador received a $250 million Chinese loan to build a nationwide surveillance system using Chinese equipment and software. The project built a nationwide network of 4,300 facial recognition cameras serving 3,000 employees from 16 centers across the country. To improve the capabilities of the system, the Chinese side provided assistance to Ecuador in the construction of an AI research laboratory. This laboratory, built and opened in less than two months, is part of a $10 million non-repayable loan provided by the Chinese government. The AI laboratory operates at the ECU 911 base in Quito, as part of the internal security management model implemented by Ecuador with the cooperation and technical and technological assistance of China.[27]

The effective cooperation between Ecuador and China in this area has led to Bolivia, Uruguay, Venezuela, Panama, and Argentina also deciding to implement large surveillance systems provided by Chinese companies.

The growing dependence of LAC countries' internal security services on Chinese technology is driven primarily by LAC governments' desire to reduce the risks of potential US interference in key security systems. China actively encourages and promotes the export of surveillance technologies at the highest level. For example, the AI research laboratory mentioned above was officially opened by Chinese President Xi Jinping.

The Chinese military and defense-industrial presence in LAC has a political significance for China, being aimed at establishing closer ties with military leaders of other countries, primarily through regular forums and seminars. This format of communication is intended to contribute to the achievement of China's broader political goals in the region. The rapidly developing cooperation in the field of dual-use technologies (especially in the field of space technologies and surveillance technologies) has led to the fact that a number of LAC countries have already become dependent on Chinese technologies in these strategic sectors. At present, China has not become the leading supplier of weapons to the LAC region, and its attempts to build a defense-industrial partnership with the countries of the region have ended in failure. China's intentions to establish a permanent military presence in this region were also unsuccessful.

From its early stages, China's cooperation with LAC in the military-technical sphere has been of serious concern to Washington. The White House fears that military ties between LAC and China will be built as quickly and unexpectedly as the Chinese economic presence in the region. This is pushing Washington to introduce new initiatives to expand its own military presence in LAC. The

---

27   http://spanish.xinhuanet.com/2018-01/19/c_136906504.htm.

Chinese factor played an important role in giving Colombia the status of major non-NATO ally in 2022.[28]

∙ ∙ ∙

Chinese–LAC interaction began in the 19th century. During the 1970–1990s China was virtually not present in the LAC region as a noticeable actor, but still managed to create the foundation for the later intensification of its presence, mainly in political ties and scientific and technical cooperation. Since the late 1990s, China has been pursuing a comprehensive strategy to increase its economic, political, and military presence in LAC. This strategy is designed to use the region's potential to develop the Chinese economy. However, China's defense cooperation with LAC is still limited and is intended to maintain political relations. Beijing is developing it gradually, avoiding steps that could cause too strong a reaction from the US. It is the clearly defined pragmatism in China's foreign policy towards LAC, characteristic of the 1970s, that continues in the 21st century.

2   Chinese Trade and Investment Presence in LAC: Main Spheres of Influence

The late 1970s marked the beginning of rapid growth for the Chinese economy, which ultimately allowed China to join the World Trade Organization (WTO) in December 2001. This gave impetus to China's development of new trade and economic partnerships with different global regions, which was facilitated by China's reduction of tariffs and the overall liberalization of its trade regime. One of the new areas of trade interaction was LAC, which received a special impetus after a reduction in the Chinese customs duties on raw materials imported from LAC. After China's accession to the WTO, the volume of Chinese exports began to increase by leaps and bounds, in 2009 surpassing Germany as the biggest exporter. This led to China becoming the largest net importer of oil, and the world's largest consumer of many types of raw materials, such as copper, iron, zinc which are goods that China had purchased from the least developed countries of Africa and the Asia-Pacific region and which it relatively recently began purchasing from LAC.

---

28   https://www.cancilleria.gov.co/newsroom/news/estatus-colombia-aliado-estrategico-no-miembro-otan-eeuu-no-solo-significa-alianza.

TABLE 5 Volume of trade turnover between China and Latin American countries (US dollars, billions)

Country	2000	2011	2022
Argentina	1,954	16,6	25,43
Brazil	2,426	79,32	157,4
Bolivia	0,075	1,448	3,32
Venezuela	0,219	6,989	3,033
Colombia	0,385	10,16	20,86
Mexico	3,188	58,21	129,5
Suriname	0,012	0,116	0,196
Guyana	0,018	0,113	0,99
Ecuador	0,134	3,517	13,52
Peru	0,731	13,33	33,22
Uruguay	0,203	1,964	4,75
Chile	1,851	31,26	64,8

SOURCE: UN COMTRADE DATABASE

2.1 Trade

In the early 2000s, China's trade turnover with LAC was extremely limited. Just five years later, however, trade began to grow at a rapid pace. By 2023, China had become the leading trading partner for nine economies in the region: Argentina, Brazil, Chile, Peru, Uruguay, Venezuela, Bolivia, Paraguay, and Cuba. In terms of trade across the entire LAC region, China has become the second-largest trading partner, after the US (Table 5).

Chile, Peru, and Costa Rica have become conduits for Chinese business in LAC by concluding FTAs with China. Chile was the first country in the region to sign an FTA in 2005, which made Chile the main exporter of copper to China.

For China, the difficult negotiations with Chile on the conclusion of the FTA became an important stage in building an effective LAC strategy, taking pragmatic national interests as a basis. China's only experience in implementing FTAs had been in the Association of Southeast Asian Nations (ASEAN). Chile was the first LAC country to recognize China as a market economy, while supporting Beijing's entry into the WTO. The Chilean experience in conducting foreign trade negotiations also played an important role: Chile had already entered into FTAs with the US, the EU, Canada, and several other LAC countries. For Chile at that time, China was seen as the entrance to the Asia-Pacific region, where Santiago sought to expand its presence. Both sides appealed to the existence of special historical relations between the countries: Chile had already had a consular representative in Hong Kong in 1842. By 2010, China had become Chile's leading trading partner, where 24% of the country's global exports were sent. However, the trade structure remained unchanged: the absolute predominance of copper in Chilean sales (more than 80%). The FTA led to more favorable terms, while opening up space for other goods that, although insignificant in the overall statistics, were extremely important in terms of their impact on Chilean development. In 2014, the Chile–Hong Kong FTA was signed, which sought to open up vast opportunities for both sides in trade and services.

An FTA between Peru and China was signed in April 2009, and entered into force in March 2010. In contrast to ties with other countries, relations between Peru and China rely on the mass of Chinese migrants, especially from the Guangdong Province, who arrived in Peru in the 19th century. These historical ties ultimately contributed to the development of modern bilateral relations. The FTA between Peru and China is believed to be the first comprehensive FTA signed by China with a LAC country. In addition to trade liberalization, it included an agreement on customs cooperation and a memorandum of understanding and cooperation in employment and job security. In addition to estimating the growth of trade exchanges, the FTA was a catalyst for increasing Chinese investment in Peru, as exemplified by the exploitation of the Toromocho and Las Bambas mines by Chinese companies. In January 2014, ICBC Peru Bank, a subsidiary of the Industrial and Commercial Bank of China, the largest bank in the world by capital, opened offices in Peru.

Costa Rica signed an FTA with Beijing in August 2011, just four years after it recognized China diplomatically. With this move, all of Taiwan's pre-existing dominance in Central America was undermined, making Costa Rica in many ways a springboard for Chinese political actions in the Central American region. A large share of Costa Rica's exports to China are fruit, leather, and dairy products. In 2014, China became Costa Rica's second largest trading partner after the US. Exports from Costa Rica to China increased from $91 million (in 2000) to $1.5 billion (in 2011). Unlike Nicaragua, China's strategy in Costa Rica has a clearly commercial nature, with a minimal political component. As the impetus for the relationship with Costa Rica came from China, it had to make a number of concessions.

In May 2022, Ecuador and China signed an FTA online. This trade agreement had been discussed for more than 10 months with four rounds of negotiations and dozens of technical meetings. In 2023, Nicaragua became the fifth Latin

American country to sign an FTA with China.²⁹ Managua and Beijing began trade talks to finalize a deal after agreeing on an early harvest deal in 2022. Colombia and Panama are also trying to follow this path, which is currently hampered by a lack of domestic political consensus.

Chile, Peru, and Costa Rica, the first in the region to sign FTAs with China, reported extremely positive results in terms of increasing mutual trade turnover. In these cases, the predominant flow of trade was determined by just a few types of goods—natural resources and mining.

The hopes of LAC countries to increase Chinese investment after the conclusion of the FTA were not justified, since the logic of investment activity does not always fit in with the logic of building trade flows. Increasing Chinese demand for a number of goods supplied by LAC, such as food products and manufacturing parts, while reflecting insignificant amounts in the total volume of exchange, represented important profit items for local LAC economies. For example, for Peru, the first five years after the signing of the FTA with China were marked by Peruvian agricultural exports to China increasing from $33 million (2010) to $142 million (2014). Exports of bottled Chilean wine to China reached $100 million per year by 2015, and cherry exports are estimated at $240 million. Progress has also been made in trade between China and Costa Rica. Despite the fact that these figures seem insignificant compared to the total volumes of exports to China from Peru and Chile, the FTAs had an extremely positive impact on LAC SME exporters who dared to enter the Chinese market. Thanks to the FTAs, the growing demand of the Chinese population, especially the middle class, for higher quality food products has created new commercial niches that LAC countries are seeking to satisfy.

The development of the first FTAs between China and LAC countries coincided with another initiative promoted by China aimed at boosting foreign trade: the China–LAC Business Summit, which is held annually, alternating between China and LAC. The first Summit took place in November 2007 in Chile, during the first presidency of Michelle Bachelet (2006–2010), who declared there that China had become Chile's main trading partner. About 400 people took part in this event.

These activities, which were seen by the LAC side as promising in terms of new deals, were, in reality, more likely to be a politically oriented mechanism consistent with China's overall strategy towards the LAC region. These activities, which were touted by LAC as particularly promising in terms of the possibility of agreeing on new trade deals, in reality rather represented a

---

29   The agreement entered into force in 2024.

mechanism with a clearly political orientation, developing in accordance with China's overall strategy in LAC.

China has repeatedly demonstrated its intentions to expand the FTA network, especially with the LAC countries whose economies are already highly diversified. However, not all countries are ready to take such steps, because it would jeopardize local producers who could not compete with an influx of cheap Chinese products. Despite the absence of an FTA, by 2010 China had already become Brazil's main trading partner, and the second largest trading partner of Argentina and Colombia.

At the beginning of 2023, the head of Brazil put forward an initiative to conclude an agreement on a free trade zone between China and MERCOSUR. However, the lack of progress in agreeing on such an agreement between MERCOSUR and the EU, which has lasted for decades, suggests that the implementation of this initiative is only possible in the long term. The proposal made to South America's leading trading bloc by Chinese Prime Minister Wen Jiabao in 2012 to create a free trade area between China and MERCOSUR ultimately remains unanswered.[30]

The sharp increase in trade turnover between China and LAC, which marked the 2000s, led to the fact that the countries of the region were able to significantly increase their foreign exchange potential, which also contributed to an increase in their influence in world politics. Between 1999 and 2008, total trade (exports plus imports) increased almost twelvefold, reaching $150 billion. At the same time, Chinese imports from LAC, primarily raw materials and food, noticeably exceeded Chinese exports to the countries of this region. Most LAC countries experienced phenomenal economic growth. However, in the 2010s, the situation changed. The slowdown in the growth rate of the Chinese economy, and the beginning of a greater focus on its domestic market, led to a progressive slowdown in China's activity in the LAC. The result of a gradual decline in world oil prices, which began in 2014, which was influenced by the overproduction of energy resources in the US and the drop in demand from China, meant that by 2016 the price of oil fell by almost half. This negatively affected the revenue of the largest LAC oil-producing corporations—the Mexican PEMEX, the Brazilian PETROBRAS, and the Venezuelan PDVSA. The interest of leading countries in investing in oil production also declined. After the commodity boom that drove the region's development from 2000 to 2015 ended, all LAC countries experienced economic contraction or at least more modest

---

30   "Los Tratados de Libre Comercio de China en América Latina: Desarrollo y Perspectivas". Fernando Reyes Matta file:///C:/Users/Ekaterina/Downloads/1448450616Fernando_Reyes_Matta.pdf

growth. In addition, the influx of cheap Chinese goods destroyed entire sectors of LAC industry, which was especially evident in Argentina, where Chinese companies developed local markets, gradually displacing local producers.

The share of LAC in China's foreign economic relations, which had shown steady growth since the 2000s, is still modest: in 2021 it was estimated at 7%. Between 2000 and 2021, trade in goods between China and LAC increased 25-fold. China, whose trade with the LAC is worth more than $450 billion, has managed to outpace the US, whose commercial exchanges with the region are valued at $295 billion. LAC has already become the leading supplier of certain commodities to China, such as sales of soybeans, which are a socially important product for the Chinese population. In the export of soybeans to China, as a key raw material for the Chinese food industry, Brazil, which is the largest exporter of this product, occupied a special place. In 2017, soybean production in Brazil reached a record of 75.3 million tons, of which 90% was exported to China.[31] China imports more than 77% of LAC soybean exports. Agricultural exports from LAC to China have become an important item of mutual trade, which has changed the geography of foreign economic interests of individual LAC countries. For example, by 2020, China had emerged as the dominant force in Chilean trade—trade with this country was double that of the US and Europe combined. In 2021, Chile became the largest exporter of fruit to China. An important factor positively affecting the rapid growth of trade between the LAC and China was the deterioration of relations of Beijing with the US, Canada, and Australia, which led to a reorientation of China towards purchasing LAC raw materials.

China's relations with Colombia were also developing rapidly by the 2020s. Colombia was already one of China's leading partners in LAC, exporting coal in significant quantities, which predetermined the continuous growth of trade turnover. Beijing built relations with Bogota very carefully. Between 1998 and 2004, Colombia's exports to China increased by almost 10%, which was twice as fast as Venezuela's exports. In the early 2000s, with waning US attention to LAC countries, the Chinese Defense Minister met with representatives of the Colombian armed forces. However, Colombia continued to be one of Washington's key allies in the region, even as the overarching US relationship with LAC faltered amid the leftward turn. For example, during his trip to Latin America in 2004, Hu Jintao did not visit Colombia because he did not want to be seen interfering with the US's closest ally LAC. This approach led to the fact that by 2010, Colombia–China trade turnover was already $5 billion,

---

31   Embrapa em numerous //https://www.embrapa.br.

which made China the second largest trading partner after the US. For China, Colombia played the role of a gateway to the rest of LAC, which was predetermined by its geographical location. This was confirmed by the desire of China to build a railway in the country that would connect the port of Cartagena, located on the Atlantic, with the Pacific Ocean, which was considered a land alternative to the Panama Canal. The cost of this project was $7.5 billion, which was to be financed by the Chinese Development Bank.

On the other hand, we can identify several weaknesses that characterize the system of bilateral trade between China and LAC. Firstly, there is the limited structure of exports and imports. Most of the LAC export basket to China consists of a limited number of commodities: soybeans, copper, and iron ore. On the Chinese side, exports to LAC are dominated by factory-made products. This makes trading unstable and dependent on changing market conditions. Secondly, trade with China is poorly diversified. For example, only four LAC countries (Brazil, Argentina, Chile, Uruguay) provide agricultural exports to China. Thirdly, mutual trade is carried out at the local level and asymmetrically. For example, LAC manufacturers of finished products have not been able to enter the Chinese market, which is explained by the fact that the reduction in customs duties on goods imported into China from LAC applied mainly to raw materials.

2.2 *Investment*

By 2022, LAC had become China's second-largest overseas investment destination and the third-largest market for the overseas projects of Chinese companies, according to Chinese sources.[32] Beijing's well-thought-out investment strategy, which went through several stages, led to similar results.

The first Chinese projects in the oil sector of LAC appeared in Peru. In 1993, the National Petroleum Corporation of China won the tender to develop block 7 of the Peruvian Talara field. This was the first time that a Chinese oil company developed an overseas field by participating in international tenders. In 1995, the company received the right to develop block 6 of the same field.[33]

A landmark date was 2004, when President Hu, during the APEC Summit, then held in Chile, gave rise to a new stage in China–LAC relations. Hu announced Beijing's plans to invest $100 billion in LAC in the 2000s, which marked Beijing's change from its low-profile policy towards the region, in which Chinese investments had not exceeded a few billion dollars.

---

32   http://world.people.com.cn/n1/2022/0919/c1002-32528808.html.
33   https://www.cnpc.com.cn/en/xhtml/images/features/CNPC_Latin_America/0-CNPC%20in%20Latin%20America.pdf.

In the early 2000s, Beijing pursued a very cautious policy in foreign markets, trying to avoid any conflict, which distinguished China favorably from the leading Western powers. In its dialogue with LAC countries, China deliberately emphasized the absence of any expansionist intentions in this region, as well as the desire to reduce the US influence.

However, the transformation of China into the world's largest oil importer (with a consumption rate of 6.4 million barrels per day) led Beijing to reconsider its strategy in LAC, based on a subtle economic calculation. The oil industries of LAC, which represent the largest group of traditional and recently discovered new rich deposits of oil, fell under the special interest of China, where it directed its investment flows. In 2005, China acquired a Canadian company that was producing oil in Ecuador, allowing Beijing to gain access to the country's richest oil reserves. The following year, China took over Guyana's bauxite mining industry by purchasing the relevant assets from another Canadian company. This made China the country's second largest producer of bauxite in Guyana.

Large-scale oil purchases from Venezuela marked the beginning of a new direction in foreign policy cooperation, which developed at a rapid pace. The Chinese presence in the Venezuelan oil sector arose even before Hugo Chavez came to power. In June 1997, the National Oil Company of China won an international tender to develop two brownfield oil fields in Venezuela at a cost of $358 million (Hongbo, 2012). At the time, it was the largest Chinese investment project in LAC. Until the end of 1999, total investment amounted to about $400 million, and 11 Chinese-financed enterprises were established in the country. At that time, Venezuela did not show interest in supplying oil to China, citing the fact that its location was not favorable.[34] The signing of a convention on economic and technical cooperation between China and Venezuela in 2000 helped strengthen the Chinese presence in the oil sector.

In 2004, Venezuela agreed to transfer to the China National Petroleum Corporation (CNPC) a license for 12 wells in the Zumano oil and gas field, which has large reserves of heavy oil. For this purpose, the company Petrozumano SA was created, which began exploration and production in the states of Anzoategui and Monagas. In September 2009, an agreement was announced between the two countries to jointly produce about 450,000 barrels per day of heavy oil in the Orinoco oil belt, Venezuela's main energy reserve. However, the Venezuelan oil sector was behind Argentina and Brazil in terms of Chinese investment during this period, (Vasquez, 2018).

---

34   https://www.igadi.gal/analise/china-and-venezuela-the-perfect-match/.

During his visit to China in 2010, Chavez announced plans to increase oil supplies to China over the coming years to a record high level of 500,000 barrels per day. As part of the strategic partnership announced between Beijing and Caracas, China received access to the development of large-scale blocks in the Orinoco River basin. The volume of Chinese investments in Venezuela was estimated at more than $2 billion, also covering other sectors of the economy. China has become the main importer from Venezuela of "orimulsion", a fuel based on heavy oil, similar in composition to fuel oil.

In 2010, China, in exchange for a $10 billion loan to Brazil, secured supplies of crude oil to the country from Petrobras Corporation over a ten-year period. A little later that year, China bought 40% of its Brazilian assets from the Spanish company Repsol. This contract, valued at $7.1 billion, was China's largest deal in the LAC region at that time. China has also invested heavily in Argentina, primarily in oil exploration and production projects.

Chinese loans to Venezuela fell between 2014 and 2017, due to repayment concerns. According to an annual report published by the Inter-American Dialogue and Boston University, Venezuela did not receive any funding from China in 2017, and in 2018 it received a single loan of $8 billion.[35] Following tightened sanctions against Venezuela in 2019, China National Petroleum Corporation stopped transporting oil from Venezuela. However, according to the Atlantic Council, China's trade with Venezuela is disguised by transit through third countries. For example, from May 2020 to June 2021, shipments of "Malaysian bitumen" to China increased thirteen-fold, but it is estimated that about 90 percent of cargo shipped between April 2020 and April 2021 were actually Venezuelan oil.[36] In the case of Brazil, Chinese loans were allocated to the state oil company Petrobras under a "loans for oil" mechanism. During the period 2009–2016, Petrobras received approximately $36 billion in loans from Chinese banks (Vasquez, 2018). At the time, the oil company was experiencing a period of turbulence and asked China for financial assistance. In 2015 and 2016, Petrobras received loans, mainly from the China Development Bank, worth $10 and $15 billion. As part of repayment of a 2016 loan, Petrobras agreed to supply 200,000 barrels of oil per day to China for ten years.[37]

---

35   https://www.thedialogue.org/wp-content/uploads/2018/03/Chinese-Finance-to-LAC-2017.pdf.
36   https://www.reuters.com/business/energy/venezuelan-oil-masked-malaysian-rushes-into-china-before-fuel-tax-2021-06-04/.
37   https://www.businesstimes.com.sg/companies-markets/energy-commodities/chinas-loan-petrobras-may-help-pay-most-2016-debt?amp.

In 2009, China joined the Inter-American Development Bank (IDB), a regional bank that financed or sponsored most investment contracts with LAC countries. Beijing contributed $225 million to the IDB. This purely practical decision significantly increased China's chances of participating in tenders, thanks to which Beijing received an advantage over other extra-regional players, such as Russia, who did not participate in IDB.

Chinese investment in the region has grown at a rapid pace. In particular in 2010, Chinese investment in the LAC increased sharply relative to the previous decade: in 2009 investment was about $15 billion, then by 2011 it was estimated at $22.7 billion. During the period 2007–2016 China's participation in the oil and gas sector of LAC countries occurred through the issuance of loans from Chinese banks, the repayment of which was made from income from future exports. The approximate amount of loans issued to LAC countries during this period is $140 billion, of which about $98 billion were allocated to the oil and gas sector.[38] The main recipients of Chinese loans in LAC in the period 2007–2016 were Venezuela, Brazil, Ecuador, Argentina, and Bolivia.

The signing in 2011 of a memorandum of understanding between the Latin American Civil Aviation Commission (LACAC) and the Civil Aviation Administration of China (CAAC), aimed at facilitating communication between citizens, businesspeople, and politicians, also gave a certain impetus to relations.[39]

2013 ushered in a new stage of increased Chinese investment in Peru. It was during this year that a number of important purchases of Peruvian companies by Chinese companies took place. In mid-November, China's largest oil and gas company, PetroChina, announced it was buying the assets of state-owned Brazilian oil multinational Petrobras in Peru for $2.6 billion. China Fishery Group bought $806 million for a 99.1% stake in Copeinca, Peru's largest fish producer, which accounts for 17% of Peru's total permitted catch quota. Chinese companies also acquired 20% of the rights to extract and export Brazilian deposits on the continental shelf.

In 2014, Chinese President Xi Jinping announced the beginning of the creation of a new cooperation structure with LAC, called "1+3+6".[40] "1" meant the development of a special cooperation program between China and LAC countries, the main goal of which is to realize inclusive growth and achieve sustainable development. "3" represented the "three big driving forces" (trade, investment, and financial cooperation), which act as the engines of partnership. In this

---

38   https://journals.openedition.org/poldev/3272.
39   https://clac-lacac.org/wp-content/uploads/2021/12/DO-AC-CHINAes.pdf.
40   https://www.fmprc.gov.cn/esp/gjhdq/ldmz/3523/3525/201407/t20140722_968717.html.

regard, China announced its intention to invest $250 billion in LAC over the next 10 years, which became the second wave of expansion of the Chinese presence in the region, and its desire to increase the volume of bilateral trade within 10 years to $500 billion. "6" meant six key areas (energy and natural resources, infrastructure construction, agriculture, manufacturing, scientific and technical innovation, and information technology), which are considered by China as priority areas of cooperation with LAC. In addition, China announced the provision of credit lines to LAC countries on preferential terms, and the creation of various Cooperation Funds with the region. All this confirmed the change in the main directions of Chinese investment: in the 2000s they were sent mainly to the extractive industries; in the 2010s they went to the electronics, telecommunications, agricultural, and automotive industries.

In July 2014, the leaders of Peru, Brazil, and China signed a memorandum of understanding to build a transcontinental railway, a project that was a long-held dream of Lima and Brasilia to connect the coasts of the Pacific and Atlantic oceans. Each participating country sought to achieve its goals through this project: Brazil gained access to the Pacific coast, which made it closer to the developing economies of Asia; for Peru, the transportation of products coming across the Atlantic Ocean, as well as other goods supplied to the countries of the Southern Cone, was facilitated; for China, the project significantly reduced the cost of transporting agricultural products imported from LAC. The initiative was part of the Initiative for the Integration of Regional Infrastructure in South America (IIRSA), which is an institutional mechanism for coordinating intergovernmental efforts among 12 South American countries to develop a common agenda for advancing transport, energy, and communications infrastructure integration projects. The estimated cost of the 5,300 km railway was about $10 billion and will be implemented by Brazilian and Chinese companies. This project was intended to complement the highway connecting Brazil and Peru, which crosses the South American region in its central part. The total cost of the project exceeded $2.8 billion, and work was completed in December 2010. On a practical level, this new route had only a minor impact on the speed of trade cooperation between Peru and Brazil: in the period 2009–2019, of the total trade turnover between Peru and Brazil, only 18% of goods passed through the new Interoceanic route.[41] Despite all the criticism, the new highway has already been nicknamed the first "gateway to Asia."

---

41   https://ac24horas.com/2020/03/14/em-dez-anos-so-18-de-tudo-o-que-o-acre-comprou-e-vendeu-passaram-pela-interoceanica/.

At the beginning of 2016, CNOOC won a major tender for the development and production of hydrocarbons in the first of ten deepwater areas of the Gulf of Mexico, the project is claimed to produce ultra-light oil. The success of this campaign was due to the Chinese proposing additional payment for subsoil development in the amount of 17.01%, which is much higher than the minimum level of 3.1% set by the Mexican government. Despite the fact that Mexico was the second most important market in LAC, and also extremely interested in foreign investment, China was in no hurry to invest its funds in this country. Over the 2010s, Chinese investment in Mexico amounted to only $530 million, which is significantly less than investments intended for Brazil ($32 billion), Venezuela ($18 billion), and Peru ($17 billion). According to official data, less than 1% of total Chinese foreign direct investment destined for LAC went to Mexico.[42] In 2022, CNOOC entered into a production sharing deal with Petrobras worth US$1.9 billion to explore Brazil's Búzios oil field.[43]

China's interest in turning Peru and Chile into "Pacific platforms" through the creation of transoceanic corridors connecting it with Brazil and Argentina, also included the development of a special level of relations with large food suppliers—Uruguay and Paraguay.

Like Argentina and Brazil, Uruguay established strong economic ties with China throughout the 2000s, based on commodity exports: in 2024, China accounted for 27% of all Uruguayan exports, mainly consisting of soybeans and beef.[44] In 2014, the Uruguayan–Chinese Chamber of Commerce was created to promote commercial exchanges and investments between companies from both countries. The creation of the Forum for Cooperation between China and LAC in 2007 became an important platform for strengthening ties between China and Uruguay. Among all MERCOSUR members, Uruguay stands out for its actively developing dialogue with China: in 2016, the countries established a strategic partnership, and in 2023 it was expanded to a comprehensive strategic partnership. The signing of the Food Security Cooperation Agreement between China and Uruguay in 2017 promoted cooperation on food security and agriculture. With MERCOSUR currently negotiating a FTA with the EU, Uruguay has taken the opposite path, instead a FTA with China.

Uruguay has also become an important destination for Chinese investment: the construction of the UPM pulp mill in Uruguay, which became one of

---

42 https://www.forbes.com.mx/mexico-brasil-y-china-tres-gigantes-enpugna/.
43 https://www.reuters.com/business/energy/chinas-cnooc-pays-petrobras-19-bln-product ion-sharing-deal-brazils-buzios-field-2022-11-24/.
44 https://www.france24.com/en/live-news/20231122-china-and-uruguay-upgrade-ties-as -leaders-meet-in-beijing.

the largest Chinese investment projects in the country and contributed to the economic and social development of LAC, and the construction of the China–Uruguay Industrial Technology Park in the department of Canelones, the purpose of which was to promote innovation and technological development in the region.

China's relations with Paraguay have been steadily developing. In 2005, Paraguay and China established diplomatic relations, which was followed by the signing of an agreement on economic and technical cooperation. In 2011, with the participation of Chinese investors, a project was implemented to build a water treatment plant in Asunción. Relations between the two countries are complicated by the fact that Asuncion recognizes Taiwan as the legitimate government of all China. Despite this, both countries are developing a pragmatic dialogue aimed at maintaining economic cooperation, which is growing at a rapid pace: in 2024, China accounts for more than 20% of Paraguayan imports.[45] The government of President Mario Abdo Benítez (2018–2023) developed a policy of "behind the scenes" dialogue with China, while focusing on maintaining the traditionally pro-Taiwan orientation of its foreign policy.

In 2018, construction began on a water treatment plant in Asunción, known as the "new Asunción Wastewater Treatment Plant." Several road and rail infrastructure projects were implemented in 2019, including the expansion of the PY02 highway and the modernization of the railway system in Paraguay. The following year, an agricultural cooperation agreement was signed, and several renewable energy projects were launched, such as the Guarambare wind farm and the Ita solar park. In 2021, agricultural cooperation programs were created, such as the Sustainable Agricultural and Rural Development Project (PRODAS), which includes the exchange of agricultural technologies with neighboring countries.

In 2010, the volume of Chinese foreign direct investment in LAC countries reached its highest level, which led to China becoming the second largest trading partner of the region, displacing the EU.[46] However, not all Chinese investment projects are successful. China's plan to become Costa Rica's largest energy partner through a joint oil refinery renovation remains up in the air. In 2008, the two countries signed a Framework Agreement that included Chinese participation in oil projects, especially the modernization and expansion of

---

45 https://www.em.com.br/app/noticia/internacional/2023/05/24/interna_internacional,1498150/paraguai-quer-fazer-comercio-com-a-china-e-manter-relacoes-com-taiwan.shtml.

46 https://www.ictsd.org/bridges-news/puentes/news/china-y-am%C3%A9rica-latina-y-el-caribe-competitividad-para-el-desarrollo.

the refinery in Moin on the Caribbean coast, with an investment of $1.5 billion. But a wave of criticism from civil society organizations, individual politicians, and citizens in Costa Rica paralyzed this initiative. The implementation of a second large-scale project with Chinese investment to expand the highway between San Jose and Limon took decades. An important Chinese investment project to build a railway system was canceled in Mexico. The plan to build a high-speed railway connecting Mexico City and Queretaro was transferred to the Chinese company China Railway and its Mexican partners GIA, Prodemex, GHP, and TEYA. However, the construction that had begun was stopped, and the tender, which would have cost $4.6 billion, was rejected, which caused sharp dissatisfaction on the Chinese side. In addition, the Mexican administration of Peña Nieto (2012–2018) also, under dubious pretexts, suspended the construction of the "Dragon Mart Cancún" project, a commercial center with an area of more than 500 hectares, in which it was planned to create exceptional conditions for presentations and sales of products from companies from all over the world.

China has gradually become one of the largest sources of FDI for LAC countries, the main volumes of capital which entered the region through two offshore territories popular for Chinese business—the Virgin and Cayman Islands. They accounted for 95.9% of all Chinese FDI in the region, from where it was then sent to other countries in LAC. According to data provided by China Investment Tracker, by 2022, accumulated Chinese investments in LAC amounted to: Brazil $63.78 billion; Peru $25.45 billion; Chile $15.9 billion; Argentina $10.65 billion; Colombia $6.35 billion; Ecuador $6.17 billion; Venezuela $4.57 billion; Mexico $4.03 billion; Guyana $1.67 billion.[47]

Meanwhile, total Chinese investment in the LAC region stood at $140 billion out of China's total overseas FDI valued at $2.5 trillion, most of which was in Southeast Asia and Europe. This confirms the fact that despite China's growing activity in this part of the world, LAC is not yet considered by Beijing as a priority direction for capital exports. From the point of view of LAC economies, the Chinese presence has become significant, shaking the influence of traditional players in this region: by 2020, China's FDI stock in the LAC was estimated at $263.4 billion (11% of total FDI stock in the region), making it the third largest investor after the EU (34.2%) and the US (20.7%).[48] In 2016, the China–LAC Cooperation (CLAC) Fund was created by the China Bank for International

---

47 China Global Investment Tracker. URL: https://www.aei.org/china-global-investment-tracker/.
48 Foreign Direct Investment in Latin America and the Caribbean. URL: https://repositorio.cepal.org/bitstream/handle/11362/47148/4/S2100318_en.pdf.

Development with a capital of $5 billion, the main goal of which was to promote Chinese investment activity in the region.[49]

It should be noted that even Chinese investments in the infrastructure of LAC countries are considered by the US as a potential security threat in the context of Beijing's desire to "militarize" seaport facilities through large-scale investments.[50]

2.3   The Belt and Road Initiative and LAC

An important impetus to the development of Beijing's relations with respect to the LAC countries was given by the global Chinese Belt and Road Initiative (BRI), aimed at developing ties between China and various regions of the world. This Chinese foreign policy strategy was first put forward by Xi Jinping in two speeches: at the end of 2013 (in Kazakhstan on the Silk Road Economic Belt) and early 2014 (in Indonesia on the 21st century Maritime Silk Road). Infrastructure projects and a continuous flow of FDI are expected to play a key role in this initiative. However, BRI, which is broadly focused on creating a new model of international cooperation through strengthening bilateral and multilateral mechanisms of interaction involving China, also includes other aspects of partnership, in particular "political coordination" and "strengthening people-to-people ties".[51]

Initially, the Latin America and Caribbean (LAC) region was not included in the Belt and Road Initiative (BRI). The original routes only extended through Eurasia to Europe and through Southeast Asia to Europe. However, as Beijing encountered difficulties in its dialogue with Western European countries, other regions, including LAC, were gradually incorporated into the BRI. LAC was one of the last to be included in the BRI coverage area. The White Paper on Chinese Policy in Latin America, published in 2016, did not contain any reference to BRI. The Chinese position regarding the potential place of the LAC in BRI changed only by 2017, which was confirmed by the participation of Argentine President Mauricio Macri (2015–2019) at the 1st Belt and Road Forum for International Cooperation, held in May 2017 in Beijing. During Macri's personal meeting with Xi Jinping, the Chinese leader made a landmark statement that Latin America is "a natural extension of the 21st century Maritime Silk Road." On a practical

---

49   The China-LAC Cooperation Fund. URL: http://gd.china-embassy.gov.cn/eng/zlhz_1/zlhzjj/.
50   Washington Must Respond to China's Growing Military Presence in Latin America. Available at: https://foreignpolicy.com/2022/03/14/china-latin-america-military-pla-infrastructure-ports-colombia/.
51   http://fec.mofcom.gov.cn/article/fwydyl/.

level, the inclusion of LAC in BRI confirmed the accession of Panama to BRI in November 2017, becoming the first LAC country to participate in this project (Jenkins, 2022). At the second ministerial meeting of the China–LAC Forum in 2018, China made a special statement emphasizing that it expects cooperation between the two regions to rapidly expand as part of BRI. This prompted other LAC countries to join the Chinese initiative: during 2018, fifteen more LAC countries announced their connection to BRI, and three more in 2019. In 2022, Nicaragua and Argentina also joined the initiative. Of the largest economies in the region, Argentina is the first and so far, the only one to join BRI, while Brazil and Mexico remain outside its framework. Chinese companies are directing investments to LAC for three main reasons: the rich natural resources and raw materials available to the countries of the region; food security; and growing geopolitical tensions. All this has led to Chinese businesses significantly expanding their presence in LAC, especially in the energy, transport, and infrastructure sectors.

Since LAC gained a place in the BRI policy, the region has seen a steady increase in investment: with Chinese investment in the region increasing by 227% since 2018.[52] However, in contrast to the flow of Chinese direct investment into developing countries in Asia under the BRI initiative, which was characterized by a decline in the 2020s, the flow of FDI to LAC remained stable.

Since the launch of BRI just over a decade ago, Beijing's sphere of influence in LAC has expanded significantly, primarily through loans, trade deals, and investments in infrastructure and mining.

As of early 2024, a total of 22 Latin American countries have joined BRI. Their decisions to move closer to Beijing in this regard was motivated primarily by expectations of a significant influx of Chinese investment in infrastructure.[53] For example, in 2022, Chinese companies invested in 32 new projects in LAC countries in areas such as electricity (50%), information technology (IT) (25%), electric vehicle manufacturing (6%)—a record high.[54]

For LAC, the BRI project is primarily a political initiative, the main goal of which is to effectively use the emerging growth in the region's economic ties with China, which makes it possible to gradually move the dissimilar countries of the region into the orbit of global Chinese politics. The practical achievements of BRI, which has very vague plans, and the absence of clear target dates and indicators are attributed to positive examples of cooperation, which in fact have nothing to do with this initiative. An example is Argentina,

---

52 https://greenfdc.org/china-belt-and-road-initiative-bri-investment-report-2023/.
53 In the summer of 2024, Brazil revealed its plan to join the Belt and Road Initiative.
54 Datos de Cámara de Comercio Brasil China. https://camarabrasilchina.com/.

which concluded its first swap agreement with China for 130 billion yuan back in 2009, when there was no talk of BRI, and extended it in 2018, two years before it joined the project. In this regard, by inviting LAC countries to join BRI, Beijing is creating conditions for increasing coordination with them on global governance issues. In addition, the Chinese project creates a favorable environment for the development of a system of agreements on trade, investment, scientific and technical cooperation, which Beijing prefers to build mainly on a bilateral basis.

Although trade between China and LAC continues to expand, the US still remains the region's largest trading partner. China's growing presence in the LAC has caused mixed reactions from countries in the region: some countries have welcomed the investment and trade opportunities offered, while others have expressed concerns about its growing influence in this part of the world. Beijing's influence in LAC has varied depending on the country's economic potential, its social and political conditions, and the availability of natural resources that China needs to meet the needs of its manufacturing sector. When China first turned its attention to LAC, the main target of the new Chinese policy was Venezuela, which was explained by its status as a major oil producer and close ties with the US.

According to the Chinese strategy, Venezuela was supposed to become the first LAC country through which Beijing could implement its "Fast and furious" strategy to which other LAC countries would gradually join. The bulk of this Chinese money was to be used in the country's oil and gas infrastructure. But all of China's plans in Venezuela collapsed. As of 2023, China had provided over $65 billion in loans and investments to Venezuela.[55] But despite this, the unique project between China and Venezuela, which would become a model of cooperation for the entire LAC, was not ultimately created. Gradually, China was forced to reconsider its strategy towards Venezuela, which became focused on gradually returning the loans issued to Caracas, while ceasing to invest its money in the country. Despite US sanctions, Venezuela used its oil to pay off billions of dollars of debt to China and millions of barrels of Venezuelan oil were sent to China.

Despite China's not very successful experience in Venezuela, the BRI cooperation model continued to attract the interest of LAC countries, primarily because the process of joining the project is very transparent and simple. Joining the BRI initiative is done through a "memorandum of understanding,"

---

55   https://thepeoplesmap.net/globalchinapulse/chinese-finance-in-venezuela-a-non-interventionist-lenders-trap/.

which does not legally obligate the parties to deepen trade or investment but represents a "gesture of approval" of China's policies by the participating country.

In the 2020s, joining BRI does not mean the allocation of large sums in the form of loans or investments by the Chinese government. For a few months after a new country's accession to BRI is signed, there is usually a slight increase in trade interaction and Chinese investment, but then relations quickly return to the regular speed. That said, recent global events, including China's strained relations with the US and the EU, the impact of the COVID-19 pandemic and China's economic slowdown, have led to lower BRI spending and a more targeted approach by Beijing in distributing funding.

However, as Beijing's desire to gain access to lithium—a valuable metal used in technical products—has increased, China's interest in LAC has renewed. Three South American countries have the largest lithium deposits on the planet, in the so-called "lithium triangle" formed between Chile, Bolivia and Argentina, where 68% of the world's reserves are located. Chinese companies are already involved in dozens of lithium projects, especially in Chile and Argentina, where lithium development has boomed over the past five years. Chinese investments, supplied by nine Chinese companies, are already involved in most of the projects launched in these countries, but only when the lithium deposits are ready for production. Unlike these countries, Bolivia's lithium reserves are not exploited at an industrial level.

In addition to lithium, China has expressed interest in developing LAC deposits of copper, iron, and zinc, which are necessary for China's industrial production. This gives a new impetus to the development of China's relations with Peru, which is already an important ally of China and has the most productive copper, zinc and iron mines in the region.

2.4   *China's Current Investment Presence in LAC*

2.4.1   Electricity

Since the start of BRI, energy has become the main area of cooperation between China and LAC countries. Beijing emphasizes the importance of clean energy development as a key goal of its new energy diplomacy and economic policy. According to China's Global Energy Finance database, Chinese investment in the energy sector in LAC during the period 2001–2022 amounted to over $49.2 billion.[56]

---

56   China's Global Energy Finance Database. https://www.bu.edu/cgef/#/all/Country.

The example of Peru stands out, where the Italian energy corporation Enel S.p.A. previously controlled almost half of Peru's electricity supply. However, in 2023, Enel S.p.A. agreed to sell two electricity assets to China Southern Power Grid International for $2.9 billion.[57] The second half of Peru's energy assets is also controlled by another Chinese company, China Three Gorges Corporation, which in 2020 acquired the assets of the Peruvian company Luz del Sur for $3.6 billion.

Peru is not the only place where there is participation of Chinese companies in the energy sector. In 2018, China Southern Power Grid International acquired a 27.7% stake of Canadian multinational company Brookfield's in Chile's largest transmission system, Transelec.[58] Two years later, the Chinese corporation State Grid International Development bought the company Chilquinta Energía, which belonged to the US energy-service holding company Sempra.[59] In 2020, the Chinese state-owned company State Grid also acquired Chilean electricity distributor CGE for $3 billion.[60] All these deals allowed China to become the owner of two of the country's four largest energy companies and control almost 57% of the Chilean energy market.

In 2008, China received a contract for the construction of the Gecelca 3 power plant in Córdoba department, Colombia. The cost of the project was $236 million. However, this project was quite problematic. The power station was supposed to be commissioned at the end of 2012, but it was opened only in 2015. In addition, due to partial failure to fulfill contractual obligations, the Colombian authorities fined the Chinese $10.5 million.

In 2013, an important Chinese investment project in Ecuador was opened: the Villonaco wind farm (Parque Eólico Villonaco).[61] This landmark $35 million Ecuadorian–Chinese project, focused on producing "clean energy" using cutting-edge technologies, ultimately providing 25% of the Ecuadorian province of Loja's annual energy consumption. This project avoids emissions of approximately 38,000 tons of CO_2, as well as the import of diesel fuel needed for thermoelectric generation, saving Ecuador about $13 million annually.

---

57   https://asia.nikkei.com/Spotlight/Caixin/China-utility-powers-up-South-America-prese nce-with-Peru-purchase.
58   https://www.reuters.com/article/chile-energy-china-idUSL1N1QX15X/.
59   https://www.latercera.com/pulso/noticia/la-china-state-grid-se-impone-a-enel-y-se -queda-con-chilquinta-en-el-mayor-negocio-del-ano-en-chile/859835/.
60   https://dialogochino.net/en/climate-energy/39680-state-grid-grows-presence-in-chile -with-cge-purchase/.
61   https://www.celec.gob.ec/gensur/noticias/central-eolica-villonaco-la-de-mayor-producc ion-por-turbina-en-el-mundo/.

The largest assets of the Chinese state-owned electric utility corporation, State Grid, are concentrated in Brazil, where the Chinese company began investing in 2010.[62] It has since invested more than $5.7 billion and operates more than 16,000 kilometers of power lines. State Grid's largest project in Brazil was a transmission line connecting the Belo Monte hydroelectric dam complex in the state of Pará.[63] The project, stretching more than 2,500 kilometers through 81 cities in five states from north to south, includes the world's longest ultra-high voltage direct current transmission line. However, on a global scale, the presence of Chinese companies in Brazil is not so large: they account for about 10% of the country's electrical capacity and 12% of the electricity transmission infrastructure.[64]

2.4.2 Infrastructure

Among the main factors that contributed to the strengthening of the Chinese influence in LAC is the participation of Chinese companies in infrastructure projects in the region. One such project aimed at changing the logistics landscape of Latin America is the port of Chancay, located in Peru. Its main shareholders are the Chinese company Cosco Shipping Ports Limited (CSPL) with a 60% stake and the Peruvian Volcan Compañía Minera with the remaining 40%.[65] The strategic geographical location of the Port of Chancay, located on the coast of Peru, 60 kilometers north of the Peruvian capital of Lima, makes it a key entry point for maritime transport into the region. The project is part of China's Maritime Silk Road project and is scheduled to begin operations in the last quarter of 2024. Chancay port is the largest Chinese investment in the LAC port network.

Another major Chinese maritime infrastructure project in the region is the port of Ensenada, located in the Mexican state of Baja California, in the northwest corner of Mexico, where container cargo handling has increased by 200% since 2014. In December 2022, the Chinese company Hutchison Ports announced plans to expand the terminal, which involves the construction of an additional 300 meters of berth for container ships, another four hectares of container yard and 80 meters of breakwater, as well as improvements to the

---

62 https://www.bloomberg.com/news/articles/2023-11-22/china-state-grid-s-brazil-unit-said-to-weigh-raising-1-billion.
63 https://www.fmprc.gov.cn/mfa_eng/topics_665678/zggcddwjw100ggs/xsd/202208/t20220829_10757157.html.
64 https://www.wilsoncenter.org/blog-post/its-electric-chinas-power-play-latin-america.
65 https://reporteasia.com/economia/2023/09/26/nuevo-puerto-multiproposito-de-chancay-un-gigante-de-la-logistica-china-en-latinoamerica/.

existing infrastructure. Work began in December 2022 and is estimated to last 22 months.[66]

Major Chinese infrastructure projects are also located in Panama, which was the first Latin American country to join the BRI Initiative. In 2016, in a deal worth $900 million, the Chinese Landbridge Group acquired control of the country's largest port on the Atlantic coast, Isla Margarita, and the Colón Free Trade Zone in Panama dedicated to re-exporting to LAC.[67] Additionally, in March 2021, the Panamanian government began renewing the lease of Hutchison Ports PPC, a subsidiary of Hong Kong-based CK Hutchison Holdings that operates the ports of Balboa and Cristobal, the two main hubs of the Panama Canal on the Pacific and Atlantic sides.

A new direction of Chinese activity in the port infrastructure of LAC is access to the south of the region, opening a route to Antarctica. The first attempt was made in 2022, when the Chinese company Shaanxi Coal and Chemical Industry Group Co., Ltd signed a memorandum of understanding with the Argentine province of Tierra del Fuego to invest $1.25 billion.[68] In addition to the construction of facilities for the chemical industry, the agreement provides for the construction of a port terminal with a berth for ships with a displacement of up to 20,000 tons. However, as of 2023, the project has been suspended due to the position of local legislators who question Beijing's plans.[69]

2.4.3 Extractable Resources

One of the key areas of Chinese investment in the minerals sector in recent years has been lithium deposits. For China, lithium is of particular strategic importance because Beijing is a leading producer of ion batteries. For example, in 2021, China was the producer of 79% of all lithium-ion batteries.[70] Although China already produces 13% of the world's lithium, this is not enough for its industry and for the energy transition that the country's leaders are committed to.

In January 2023, Chinese company CATL, the world's largest manufacturer of automotive batteries, signed a contract with the Bolivian government to

---

66 https://www.forbes.com.mx/hutchison-ports-eit-invierte-2300-mdp-en-su-terminal-en-el-puerto-de-ensenada/?__cf_chl_rt_tk=Odo8t8C5b4ySyubE8Ow4S7Hp3VZVwNXyy2Bk PmZs104-1708333295-0.0-4882.
67 https://www.csis.org/analysis/key-decision-point-coming-panama-canal.
68 https://dialogo-americas.com/articles/china-refuses-to-back-down-in-port-plan-in-argentina/.
69 https://www.bloomberglinea.com/latinoamerica/argentina/puerto-chino-en-tierra-del-fuego-que-se-sabe-del-proyecto-y-que-dijo-el-gobernador/.
70 https://www.statista.com/statistics/1249871/share-of-the-global-lithium-ion-battery-manufacturing-capacity-by-country/.

invest $1.4 billion to build two direct lithium mining facilities.[71] Despite having the world's largest lithium reserves, processing in Bolivia remains underdeveloped. The arrival of Chinese companies was the first time a foreign country has intervened in Bolivia's lithium industry.

Chinese companies are also active in Chile. In 2018, the Chinese mining and manufacturing company Tianqi acquired a 23% stake in the largest Chilean lithium producer Sociedad Química y Minera. The same year it announced plans to expand its stake in various Chilean lithium projects, as a reaction to the decentralization of the market and the emergence of new players. The lithium industry in Chile has grown from a market with about 10 competitors in 2018 to about 24 by 2025.[72] The company is also asking local authorities to lift antitrust restrictions that prevent it from appointing its executives to the board of directors of the Chilean company.[73]

In addition, Chinese multinational conglomerate BYD, one of the world's largest automakers, announced plans this year to build a lithium cathode plant in the northern Chilean region of Antofagasta. Once a specialized lithium producer, BYD will be able to receive preferential prices for 11,244 metric tons per year of battery-grade lithium carbonate through 2030.[74] In October 2023, the leadership of BYD announced plans to build an electric vehicle plant in Brazil, which would include a lithium and iron phosphate processing plant for the international market.[75]

The presence of Chinese lithium players in Argentina is also gaining momentum. In June 2023, it was reported that the Chinese mining company Tibet Summit Resources would immediately invest $1.7 billion in two mines: Arizaro and Diablillos salt flats in Salta province. The Argentine Ministry of Economy estimates that these mines will produce between 50,000 and 100,000 tons of lithium. Ganfeng Lithium, China's largest lithium producer, has also expanded its involvement in Argentine projects. In 2022, the company acquired 100% of the shares of LitheA Argentina for $962 million. The capacity of the first stage of production is expected to be 30,000 tons of lithium carbonate per year.

---

71 https://www.reuters.com/markets/commodities/chinese-battery-giant-catl-seals-14-billion-deal-develop-bolivia-lithium-2023-06-19/.
72 https://www.elmostrador.cl/mercados/2023/08/28/tianqi-presiona-para-aumentar-participacion-en-sqm-apunta-a-nuevos-actores-en-industria-del-litio/.
73 https://www.latercera.com/pulso/noticia/tianqi-quiere-intervenir-mas-en-sqm/BKRWTAD73VH2TK5D7FSOTLE3HQ/.
74 https://www.bloomberg.com/news/articles/2023-07-04/china-byd-se-une-a-la-fiebre-del-litio-en-latinoamerica.
75 https://www.bnnbloomberg.ca/byd-looks-to-buy-lithium-assets-in-brazil-in-ev-raw-material-push-1.1983945.

This transaction complements the existing joint venture with the Canadian company, Lithium Americas—called the Cauchari Olaroz salt flat project—a lithium mining project located in the Susques department, in the province of Jujuy.[76]

2.4.4 Agriculture

China's presence in the LAC agricultural sector began after the 2008 crisis. Although China increased grain production by 41% between 2003 and 2014, soaring domestic demand exacerbated the supply gap (Zhang, 2016). Since then, FDI has become an instrument for domestic food supply.

In 2008, agricultural exports from LAC were mainly directed to the EU (25%), US (15%) and China (9%). By 2018, the US (22%) and China (17%) had increased their share, while the European Union's share had declined (17%). The rise in the share of LAC agricultural exports going to China becomes even more pronounced when looking back several decades, as it was only 1.1% in 1990 and 2.5% in 2000 (Boza, 2022). In 2008, Argentina and Brazil accounted for over 50% of LAC agricultural exports to China.[77] In 2018, the main source of Chinese agricultural imports from Latin America was Brazil, accounting for about 76% of the total, followed by Chile (7%), Argentina (5%), Peru (4%), Ecuador (2%) and Mexico (2%).

However, Chinese FDI in agriculture is not as significant compared to other sectors of the economy. During the most rapid growth years of Chinese FDI in LAC (2010–2016), agriculture accounted for about 1–2% of total investment (Gooch, 2018). As of 2015, Chinese companies had purchased or leased less than 0.2% of all arable land in LAC (Myers, 2015). Researchers suggest that the reason lies in the difficulties that the Chinese have in adapting to local environmental legislation (Zhang, 2019). Another format of participation of Chinese business in the agricultural sector of LAC is the commercialization of this sector.

China's largest food processing and trading company, China Oil and Foodstuffs Corporation (COFCO Group), gradually acquired all the agricultural assets of the large traders Noble and Nidera by 2016. In this way, COFCO guaranteed access to a supply, storage, and logistics network in key production regions. Another example of Chinese investment expansion was the

---

76 https://www.reuters.com/article/argentina-lithium-idUSKBN2XM1SU/.
77 OEC. Country profile: China https://oec.world/en/profile/country/chn?subnationalFlowSelector=flow1&subnationalTimeSelector=timeYear&yearlyTradeFlowSelector=flow1&depthSelector1=HS2Depth&yearSelector1=2008.

acquisition by Shanghai Pengxin Group Co of the agro-industrial producers Fiagril and Belagricola in Brazil for more than $500 million.[78]

•••

During the period 1970–1990s China, while practically absent from the region, had created the groundwork for an increase in its activity in the future, primarily in the field of political ties and scientific and technical cooperation. In the 2000s, LAC established itself as one of the important and promising areas of Chinese foreign policy, where Beijing saw significant potential for increasing economic and political influence. This potential is based on China's role as the region's largest trading partner, which continues to grow, the increase in Chinese investment, and the interest of a number of LAC countries in China in the investment, economic, and political spheres. A turning point came in the 2010s, when China began to involve LAC in its global initiatives, motivated by securing their support for Beijing's growing role in global governance and world politics in general.

Currently, China's participation in the LAC region goes far beyond just the economic, trade, and investment spheres, covering increasingly broader and more diverse areas of cooperation. Every year, China's growing involvement in political, social, cultural, academic, and environmental issues of LAC countries is becoming more visible. Nowadays, China's political and strategic actions necessarily accompany all measures and projects of an economic nature.

At the present stage, the main platform for political exchange between China and LAC is the China–CELAC Forum, established in 2014 and operating since 2015 with the official goal of promoting the development of the China–LAC Comprehensive Cooperation Association. In turn, China's implementation of BRI in LAC also occurs through the China–CELAC Forum. Today, China and LAC are building regional cooperation with a strategic perspective. For this reason, China has expanded its strategic interests in the region, which is reflected in China's greater presence in multilateral regional arenas. For example, it joined as a permanent observer member of OAS in 2004 and became a non-loaning member of the Inter-American Development Bank in 2009.

In the 21st century, China has successfully developed and effectively implemented a comprehensive and multifaceted policy towards LAC, which goes beyond just economic and trade and includes such diverse areas as cultural, academic, social, technical, communication and environmental investment.

---

78   https://news.agropages.com/News/NewsDetail---47435.htm.

CHAPTER 4

The European Union as a Player in Latin America

1   Three Institutions for Multilateral Cooperation in EU-LAC Relations

The relations between the EU and LAC have been unstable for several decades. The LAC was virtually absent from Europe's international agenda until the early 1980s, when Europe began to become involved in the peaceful resolution of the Central American conflict. Until the mid-1990s, the European Community's relations with LAC countries were limited to agreements on cooperation, financial and technological assistance, and tariff preferences under the Generalized System of Preferences (GSP).

The last years of the 20th century took place under the auspices of the end of the Cold War, the emergence of the EU's Common Foreign and Security Policy (CFSP), and the rise of LAC regionalism. The inclusion of LAC in the internationalized neoliberal economy allowed the states of the region, not themselves among the global leaders, to gradually acquire a nascent autonomy in world politics. An important boost for a number of LAC countries has been the adoption of a foreign policy strategy based on open regionalism, the availability of mineral resources in strong demand from the world's most powerful economies, and increasing subregional influence. All this prompted the EU to develop a new interregional strategy regarding LAC. In 1999, at an EU–LAC summit, the formation of a "strategic association" was announced, which became a qualitative leap in interregional relations. This leap contributed to a noticeable intensification of bilateral relations, supported by the total of 60 countries that entered the association: 27 states from the EU and 33 from LAC.

The EU–LAC summits created the basis for a rapprochement between the two regions. However, in reality success was mostly declarative rather than practical. The lack of stability in the dialogue between the regions was confirmed by the fact that the negotiation processes on agreements between Brussels and MERCOSUR, the Caribbean Forum (Cariforum), and the Central American Common Market (MCCA), which began at the turn of the millennium, were repeatedly stalled, causing acute discontent from LAC.

Tangible transformations in EU–LAC dialogue began in the 2000s. The terrorist attacks of September 11 and the subsequent invasion of Iraq by US forces and their allies changed the global trends in the development of multilateral cooperation even without bloc divisions. The global economic crisis of 2008 brought renewed attention to the gap between the two worlds, developed and developing, highlighting the need to create new global governance frameworks (Lechini, 2009). Gradually, the increased presence of new global economic and political players in the Western Hemisphere began to have a noticeable influence on EU–LAC interregional relations. This was largely a consequence of the fact that since the end of the 20th century, LAC has steadily sought to expand its extra-regional ties. Efforts made in this direction allowed the region to balance the influence of the US (Bernal-Meza, 2005). Ultimately, all this led to the traditional presence of the EU and the US in this region being gradually supplemented by the expanding economic presence of China.

The vision of interregional cooperation between the EU and LAC was different. For the EU, interaction with LAC was important, both from the point of view of greater consolidation of the CFSP and in order to deepen its own inclusion in the world agenda as a prominent actor. Broadcasting its authority beyond the traditional sphere of influence, for LAC, relations with the EU were considered as a mechanism capable of activating bilateral cooperation. LAC sought in dialogue with the EU to expand trade and investment cooperation with a greater emphasis on development, which contrasted with the LAC–US relationship, which emphasized national security (Arenal, 2009).

Despite different visions of the main goals and objectives of interregional ties, relations between the EU and LAC are built around three main institutions of cooperation: political dialogue, assistance, and trade. These three thematic vectors were identified at the summit held in Rio de Janeiro in 1999 as the basis for bilateral interaction.

1.1   *Political Dialogue*

The political dialogue between the two regions began in 1984 with the initiation of interregional negotiations through the San Jose Process to pacify Central America. This was the first step towards rapprochement between the EC and LAC. As Mexican researcher Lorena Ruano notes, it was in relation to the Central American crisis that the Europeans initiated their first "foreign policy project" in LAC, formed jointly (Ruano, 2018). The experience gained allowed, by 1990, the institutionalization of dialogue between the EU and the Rio Group, followed by the creation of a number of independent subregional and bilateral dialogue forums with the Andean Community (CAN),[1] MERCOSUR, Chile, and Mexico.

---

1   The Andean Community (CAN) is one of the main integration associations of LAC, pursuing the goal of improving the quality of life of 111 million Andean citizens. Created in 1969, it consists of Bolivia, Colombia, Ecuador, and Peru.

The key themes of political dialogues held between the EU and LAC at different levels have traditionally been social cohesion, the respect and protection of human rights, democracy and democratic governance, strengthening the rule of law, combating corruption, and defending multilateralism (Serbin, 2012). Over time, the following issues were added to the agenda: the fight against drugs, climate change, migration, sustainable development, overcoming the consequences of economic crises, and science and technology. In 2004, the EU began to develop public dialogue with civil society in order to provide an alternative vision to the official approach of interregional relations. In the decade of the 2010s, a key theme of the dialogue was the issue of social cohesion, on which the EU and LAC had different positions.

In terms of political dialogue, the launch of a strategic association, based on the idea of a "common cultural universe," was given special significance. Spanish political scientist Celestino del Arenal emphasizes that the political dialogue between the EU and LAC is largely based on the historical and cultural heritage that unites the regions, which allows them to share common values and principles, responding to the needs of both sides in terms of strategically aligning common positions and strengthening their leading roles in various international forums (Arenal, 2010). In this context, for LAC, the institution of political dialogue with the EU was seen as an important tool aimed at increasing the autonomy and diversification of the region's international relations.

Political dialogue has become a mechanism to ensure the effective implementation of agreements signed between the EU and LAC at the regional, subregional, and bilateral levels. Its main goal is to deepen the level of interregional relations. Within the framework of the political dialogue, issues were considered that were not covered by agreements in the sphere of trade and the provision of assistance from the EU. The institution of political dialogue is a distinctive element of the foreign policy of the EU, characterizing its interaction at the interregional level (Coral, 2007).

The holding of EU–LAC summits to address key issues on the joint agenda led to the institutionalization of interregional political dialogue at the highest level. Since the first EU–LAC summit in 1999, a total of nine meetings have been held, first in the EU–LAC format and then in the EU–CELAC format.[2] The last EU–CELAC summit was held in 2023. However, the summit which

---

2   The Community of Latin American and Caribbean States (CELAC) was created in 2011. Since then, it has been the only regional association that speaks on behalf of the entire LAC region. The Community was created by the Caracas Declaration and replaced the Rio Group, which had existed since 1986 and the short-lived Latin American and Caribbean Summit on Integration and Development (CALC). CELAC unites 33 sovereign states in one regional

was supposed to take place in El Salvador in October 2017 was eventually postponed indefinitely due to differences between LAC countries regarding the Venezuelan crisis. Despite the instability of this format of interaction, it should be recognized that all nine summits made a significant contribution to strengthening interregional relations. During the meetings, the main areas of cooperation were outlined and the main guidelines for the development of interaction were determined. In addition, the summits created platforms for developing dialogue between businesses and public associations representing both regions.

Political dialogue at the highest level made it possible to gather at one table all the key actors making decisions on behalf of the regions. Thanks to this, a favorable atmosphere was created for agreeing on issues of mutual interest—something that did not exist throughout almost the entire 20th century, since there were no platforms for discussions at the regional level. A feature of the format of the EU–CELAC summits was the inclusion in this dialogue of all LAC countries with their characteristic differences, heterogeneity, and divergence of positions, as a result of which the practical outcomes of this mechanism were quite modest (Partiño, 2015).

The first EU–LAC summit marked the beginning of a new forum for interregional dialogue at the highest political level. Gradually, it was joined by a number of industry, governmental, and non-governmental formats of interaction, as well as bilateral strategic associations. The EU has been quite successful in building a dialogue with individual LAC countries: EU association agreements were signed with Mexico (2000) and Chile (2002); strategic partnership agreements were signed with Brazil (2007) and Mexico (2008). The EU has also taken steps to institutionalize high-level political dialogue with Argentina. An important step towards bringing the two regions closer was the signing in 2016 of the bilateral Agreement on Political Dialogue and Cooperation between the EU and Cuba—an initiative first voiced back in 2008.[3] All this made the joint interregional agenda noticeably more complete.

An important feature of the EU policy in this region is that Brussels has always been extremely wary of rapprochement with a large number of LAC countries at the same time because LAC itself did not have clear mechanisms for agreeing on common positions and coordinating steps in the multilateral

---

intergovernmental organization with a fairly low level of institutionalization and the absence of permanent structures and mechanisms for the implementation of common decisions.

3 ACUERDO DE DIÁLOGO POLÍTICO Y DE COOPERACIÓN entre la Unión Europea y sus Estados Miembros, por un lado, y la República de Cuba, por otro. Available at: https://eur-lex.europa.eu/legal-content/ES/TXT/?uri=celex%3A22016A1213%2801%29

arena; and LAC was perceived by the EU as a very heterogeneous region, in terms of their degree of development, leading to different opportunities for economic cooperation on a regional basis.

In this context, the EU "divided" LAC into several groups, based on the level of its interest and potential for economic interaction: the priority group included Mexico, Chile, MERCOSUR member countries, CAN member countries, as well as countries of the Central American subregion; The low-priority group included the Caribbean, which were considered by the EU primarily as part of the African, Caribbean, and Pacific Group of States (ACP), and not as an integral part of Latin America. In its foreign policy discourse, the EU has traditionally emphasized the importance of greater integration of Latin American countries. However, this "mapping" of LAC into priority groups, which in practice manifested itself in differentiated proposals from the EU in relation to individual countries, ultimately led to increased disagreements within the Latin American region.

In addition to dialogue at the highest level, several more levels can be identified at which the EU–LAC political dialogue developed most effectively.

One of the most significant mechanisms in EU-LAC political dialogue is inter-parliamentary dialogue, which has existed for more than forty years and has been developing between clearly defined actors: the European Parliament and the Latin American Parliament (Parlatino). This mechanism of interaction is well institutionalized. In particular, its meetings, which became the first official interregional political dialogue, are regular. The entities representing the EU and LAC within this interaction, however, differ in their powers and prerogatives. The European Parliament is the legislative and representative body of the EU and Parlatino is an intergovernmental body that is not assigned to any integration association and does not have any special powers. In 2006, the Euro-Latin American Parliamentary Assembly (EuroLat) was created. Within EuroLat, a special working group was created consisting of representatives of the European Parliament, Parlatino, Parlandino (Andean Parliament) and Parlacen (Central American Parliament). The inter-parliamentary dialogue has already produced results: through this institution of interaction, the EU has contributed to the protection and promotion of human rights, the preservation of peace, and the strengthening of democratic institutions in LAC.

Another important format of interaction is the ministerial dialogue between the EU and the Rio Group, which made it possible to create a unique regional negotiating platform. It represented a united Latin America and contributed to the formation of an institutionalized dialogue between the two regions. As part of this dialogue, starting with the adoption of the Rome Declaration in 1990, ministerial meetings were held every two years, the objectives of which were to promote the consolidation of democracy, to ensure security, and to support peace processes in the region. The emergence of EU–LAC summits eventually replaced this mechanism of interaction.

Political dialogue is also developing at the subregional level. An example of this is the EU–Central America political dialogue, which was fruitful in the 1980s and early 1990s. However, the failure of negotiations to conclude an EU–Central America association agreement and Central America's refusal to conclude a "third generation" agreement in 2003, as not meeting the expectations of the countries of this subregion, led to a freeze in contacts. The period of stagnation continued until the Vienna Summit in 2006, which restarted negotiations on the EU–Central America Association Agreement, which was eventually signed in 2013.

The political dialogue between the EU and CAN developed according to a similar scenario, noticeably intensifying after the signing of the agreement on political dialogue and cooperation in 2003. Despite the fact that the agreement was an important step towards rapprochement, it still did not fully meet the expectations of the Andean countries: their access to the EU market was never expanded. Thanks to this agreement, however, the bilateral political dialogue became much more institutionalized, and the list of issues for interregional cooperation was expanded, facilitating the participation of civil society. In particular, Article 52(3) of the agreement provides for the establishment of a Joint Consultative Committee to promote dialogue with the economic and social entities of civil society.[4] In July 2007, the EU and CAN began negotiations on an association agreement capable of taking into account the different geopolitical and economic weights of the parties. However, a political split within CAN and the inflexible position taken by the EU, led to the fact that the negotiation reached a dead end a year later. The EU was forced to move the dialogue to a bilateral level with individual Andean countries. The result was FTAs with Colombia, Peru, and Ecuador, where mechanisms of political dialogue and facilitation became secondary objectives compared to trade.[5]

The EU–MERCOSUR political dialogue, the fifth largest trading area in the world, was launched in 1995 after the conclusion of the "fourth generation" framework agreement. Despite the fact that the parties announced the signing of the Agreement back in 2019, at the time of writing it still remains

---

[4] Acuerdo de Diálogo Político y Cooperación entre la UE y la CAN. El 15 de diciembre de 2003. Available at: https://gredos.usal.es/bitstream/handle/10366/129066/Acuerdo_de_dialogo_po litico_y_cooperacio.pdf;jsessionid=FF29D966D6BF096E6D8ECEDFB08CFEFF?sequence=1.

[5] Acuerdo Comercial entre la Unión Europea, Colombia, Perú y Ecuador. Available at: https://www.tlc.gov.co/acuerdos/vigente/union-europea.

a non-legally binding pact. The text of the document is still subject to legal adaptation, legal clearance, and there has been varying levels of ratification on the part of both the EU and the MERCOSUR member states. The director of the Spanish Carolina Foundation, José Antonio Sanahuja, notes that the main paradox of the EU–MERCOSUR agreement is that at the time of its signing in 2019, the document was built functionally taking into account the features of regional globalization of the previous decades, when it had already entered into crisis and lost the political support of many European countries (Sanahuja, 2019).

In contrast to the dialogue between the EU and MERCOSUR, bilateral dialogues between the EU and Mexico, as well as Chile, based on association agreements signed in the early 2000s, demonstrate noticeably greater effectiveness. This confirms the thesis that it is the bilateral format of interaction that is preferable for the both sides, taking into account its more effective coordination in the ideological fragmentation of LAC.

The initiative to launch dialogues with civil society, as an important tool for the development of interregional relations and the effective implementation of many cooperation programs, was first voiced during the III EU–LAC summit held in 2004. Before then, this level of interaction did not practically exist. The following formats of dialogue with civil society were gradually formed: EU–Central America civil society dialogue forums on regional integration (2004), EU–CAN (2005), and consultations with civil society in delegations on draft country concept notes, conducted between 2007 and 2013.

It can be concluded that the EU–LAC political dialogue, developing at different levels, has led to an expansion of the thematic agenda, and has had a positive impact on increasing the scope of cooperation programs and in terms of involving civil society in the discussion. There is, however, no consensus among experts regarding the effectiveness of this interaction mechanism. For some, the institution of political dialogue is effective in the traditional system of managing bilateral relations (Freres, 2007); others view it primarily as a declarative rather than a practical institution, taking into account the ignorance of each of the parties of all powers and mechanisms, which does not allow all the agreements reached to be put into practice (Torrent, 2005).

1.2   *Assistance*

The second institution of EU–LAC multilateral cooperation is "assistance", which refers to that provided by community institutions and individual member states. In general, EU policy regarding LAC assistance is focused on the following areas: counter-narcotics, including in the Caribbean; cooperation in security and border management; promoting social cohesion, gender equality, and digital sovereignty; securing investments through the Latin America Investment Facility (LAIF); combating climate change and environmental protection; and assistance programs in the field of education and culture.

Coordination of the content and budget of EU assistance occurs at the internal political level and is formed based on the priorities of the "new support architecture" enshrined in a number of documents: in particular the Millennium Development Goals (MDGs), the 2002 Monterrey Consensus, the 2003 Rome Declaration on Harmonization, and the 2005 Paris Declaration on Aid Effectiveness. The creation of the "new support architecture" entailed a revision of the cooperation policy for the development of the EU. Priorities were shifted towards the "least developed countries" and "low-income countries" and EU aid was gradually redirected to sub-Saharan Africa and East and South Asia, to the detriment of the group of "middle income countries", which included all LAC countries with the exception of Haiti.

In this context, since 2014, most Latin American countries have ceased to receive official development assistance (ODA) from the EU, since they were classified by the OECD as "upper middle-income countries" without rights to this type of support. In particular, bilateral cooperation was completely suspended with eight LAC countries that have the highest level of development in the region: Brazil, Mexico, Argentina, Chile, Costa Rica, Panama, Uruguay, and Venezuela. With regard to Venezuela, this decision was later revised: since 2018, the EU has continued to provide humanitarian and emergency assistance to the country.

During the period 2007–2013, 18 LAC countries received financial assistance from the EU under bilateral development cooperation. However, during the next period, 2014–2020, this list was reduced to 10 countries: Bolivia, Cuba, Paraguay, El Salvador, Guatemala, Honduras and Nicaragua, Colombia, Ecuador, and Peru. Despite this, the EU remains the largest donor of ODA in LAC. In the early 1990s, the region accounted for 9.1% of total EU aid and 7.5% in the period 2010–2011.[6] Financial flows of ODA allocated to LAC by the EU in the period 1990–2020 fluctuated (Figure 4).

ODA allocated since 2000 from the EU to LAC, amounted to almost 50% of the total ODA received by countries in this region.[7] Much of this funding was directed towards social and economic development and trade, and

---

6 CEPAL Datos. Available at: https://www.cepal.org
7 UE, América Latina y el Caribe: asociación para la prosperidad, la democracia, la resiliencia y la gobernanza mundial. Available at: https://ec.europa.eu/commission/presscorner/detail/es/IP_19_2137.

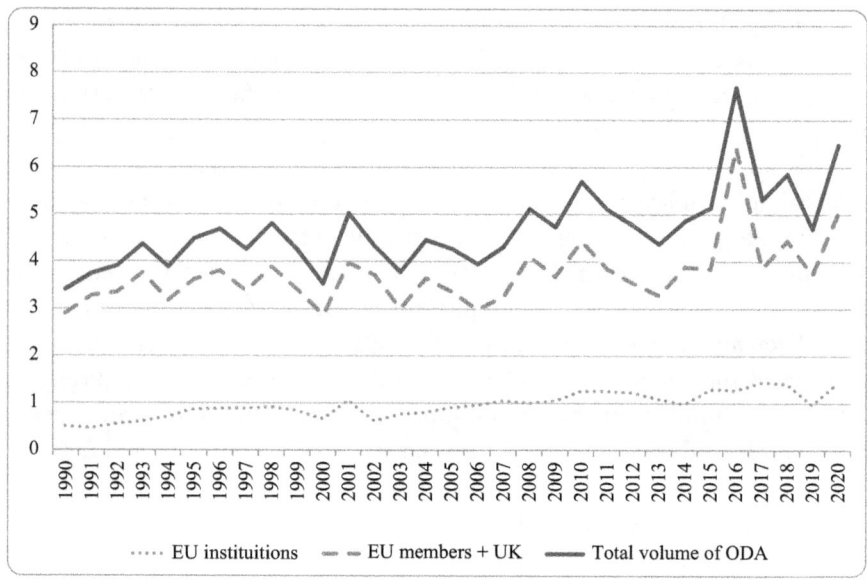

FIGURE 4 Volumes of official development assistance (ODA) provided by the EU and its member states to LAC countries in the period 1990–2020, EUR, billions
SOURCE: OECD STATISTICS

environmental protection. Geographically, this funding was distributed as follows: Central America accounted for 41% of all funds; Andean community 36%; MERCOSUR 15.5%. Of the total funds allocated, almost 80% went to 9 countries: Bolivia, Honduras, Nicaragua, Colombia, Guatemala, Ecuador, Peru, Paraguay, and El Salvador. In the 2010s, ODA decreased markedly compared to previous periods in favor of other regions such as Asia, Europe, and Africa.[8] In addition, a number of EU donor countries have gradually reduced ODA to LAC. Sweden and Denmark have followed the path of the UK by closing almost all of their offices in LAC, and the Netherlands and Italy have significantly reduced their ODA budgets in recent years.[9] Germany and France made the largest contributions to ODA for LAC.

The EU institution of assistance to LAC is characterized by a lack of complementarity and coordination between regional, subregional, and bilateral cooperation programs, which are dominated by approaches that are inflexible

---

8 Data and metadata for OECD. Available at: https://stats.oecd.org.
9 Geographical Distribution of Financial Flows to Developing Countries 2022 Available at: https://read.oecd-ilibrary.org/development/geographical-distribution-of-financial-flows-to-developing-countries-2022_6de17bb2-en-fr#page831.

to the transforming regional conditions. The EU has not yet been able to adapt its assistance policies to multilateral, regional, and subregional frameworks. Such policies were never adapted to the horizontal model of relations characteristic of the chain of already concluded association agreements with the EU, which was a consequence of the lack of a unified policy of European countries in the Latin American direction. LAC assistance programs have not come close to the level of resources allocated to similar initiatives implemented by the EU in other regions, such as the PHARE Program for Central and Eastern Europe, Tacis for the CIS countries, or the EU Cooperation Line with ACP countries.

On the other hand, it was thanks to the assistance mechanism that the EU managed to secure a privileged place among other extra-regional actors expanding their presence in LAC. In this regard, the launch in 2018 of the European Fund for Sustainable Development of Latin America is indicative.[10] Although the EU had previously announced similar programs, the new initiative was truly innovative, as it confirmed the transition from the outdated donor-recipient model of cooperation to a progressive form of peer-to-peer partnership.[11] This evoked an extremely positive response from LAC, for which the issues of dependent development and models of Center-Periphery relations have traditionally been extremely sensitive.

1.3   *Trade*

Trade traditionally occupies an important place in relations between the EU and LAC. Economic cooperation was at the center of discussion at the II (2002) and IV EU–LAC summits (2006). At the 2008 summit, the goal was again set to achieve a noticeable expansion of trade cooperation.

Mutual trade in the period 1990–2010 developed at a slow pace, and was poorly diversified and asymmetrical. In the late 1990s, imports of EU goods into the LAC significantly exceeded LAC exports to the EU. The economic crises that engulfed several LAC countries in 2000–2002 had a negative impact on mutual trade, which remained frozen at the same level. Against the backdrop of steady economic growth in LAC countries, characteristic of the period 2003–2008, the volume of mutual trade began to increase. The increase in the cost of raw materials led to the fact that exports from LAC to the EU began to

---

10   Relación UE—América latina y el Caribe es fuerte, profunda e inalienable. Available at:. https://www.eeas.europa.eu/node/48669_en.
11   The implementation of this project is supported by the OECD and the United Nations Economic Commission for Latin America and the Caribbean.

outstrip EU imports. However, by the end of 2008, the global economic crisis interrupted the phase of active growth of interregional trade.

The low economic growth rates of most EU countries after the onset of the financial crisis led to a decline in their interest in the development of extra-regional areas of cooperation, which was accompanied by a gradual decline in trade turnover. By the end of the 2020s, LAC accounted for only 6% of the total value of EU exports globally and 5% of imports. The trade niches vacated in LAC were quickly filled by China. In 2014, China displaced the EU as the region's second-largest trading partner. In 2017, China accounted for 14% of the region's total foreign trade (including exports and imports), while the EU accounted for less than 12%.

EU–LAC trade is characterized by: 1) insufficient diversification, which is manifested in the fact that trade is dominated by only a few countries: Germany, France, the UK, Italy, and Spain in the EU and Brazil, Mexico, Argentina, Chile, and Colombia in LAC side; 2) lack of sustainable growth; 3) a gradual decline in EU participation in LAC trade, first as a result of economic crises and then due to the increasing presence of China in the region; and 4) limited demand and interests of both parties in terms of the structure of mutual trade: 85% of Latin American imports from the EU are manufactured goods, and more than 40% of LAC exports to the EU are raw materials (Figure 5).

Investment cooperation demonstrates fairly stable growth. EU FDI into the LAC has gradually acquired a more prominent role. It increased sharply in the

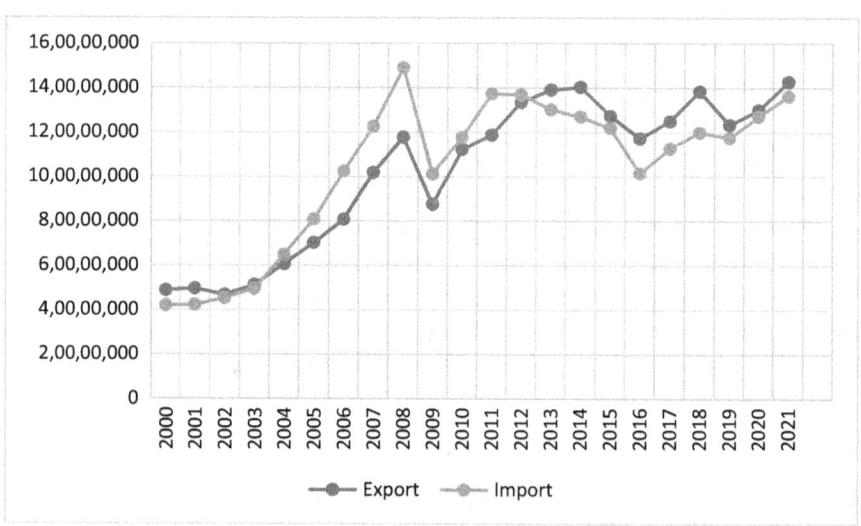

FIGURE 5   EU imports from LAC and EU exports to LAC, 2000–2021, EUR, billions
SOURCE: COMPILED BY THE AUTHOR BASED ON TRADE MAP DATA

1990s when economic conditions developed in such a way that LAC and the EU were able to effectively complement each other, which allowed for a significant increase in mutual FDI. To accelerate international integration, structural reforms were carried out in LAC countries, eliminating many restrictions on foreign capital in the hydrocarbon, mining, and service sectors of the economy, which had previously been monopolized by the state. This resulted in FDI inflows increasing sharply, allowing many EU companies to penetrate into sectors opened up by privatization. Meanwhile, in the EU, the formation of a single internal market led to the fact that companies from individual EU countries were forced to grow to a size necessary to compete in the European space. As a result, many companies chose to "grow abroad" through mergers and acquisitions, some of which have taken advantage of new opportunities in LAC. The expansion of investments of Spanish origin played a significant role in these processes.

However, this phase of the investment boom, which peaked in 1999, unexpectedly gave way to a recession phase the following year, which continued until 2003. Since 2004, EU FDI has again increased in LAC, mainly due to the interest of international investors in the natural resources of LAC, fueled by an increase in commodity prices. Under these conditions, the structure of EU FDI had slightly different characteristics compared to the previous decade. The sharp rise in EU FDI in the 1990s was primarily due to the one-time privatization processes that took place in a number of LAC countries, thanks to which the region became a priority area for EU investment activity compared to other developing regions. Unlike the first, during the second phase of the boom in 2004–2008, LAC already occupied a secondary place in matters of investment compared to Asia.[12]

The global financial crisis of 2008 led to the volume of investment from the EU, especially from Spain and Portugal, which had plunged into recession, falling sharply and significantly. Despite this, not a single major EU company abandoned its investment in LAC, even during the crisis. This was explained by the fact that in 2008–2009 the economies of the LAC countries outpaced the EU countries in terms of economic growth. The subsidiaries of EU companies located in LAC were among the most profitable globally, which strengthened the importance of this region compared to other developing countries.

In the 2010s, the volume of investment from the EU in LAC gradually reduced: in the period 2010–2014 FDI from the EU accounted for more than

---

12   Comisión Económica para América Latina y el Caribe (CEPAL), La Inversión Extranjera Directa en América Latina y el Caribe, 2018 (LC/PUB.2018/13-P), Santiago, 2018.

53% of total FDI in the region; in the period 2015–2019 it was estimated at 51%; and in 2020 it was 38%.[13] The geographical distribution of US investments was heterogeneous, since they were concentrated in the countries of South America. In Mexico, Central America, and the Caribbean, investment from the US dominated. Most EU FDI is concentrated in three sectors of LAC economies: renewable energy, telecommunications, and the automotive sector.

During the period 2000–2020, the EU formed the widest network of trade agreements with LAC in the world, ahead of even the US. The lack of a coordinated EU policy on trade issues with LAC has more than once acted as a factor weakening the mechanisms of LAC integration. Examples of such an effect were the stalled negotiations on the EU–CAN and EU–MERCOSUR agreements.

1.4 Cooperation during New Global Challenges

By the beginning of the 2020s the relations between the EU and LAC experienced a period of stagnation. The impetus for a relative decrease in cooperation was the COVID-19 pandemic. The coronavirus crisis led to the largest economic downturn in the recent history of LAC, further exacerbated by the ideological fragmentation and economic disintegration of countries in the region. The pandemic has set LAC back decades, exacerbating unresolved problems of inequality and poverty (Kosevich, 2021).

EU–LAC cooperation in the fight against COVID-19 combined several directions. The EU, as a promoter of the 2030 Agenda for Sustainable Development, sought to prevent the collapse of health systems and the emergence of new social crises in the LAC countries; the EU also saw assistance in the fight against COVID-19 as an opportunity to advance its strategic and trade interests in LAC, and strengthen its position as a global player.

During the COVID-19 pandemic, there was a reorientation of existing programs and funds already established previously as part of EU–LAC cooperation. The first step towards uniting efforts to find effective and efficient mechanisms to confront the crisis was the initiative "COVID-19 Tables" (Spanish: Mesas COVID-19), which was launched in 2020 by the European Commission in Argentina, Ecuador, and Costa Rica. In LAC, the geographic spread of the virus has been as patchy as government measures aimed at controlling the spread of the infection.[14] In this regard, the main objective of this initiative was to

---

13 La Inversión Extranjera Directa en América Latina y el Caribe 2021. Available at: https://www.cepal.org/es/publicaciones/47147-la-inversion-extranjera-directa-america-latina-caribe-2021

14 Sistema Económico Latinoamericano y del Caribe, SELA, Las relaciones económicas recientes de América Latina y el Caribe con la Unión Europea en vísperas de la Cumbre de Madrid, SP/RR-REALCUE-VICBM/DT núm. 2–10. Caracas, Venezuela, 2010, pp. 15–17.

identify the needs in order to prioritize them, coordinate actions and thus direct EU assistance in the most structured and coordinated way.[15]

The EU reconsidered its approach to the LAC, which was in great need of international support (Kosevich, 2021). As part of the Team Europe initiative as the EU's global response to the COVID-19 crisis, a total of €918 million was allocated to the region by the European Commission, with a further €325 million allocated by the European Investment Bank.[16] In addition, the EU made previously launched programs more flexible, reorienting them to a new context. Examples include EUROsociAL—an EU program to promote social cohesion in LAC, and Euroclima, a project to help the region improve its resilience to climate change. As part of the EUROsociAL program, some of its tools were activated to speed up decision-making processes and management of health emergencies.[17] To support countries in the region, the EU began to collaborate with regional organizations such as the Pan American Health Organization (OPS) and the Caribbean Public Health Agency (CARPHA).[18]

A range of new initiatives was launched in 2020–21, specifically focused on providing urgent assistance to LAC. In particular, Humanitarian Air Bridge[19]—an EU project to deliver humanitarian aid to countries most affected by COVID-19;[20] *NDICI*[21]—a program aimed at supporting countries most in need to overcome long-term development challenges; and *The Horizon Europe programme*[22]—an initiative promoting collaboration in education and research. All these programs became part of the EU foreign policy assistance institution in LAC.

---

15 El Equipo Europa ha celebrado el segundo encuentro de la Mesa COVID-19. Available at: https://www.fiiapp.org/de-las-mesas-covid-19-a-las-mesas-equipo-europa/.
16 La UE y América Latina y el Caribe: aunar esfuerzos frente a la COVID-19. Available at: https://www.fundacioncarolina.es/la-ue-y-america-latina-y-el-caribe-aunar-esfuer zosfrente-a-la-covid-19/.
17 Cohesión social frente a la COVID-19. Available at: https://eurosocial.eu/covid-19/.
18 COMUNICACIÓN CONJUNTA AL PARLAMENTO EUROPEO, AL CONSEJO, AL COMITÉ ECONÓMICO Y SOCIAL EUROPEO Y AL COMITÉ DE LAS REGIONES. Available at https://eur-lex.europa.eu/legal-content/ES/TXT/PDF/?uri=CELEX:52020JC0011&from=EN.
19 European Civil Protection and Humanitarian Aid Operations. Available at: https://civil-protection-humanitarian-aid.ec.europa.eu/what/humanitarian-aid/eu-humanitarian-air-bridge_.
20 Peru, Haiti and Venezuela received assistance under the program.
21 The Americas and the Caribbean Regional Multiannual Indicative Programme 2021–2027. Available at: https://international-partnerships.ec.europa.eu/system/files/2022-01/mip-2021-c2021-9356-americas-caribbean-annex_en.pdf.
22 https://euraxess.ec.europa.eu/worldwide/lac/horizon-europe-work-programme-2021-2022-whats-it-brazil-and-lac.

In 2023, the EU launched the *EUROFRONT program*,[23] aimed at enhancing regional security and protecting human rights in the LAC. In contrast to the programs listed above, this initiative was aimed at revitalizing the institution of EU–LAC political dialogue.

1.5 Perception of the EU's Regional Policy by Residents of Latin America

Historically, LAC has had strong ties with Europe, covering a range of areas of cooperation from political to cultural. Little is known, however, about exactly how people in LAC perceive the Old World. Understanding the place of the EU in the international context from a LAC perspective is the focus of this part of the section. The author turns to the results of public opinion polls conducted by *Latinobarómetro*[24] in 2004 and 2021, which were devoted to assessing the role of the EU in regional and international affairs.[25]

The survey conducted in 2004, when a leftist turn was gaining momentum in the LAC with anti-American sentiment emerging, demonstrated that residents of the region viewed the EU as a "civilized force" that would not turn into the aggressive military force that the US represented (Noya, 2005). At the beginning of the 21st century the 60% of LAC residents were pro-European. A large majority still recognized US leadership on issues such as development assistance, trade, maintaining peace, and promoting democracy (Table 6).

For Mexico and South American countries, assessments of EU influence in promoting democracy and maintaining peace were ahead of assessments of US influence in these areas. The same survey showed that the EU is associated primarily with two topics: football and wars.

The survey conducted in 2021 demonstrated that the idea of creating an interregional strategic association with the EU was seen as a feasible and not a utopian goal. The majority described the EU as an influential player in international affairs, and also recognized its strategic independence.

In 2021, respondents agreed that the EU is a preferred partner for LAC compared to China and the US in 5 areas: protecting the environment, protecting human rights, promoting world peace, fighting poverty and inequality, and humanitarian assistance. These data are consistent with the fact that it is these areas that receive primary attention in the programs that the EU is currently developing in LAC. The EU is not seen as a priority partner when it comes to

---

23   https://programaeurofront.eu/en/page/que-es-eurofront.
24   Latinobarómetro—non-governmental research organization, the largest independent survey center in Latin America.
25   América Latina—Unión Europea: miradas, agendas y expectativas. Available at: https://colombia.fes.de/detail/america-latina-union-europea-miradas-agendas-y-expectativas.

TABLE 6 Assessment of the presence and influence of the EU and the US in certain areas through the eyes of Latin Americans, % of the number of respondents (Results of a Latinobarómetro survey conducted in 2004)

%		South America	Central America	Mexico	Average
Democracy	EU	33	16	54	27
	US	28	54	20	37
Preserving peace	EU	29	16	46	24
	US	27	52	20	36
Development	EU	19	11	24	16
	US	28	51	29	36
Free trade	EU	16	8	21	13
	US	33	60	33	43

SOURCE: COMPILED BY THE AUTHOR BASED ON DATA FROM A LATINOBARÓMETRO SURVEY CONDUCTED IN 2004

security, military power (US primacy was noted in these areas), or economic cooperation, technological progress, and science and education, since the dominant role of China is recognized here (Figure 6).

The data shows that Latin Americans in 2004 and 2021 had a fairly high level of knowledge about the EU and its internal leadership hierarchy: they recognized the leadership roles of Germany and France. In the third place of the "leading countries of the EU", according to LAC residents, is Spain. Regarding the assessment of the economic presence of EU countries, the 2021 survey confirms that, in comparison with the US and China, it is minimal. The majority of respondents (69%) expect a sharp increase in the influence of the EU in global politics and economics in the near future. The presence of the strategic independence of the EU is recognized by 52% of respondents (according to 34% of respondents, the EU directly follows the US in its policy).

∙ ∙ ∙

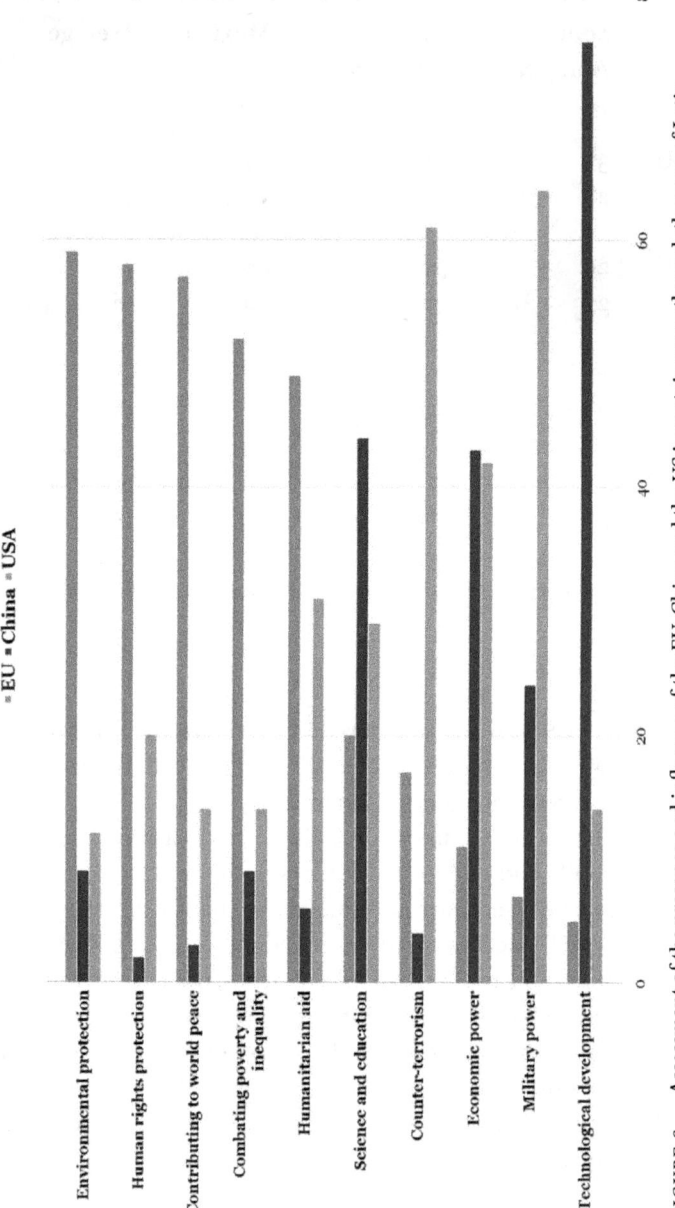

FIGURE 6 Assessment of the presence and influence of the EU, China and the US in certain areas through the eyes of Latin Americans, % of the number of respondents (results of a Latinobarómetro survey conducted at the end of 2021)
SOURCE: COMPILED BY THE AUTHOR BASED ON DATA FROM A LATINOBARÓMETRO SURVEY CONDUCTED AT THE END OF 2021

Interregional relations between the EU and LAC are based on the idea of dialogue between equal parties, where three main areas are distinguished: political dialogue, assistance programs, and trade. The presence of common values and a long history of close cooperation makes the EU–LAC relationship truly "special", which is characterized by a dual nature. While the EU is the largest investor, the largest source of development finance and also the third trading partner of LAC countries, Europe is not yet ready to recognize LAC as a significant actor in international relations, which ultimately led to a decline in European influence in this region.

At the beginning of the 21st century LAC and the EU built their interaction mainly according to the old model without taking into account the fundamental transformations that the world, Europe, and LAC were undergoing. This makes the entire multi-level system of interregional relations unstable to new global and regional challenges. In particular, EU policy has so far been unable to take into account the specificities of the new ideological landscape of LAC with leaders who are characterized by a personalist, populist, and even "anti-system" style of government. A clear example is the cooling in relations between Spain and Argentina, which arose in May 2024 after accusations made by the anti-system populist Argentine President Javier Milei against the wife of Spanish prime minister, Pedro Sánchez.[26] The diplomatic crisis is striking in the harshness of the positions of both sides, the fact that it took place between two countries that are deeply connected historically, and the change in EU interactions with LAC.

An important characteristic feature of the new LAC governments was that their foreign policy was much more open to extra-regional alternative cooperation to the detriment of the traditional Atlantic direction. All this creates serious obstacles to the interests of the EU in this region.

2 EU–LAC Relations: the Priority of Economics over Politics

The III EU–CELAC Summit, held in July 2023 in Brussels, left an ambivalent impression. The event brought together representatives of 27 EU countries and 33 LAC countries at one table, which became a long-awaited event after eight years since the last event of this format (Kosevich, 2024). The 2023 Summit was not without scandal: on the eve of the event, the head of the Cuban

---

26   https://elpais.com/argentina/2024-05-22/la-crisis-diplomatica-con-espana-ayuda-a-milei-a-tapar-sus-frentes-internos.html.

Foreign Ministry publicly pointed out the lack of transparency and manipulative behavior of the EU during the preparation of the III Summit, noting that Brussels was trying to "impose a Europeanized vision on bi-regional relations, ignoring the priorities and interests of LAC countries."[27]

The renewed interest of the EU in the LAC, which emerged in October 2022 when the meeting of the EU and CELAC foreign ministers took place, is explained by a number of factors: the reduction of the EU influence in LAC, which was the result of China's expanding presence there, the growing US–Chinese competition; the escalation of the Russia–Ukraine conflict; and the need for an energy and digital transition.

New global challenges have once again drawn the attention of the EU and LAC to the need to renew cooperation. The COVID-19 pandemic confirmed that the state remains the main actor in international relations, but its actions alone are not enough to solve global problems. The pandemic drew attention to the world's unresolved problems, such as climate change, social inequality, and the fight against poverty, emphasizing the importance of creating multilateral alliances that allow us to move towards overcoming them. The escalation of the Russia–Ukraine conflict and the outbreak of the war in Gaza also emphasized the importance of having a strong strategic partnership between the EU and the LAC, where the presence of a multi-level and effective dialogue capable of withstanding increasing global pressure has acquired particular importance. In this context, the EU's most effective tool has been to promote multilateralism, built around common interests and a common understanding of the mechanisms of interregional dialogue, where economic cooperation plays an important role.

The EU and LAC have developed their own understanding of multilateralism. Multilateralism, as one of the key principles of EU foreign policy towards the LAC, is based on the idea of promoting global and regional governance through the convergence of legal frameworks and the creation of facilitation mechanisms that allow the formation of common proposals submitted for discussion in international forums to address the main challenges of the future, primarily in the field of sustainable development (Beaumont, 2020).

The main foreign policy instrument of the EU in promoting multilateralism is diplomacy, using which Brussels is able to bring divided LAC countries to the negotiating table. Diplomacy is helping to "unfreeze" the work of such multilateral regional institutions as CELAC, UNASUR, and OAS, which by the beginning

---

27   https://www.prensa-latina.cu/2023/07/10/cuba-denuncio-conducta-manipuladora-de-la-ue-en-cumbre-con-la-celac

of the 2020s found themselves paralyzed by intraregional disagreements. The EU, perceived by LAC countries as a "civilized force" and a trustworthy actor, is able to resume dialogue even on particularly difficult issues such as the crisis in Venezuela and the recent political instability in Bolivia (Pietikäinen, 2020). The EU views its relationship with LAC as "a platform capable of coordinating and projecting common interests on the international stage", in which multilateralism acts as a unifying factor to promote more sustainable and equitable development (Ayuso, 2021).

Extra-regional trade traditionally occupies an important place in the foreign policy of LAC, considered by LAC countries as an important tool aimed at increasing the autonomy and diversification of the region's international relations. This led to the fact that multilateralism was interpreted precisely from the standpoint of economic cooperation, as "a system of principles, rules of the game, and institutions aimed at shaping collective global trends in world trade" (Peña, 2000). This correlated with the fact that, despite the traditions of multilateral cooperation over the past decades, distrust in international organizations has become entrenched in LAC. For example, during the pandemic, LAC governments emphasized measures at the national level to the detriment of joint actions with regional coverage (Kosevich, 2020).

In terms of expanding interregional cooperation in the first quarter of the 21st century, where trade occupies a special place, the EU and LAC experienced a situation similar to the second half of the 1990s. The EU followed the path of developing bilateral relations, rather than a unified regional strategy.

2.1 Trade and Economic Relations between the EU and LAC

The EU began negotiation processes on agreements with LAC regional associations back in the 1990s. Several treaties were developed almost simultaneously, which predetermined their certain similarities.

The reasons that pushed the EU to conclude such agreements were primarily political rather than economic. The EU developed external relations during the conditions of relative global stability that emerged after the end of the Cold War, while trying to take advantage of the moment when LAC countries, having just experienced democratization, showed increased interest in diversifying extra-regional areas of cooperation.

Since the end of the Cold War, LAC has seen a reconfiguration of intra- and inter-regional ties. The new system of international relations that emerged in LAC was characterized by the presence of two opposing blocs that emerged after the failure of the Free Trade Area for the Americas (FTAA), an initiative promoted by Washington, and the creation of the ALBA, led by Caracas. In the new reality, increased attention began to be paid to the integration processes developing in the region and driven primarily by internal rather than international goals, taking as a basis the idea of combining the efforts of all LAC countries (Lechini, 2009). For the EU, such a new alignment in LAC significantly facilitated the development of agreements with several countries and integration associations at once, which was facilitated by the strong negotiating position of the EU, taking into account high rates of economic growth. Brussels did not have any particular economic interest in such agreements, given that the LAC has never been its priority foreign policy.

In 1994, the EU announced a new strategy for the development of relations with LAC, according to which two priority areas of cooperation between the EU and LAC were identified: building constructive political dialogue at different levels and the formation of a more effective model of economic interaction. Interest in trade with LAC was caused by the increased attractiveness of LAC markets, which were emerging with new integration models, in particular MERCOSUR, NAFTA, and FTAA. The EU's fears that NAFTA and FTAA would reduce the EU's share of trade with LAC in favor of the US led to the activation of the economic wing of interregional relations. The EU's attention to the MERCOSUR bloc increased, including thanks to the proposal for the formation of a Free Trade, Cooperation and Technology Transfer Zone. This project was put forward during the EU–MERCOSUR meeting at the level of foreign ministers, held in Sao Paulo in 1994 (Bizzozero, 2001).

The EU's desire to create free trade zones with MERCOSUR, Mexico, and Chile was received extremely positively in LAC, since for the first time it opened up the region's access to the EU market without traditional protectionism. The EU's increased interest in the LAC has gradually led to the signing of a number of trade agreements.

2.2   The EU, Mexico, and Chile

In 1997, Mexico became the first LAC country with which the EU signed an association agreement, which, in addition to agreements on new terms of trade and assistance from Europe, provided for political dialogue with European partners, eventually receiving the name "global agreement". This pact soon turned into a free trade agreement; in 2000 it extended to trade in goods, and in 2001 it extended to trade in services. In 2008, Mexico was declared a strategic partner of the EU.

The new level of relations led to the fact that by the beginning of the 2020s, the EU had become Mexico's third largest trading partner, after the US and China which account for more than 80% of Mexico's total trade. Mexico is the EU's 13th largest trading partner.

In 2013, a decision was made on the need to modernize the EU–Mexico global agreement: the trade part was updated in 2018, and the government procurement part was updated in 2020. The EU side requested a special study reflecting the real social, economic, and environmental consequences of this agreement. In addition, there was no consensus on the procedure for ratifying the updated treaty for each section of the document separately or simultaneously for the entire text. Despite announced statements that the parties had reached a consensus, the agreement was not fully ratified by 2024, encountering resistance from a number of EU countries.

The 1997 agreement was considered the foundation for building strong relations on an equal basis; the renewal of this agreement in the 2020s took place in a completely different context. The EU became more focused on better controlling the geopolitical changes taking place in the Western Hemisphere, using every opportunity to strengthen its role in international trade. Mexico viewed the agreement with the EU as a tool to strengthen the country's internal stability, both economically and politically (Domínguez, 2022).

The stalled negotiations on the EU–Mexico agreement were caused by the fact that the parties could not reach a consensus on issues such as the legal protection of geographical indications, investment protection, and a ban on the sale of Mexican beef in the EU. If concluded, the updated agreement would make trade between Mexico and the EU free of customs duties on almost all goods, which angered European farmers. As with the EU–MERCOSUR agreement, the European side pointed to the increasing risks threatening sustainable development and environmental management in Mexico, and the inability of Mexico to cope with a range of new challenges, such as the digital economy, corruption, and migration. That criticism obscured the fact that the renewed agreement could triple trade between Mexico and the EU.

The EU–Chile Cooperation Framework Agreement was signed in 1996 and entered into force in 1999. The stated purpose of this agreement was to form a basis for building an effective partnership of a political and economic nature, and the creation of a bilateral free trade zone. In 2002, the EU and Chile concluded an association agreement that included three areas of cooperation: political dialogue, assistance, and trade.

The signing of the association agreement initiated a new stage in the development of trade and economic relations between the EU and Chile, becoming one of the most extensive, deep and modern, standing out favorably against other similar documents signed at that time by the EU. The result was a noticeable increase in mutual trade flows: the EU became the main foreign investor in Chile and its third largest trading partner. In 2020, mutual trade turnover between the EU and Chile was 13.4 billion euros, and EU FDI was 89.8 billion euros, accounting for 36% of total foreign investment in Chile. In addition, the new terms of trade enshrined in the agreement contributed to the diversification of Chilean exports to European markets, and also expanded the presence of Chilean SMEs in the eurozone.

As in the case of Mexico, the renewal of this agreement also faced a number of obstacles. In particular, EU Trade Commissioner Cecilia Malmström proposed including a new chapter on gender equality in the document. New aspects that were reflected in the modernized agreement were the protection of investments, the protection of geographical indications, the fight against corruption, and ensuring sustainable trade.

Despite the positive economic relations between Santiago and Brussels, Chile became the first LAC country to sign an FTA with China in 2005. For Chile, this agreement was the fruit of the "openness policy of open regionalism" that the Chilean government had begun to build since the 1990s. Chile unilaterally reduced its customs duties, signed important trade agreements with a number of countries, and took part in multilateral forums such as APEC. Capitalizing on 42 years of officially positive diplomatic relations with China, Chile became the first non-Asian country to sign a free trade agreement with China. This led to China becoming the dominant force in Chilean trade by 2020. Trade with China was double that of the US and the EU combined.

The lack of ratification of modernized agreements between the EU and Chile and Mexico has become the focus of the EU's attention. At the height of the COVID-19 pandemic, the French President stated that delegating food production to other countries would be an irresponsible step, which led to the stalling of these negotiation processes, but in 2022, Europeans again began to lean towards ratifying agreements with Mexico and Chile, given the increasing influence of China in these countries. In February 2024, the EU Council adopted a decision on the conclusion of the Interim Agreement on trade between the EU and Chile, marking the end of the internal ratification process within the EU.

2.3 The EU, Colombia, Peru, and Ecuador

The EU began developing a free trade agreement with Colombia and Peru after the failure of negotiations on a comprehensive agreement between the EU and CAN, reached an impasse after irreconcilable political differences arose between the members of this association. In particular, Venezuela's withdrawal from CAN in 2006 significantly reduced the EU's economic interest in concluding an association agreement with this bloc.[28]

---

28 Caracas justified its withdrawal from CAN by the free trade agreements signed by Peru and Colombia with the US, which entailed economic losses for all other members of the

Another obstacle to EU negotiations with Andean countries was the banana war,[29] which had regional consequences. In particular, the EU–Central America agreement could only be concluded after the banana conflict between LAC and the EU was resolved. Despite all this, Colombia and Peru, as states actively developing their foreign economic relations, were interested in concluding a trade agreement with the EU much more than other Andean countries. Colombia and Peru themselves expressed interest in pursuing a separate agreement with the EU; they were also motivated by their intention to become members of the OECD and an increased focus on protecting workers' rights.

The interest of all parties in concluding such a pact influenced the speed of the negotiation process on this agreement: it was agreed upon in 2011, signed in 2012, and came into force a year later. In 2017, Ecuador officially joined the trade agreement concluded between the EU and Colombia and Peru (EU-C-P-E agreement).[30] Bolivia also plans to join the treaty.

The main goal of the EU-C-P-E agreement was the gradual opening of markets, where a special emphasis is placed on achieving sustainable development and complying with environmental obligations. An important role is assigned to the greater involvement of civil society in interregional dialogue, expanding cooperation in the field of technology transfer and the protection of geographical indications.

Thanks to the EU-C-P-E agreement, preferential treatment was created in trade between the EU and three CAN member countries, with the exception of Bolivia, which is a beneficiary of the GSP+ system—a system of unilateral trade preferences provided by the EU to developing countries as part of its obligations to the WTO. The treaty provided better market access by reducing or eliminating tariffs on goods that are most important to bilateral trade. This led to the formation of a more stable and predictable business environment, the creation of better conditions for mutual trade using non-tariff barriers, the formation of transparent systems for the movement of capital, access to public procurement, and the protection of intellectual property.

---

community, thanks to them it became a "dead" and therefore meaningless association.

29   The Banana War was a conflict that arose over the preferential treatment that the EU granted to banana imports from some ACP countries to the detriment of the economies of Latin American states. The dispute, which began in 1993, finally came to an end in 2012 after being resolved through the Dispute Settlement Body of the World Trade Organization (WTO). The conflict was an important precedent that demonstrated to the world how developing countries could benefit from the dispute settlement system.

30   On July 17, 2014, after four rounds of negotiations, Ecuador and the EU concluded a treaty allowing Ecuador to join the multilateral trade agreement signed by Colombia and Peru with the EU. In 2017, this agreement officially came into force.

Since the signing of the EU-C-P-E agreement, all three Latin American countries have experienced economic benefits. The sector of the LAC economy that benefited most from the EU trade agreement was agriculture, with the sales of LAC food products to the eurozone increasing significantly. Ecuador has become an important agricultural supplier to the eurozone. By 2022, every third banana sold in an EU member state was Ecuadorian. Micro, small, and medium-sized enterprises in Ecuador, Colombia, and Peru entered the EU markets at a very slow pace, due to the need to meet high quality and safety standards for their products, for which many of them were not prepared.

The EU is not among the priority trading partners of the countries of the Andean subregion: the US and China are the main trading partners of Colombia and Ecuador; China has already become Peru's largest export and import market, followed by the US. The high and stable rate of development of commercial relations between China and Peru is the result of a bilateral free trade agreement signed in April 2009. Peru, together with Chile, have already become "Pacific platforms" connecting China with the largest economies of South America.

2.4   The EU and the Caribbean

The Caribbean was initially considered by the EU as part of ACP, and not as an integral part of Latin America, which explained the existence of a separate dialogue between the EU and these countries.

The Caribbean as part of the ACP association, gives it significant advantages over the rest of the LAC in terms of receiving ODA from the EU, and the level of intensity of political dialogue with the EU. Promoting development through expanding economic ties between the EU and ACP countries was the main purpose of the creation of ACP.

The development of trade relations between the EU and ACP was facilitated by the signing of the Lomé Conventions; I Convention was signed in 1975 (with the participation of 46 ACP countries), II Convention in 1979 (58 ACP countries), III Lomé Convention in 1984 (65 ACP countries), and the IV Lomé Convention in 1989 (68 ACP countries, which were joined by 2 more countries in 1995). In 2000, the EU and 78 ACP countries, including 15 Caribbean countries, signed the Cotonou Agreement,[31] governing relations between the Caribbean Community (CARICOM)[32] and the EU. All CARICOM members,

---

31   The Cotonou Agreement is designed for twenty years and contains a clause allowing it to be revised every 5 years.
32   CARICOM is an international organization created to strengthen relations within the Caribbean subregion.

with the exception of Montserrat, signed and ratified the Cotonou Agreement. Article 37 of the Cotonou Agreement provided for the conclusion of economic partnership agreements aimed at strengthening the integration of ACP countries into the world economy and regulating trade cooperation between the EU and ACP. This prompted the parties to begin negotiations with a view to concluding similar agreements.

Negotiations for an Economic Partnership Agreement between the Caribbean and the EU began on 16 April 2004 in Kingston, Jamaica. The negotiation was repeatedly stalled, causing acute discontent in the Caribbean. As a result, having gone through four stages of approval, the economic partnership agreement between the EU and the Caribbean Forum (Cariforum)[33] was signed in October 2008.[34] A year later, Haiti joined the agreement.

The terms of trade exchange enshrined in the EU–Cariforum agreement led to the fact that trade between the countries of the Caribbean and the EU developed asymmetrically in favor of Cariforum, which could export unhindered to the EU, while European imports to the Caribbean face a number of obstacles.[35]

Thanks to this agreement, sales of professional services provided by Caribbean states were transferred to lighter terms. The EU assists countries in this subregion in providing technical assistance and strengthening their capacity to comply with European standards in health, safety, and the environment. The EU also supports the formation of a single economic space between the Dominican Republic and Haiti, promoting integration within CARICOM.

Following the UK's exit from the EU in 2020, the six British overseas territories located in the Caribbean found themselves in a special situation.[36] From that moment on, the overseas territories of the UK began to be considered by the EU as part of a single Caribbean basin. This led to the fact that as Brexit negotiations progressed, the UK actively negotiated new trade agreements with Latin American states representing different subregions, trying to maintain its economic contacts in this area. In particular, in 2019 the UK signed

---

33   Cariforum is an association of Caribbean states, which includes Antigua and Barbuda, the Bahamas, Barbados, Belize, Dominica, the Dominican Republic, Grenada, Guyana, Haiti, Jamaica, Saint Keats and Nevis, Saint Lucia, Saint Vincent and the Grenadines, Suriname and Trinidad and Tobago.
34   SICE. (2008) *Acuerdo de Asociación Económica CARIFORUM-Comunidad Europea.* http://www.sice.oas.org/Trade/CAR_EU_EPA_s/careu_in_s.ASP.
35   Most of the trade flow from the EU to the Caribbean is in the industrial sector, primarily cars, vehicle parts and boats. Caribbean countries sell fuel, mining products, and agricultural products such as bananas, sugar, and rum to the EU.
36   The British Overseas Territories in the Caribbean are Anguilla, Bermuda, the British Virgin Islands, the Cayman Islands, Montserrat, and the Turks and Caicos Islands.

trade agreements with Peru, Chile, Colombia, Cariforum member countries, and Central America. By the time the UK left the EU, it had been able to secure a chain of trade agreements with the LAC, which were already in use thanks to the mechanisms of "bridges", allowing for their temporary validity without ratification. In December 2020, the UK and Mexico signed a business continuity agreement, which preserved the preferential trade regime enshrined in the EU–Mexico free trade agreement. All this was a confirmation of the UK's interest in expanding both trade cooperation and political interaction with the LAC in general and the Caribbean in particular, while emphasizing the existence of a common history.

China is interested in expanding its relations with the Caribbean, which is geographically very close to the US, making it strategically important for Beijing in the areas of logistics, trade, and banking. In particular, China has already "donated" special weapons and security equipment for the military and law enforcement forces to the entire Caribbean region, created a network of Chinese cultural centers, and issued loans to a number of Caribbean countries for the construction of kilometers of new highways. During the pandemic, the Chinese government made large-scale supplies of COVID-19 tests, masks, and ventilators much needed to protect the population of this poor subregion. Unlike other LAC subregions, one of the main actors in relations between China and Caribbean countries are not only governments, companies, and banks, but also Chinese immigrants. However, despite the fact that China has already become a significant trading partner of this subregion, a general distrust of China has taken hold in Caribbean society, which significantly limits its capabilities in this area.

The Caribbean is integrating quite slowly and difficultly with the rest of Latin America, which is the result of several factors: underdeveloped infrastructure and transport networks in this subregion; an extremely high level of dependence on trade with the US; and despite the fact that the most common language in this subregion is Spanish, virtually all Caribbean islands are characterized by African culture, which sets them apart from the rest of the LAC countries, which have inherited the so-called "direct Latin tradition".[37] This results in the Caribbean existing and developing in parallel with the rest of the LAC, but not with it. However, this gap has been further exacerbated since 2020, with the Caribbean being disproportionately affected by the COVID-19 pandemic as a result of weak health systems. The format of parallel cooperation that the EU

---

37 The languages spoken in the Caribbean are Papiamento, Creole, Pidgin English, Patois, Garifuna (which is a mixture of Arawakan and Spanish), French and English.

is developing with the Caribbean also partially contributes to further polarization of this subregion from the rest of the LAC.

2.5 The EU and Central America

The dialogue between the EU and Central America has become another important separate direction in the growing activity at the end of the 20th century within the EU Latin American policy: in 1993, the EU and Central America signed a framework agreement on cooperation, and in 2003, an agreement on political dialogue and cooperation. The parties voiced their intention to conclude a comprehensive association agreement during the EU–Central America summit held in Vienna in 2006, after which a rapid negotiation process began: it began in 2007, ended in 2010, and in 2012 was signed by all parties. The conclusion of this agreement was partially facilitated by the fact that the Central American group had already signed a similar agreement with the US, which established the need for a number of structural reforms at the national level, which were subsequently requested by the EU.

The Association Agreement between the EU and the Central American countries (Costa Rica, El Salvador, Guatemala, Honduras, Nicaragua and Panama) was the first agreement concluded between the EU and a group of Latin American countries. For Central America, the agreement opened up new opportunities for the inclusion of the countries of this subregion in the world market, and for the EU it became the practical implementation of its updated strategy of pivoting towards the developing world.

The agreement outlines three main areas of cooperation: trade, where the focus was on the access to sensitive goods from Central America (such as bananas, sugar and meat products) to the EU market; assistance which is primarily related to supporting integration processes in the countries of Central America; and political dialogue aimed at reconciling the parties' common positions on issues of multilateralism, democracy, and human rights. Taking into account the fact that in the 21st century the human rights problem in Central America has become particularly acute, the EU became committed to developing close cooperation with the countries of the subregion in this area. Thus, the EU provides financial and technical assistance to civil society and human rights organizations that contribute to the protection of human rights and the rule of law in vertical regulation. This support is aimed at strengthening the capacity of these institutions to protect human rights, especially the rights of women, children, indigenous communities, and the poorest people.[38]

---

38 In this regard, a number of related initiatives have been launched: the EU–Central America regional program for promoting human rights and strengthening the rule of law,

As a result, the EU–Central America agreement brought tangible benefits to the national economies of the Central American countries, thereby giving impetus to the development of regional integration and interregionalism. An important achievement was that it was possible to achieve relative unification of law in the member countries of the Central American Common Market (CACM),[39] especially in terms of the legal regulation of the service sector. The agreement allowed Central American countries to reap the benefits of access to the liberalized EU market, while also bringing LAC-wide attention to the policy of "merging the commercial, environmental and social agenda" promoted by the EU.

The EU–Central America agreement enshrines the Generalized System of Preferences Plus (GSP+). This mechanism has become a kind of reward for responsible compliance with international conventions,[40] allowing developing countries to receive tariff breaks on critical exports from Central America to the eurozone, which must meet certain requirements set by the EU, such as origin requirements. These conditions are unilateral and can be terminated by the EU at any time.

In fact, the EU–Central America Agreement had one main goal—to help Central American countries, through increased trade, move towards sustainable development, which found an immediate response in this subregion, for which the problem of development is pressing. This goal is achieved by gradually eliminating barriers to industrial goods and products from the agricultural and fishing sectors; complying with general standards for the protection of intellectual property rights and the recognition of geographical indications; accelerating the movement of goods in Central America through greater integration at the subregional level, and reducing administrative burdens for exporters.

In Central America, which occupies an important economic and geographical position in the Western Hemisphere, as a bridge between North and South America, the influence of China is increasingly felt. In particular, Panama, due to its strategic location, has become the main port of entry for goods moving along the Chinese "Silk Road" to the American continent. In 2017, Panama established diplomatic relations with China, while severing them with Taiwan,

---

and the EU Support for the Protection of Human Rights Defenders in Central America and the Support for Gender Equality and Women's Empowerment programs.

39 Central American Common Market (CACM) is a regional integration association created in 1960 and includes Costa Rica, El Salvador, Guatemala, Honduras, Nicaragua, and Panama.

40 First of all, conventions relating to the protection of human rights and freedoms.

which was one of its oldest reliable partners. Beijing has significantly increased its presence in Nicaragua, becoming one of the largest trading partners and sources of investment. China is involved in a number of projects in Nicaragua aimed at accelerating economic growth and the development of the state. The construction of the Nicaraguan Canal, which should become an alternative to the Panama Canal, large-scale programs for modernizing ports and highways, projects in the field of renewable energy sources (including wind and solar energy projects), programs for the construction of affordable housing and support for agricultural development. For the sake of rapprochement with China and attracting Chinese investment, El Salvador, Costa Rica, and the Dominican Republic also changed their positions towards Taiwan, despite the fact that this immediately negatively affected the dialogue with their traditional patron, the US. Unlike the Caribbean, Central America is ready to completely pivot towards China, while the US still retains its primacy in trade in Central America.[41]

2.6 The EU–MERCOSUR Agreement

An important role in the updated EU strategy in LAC, launched at the turn of the century, was played by support for the integration processes that were developing at that time in the region, where MERCOSUR, led by the Latin American giants Argentina and Brazil, occupied a special place. MERCOSUR was created in 1991 by the Treaty of Asunción and included Argentina, Brazil, Paraguay, and Uruguay as founding members. Venezuela joined the trade bloc in 2006 when Paraguay's membership was temporarily suspended amid the country's declining levels of democracy. Bolivia's accession protocol was signed in 2015, but the country is still in the process of joining the bloc. Bolivia's interest in joining MERCOSUR has temporarily dropped due to the internal crisis caused by the resignation of President Evo Morales (2006–2019), which ultimately froze the Andean country's participation in regional integration processes. The rise to power of Luis Arce in 2020 saw Bolivia turn again to MERCOSUR, which La Paz views as a "natural process". In December 2023, Bolivia joined the organization as the fifth country, only the last ratification is pending at time of writing.

The Ushuaia Protocol on democratic commitment under MERCOSUR, signed in 1998, established the presence of democratic institutions as a prerequisite for a member country of this trading bloc. In this regard, since April 2017, MERCOSUR has hold consultations with Venezuela, whose regime has been accused of violations of democratic principles of governance. However, all the recommendations voiced were not accepted by Venezuela, which led to

---

41 UNCTAD. *Statistics*. Available at: https://unctad.org/statistics.

the fact that in August 2017 Caracas was deprived of membership in the bloc. Despite the fact that Venezuela does not participate in the EU–MERCOSUR Association Agreement, the internal socio-economic crisis that has gripped the country also affects other members of this trading bloc. Although the domestic situation in Brazil is far from what Venezuela is experiencing, the presidency of Jair Bolsonaro (2019–2022) has also led to political instability in Brazil. It is worth mentioning separately the tension in relations between Brazil and Argentina, which at the beginning of the 2020s has grown to levels not seen since the 1980s (Stuenkel, 2019).

It was the gradual formation and strengthening of the Brazilian–Argentine axis, which set the trajectory of the economic and political development of all of South America, that ultimately contributed to the emergence of the MERCOSUR bloc, which pursues three main goals: the democratization of South America; the transition from a protectionist economic model to a more open economy; and the formation of a foreign policy aimed at greater inclusion in the system of international relations. It was these that prompted MERCOSUR to agree on a trade agreement with the EU, discussions on which began in 2000.

EU–MERCOSUR relations have been governed by the Cooperation Framework Agreement, signed on 15 December 1995 and which entered into force on 1 July 1999. The EU viewed negotiations on a trade agreement with MERCOSUR as part of a strategy to defend the liberal world order. The impact of this pact on the level of trade relations was of secondary importance for them. For the EU, the agreement with MERCOSUR was another opportunity to establish itself as a normative actor fighting against growing protectionism and economic nationalism. MERCOSUR perceived this agreement as a continuation of its policy of "openness" in the context of the course taken by the new liberal and right-wing governments of Argentina and Brazil to build a "commercial MERCOSUR". For the South American bloc, this treaty represented an opportunity to deepen regional integration. One common goal that was associated with the conclusion of the agreement by both the EU and MERCOSUR was to ensure greater inclusion in interregional interaction of the most "intractable countries", such as Brazil and France.

Despite Bolsonaro's criticism of MERCOSUR, and his promise of Brazil's exit from the bloc, the EU–MERCOSUR trade agreement was signed during his presidency, becoming a symbol of the defense of economic globalization and a multilateral system already bursting at the seams. In 2019, through the EU–MERCOSUR agreement, the Latin American and EU parties declared their rejection of protectionism and their readiness to trade and cooperate in compliance with the highest standards. It was the EU here that acted as the defender of free trade in the Global West, which contrasted with the protectionist policies of the Donald Trump administration.

On the other hand, by agreeing to this pact, the EU tried to stop China, which was actively expanding its presence and influence in MERCOSUR countries. During the 2010s, China's trade volumes with MERCOSUR have approached the bloc's trade volumes with the EU and the US combined, leading to a rapid decline in the EU's influence in South America. China was noticeably ahead of the EU in terms of investment in this subregion. In particular, in the period 2008–2018, Brazil ranked fifth in terms of Chinese investment globally. China's interest in Latin America increased as tensions between Washington and Beijing grew. By the beginning of 2022, China had become the main trading partner of Brazil and Argentina, which was the result of the leadership of these countries in soybean production.

The conditions set out in the EU–MERCOSUR agreement made it much easier to export MERCOSUR to the EU by integrating dynamic sectors of the South American economy into the EU's value chains, thereby helping to diversify the trading bloc's economy and make it less dependent on certain types of exports. The agreement also contributed to the creation of a favorable business environment for the EU in MERCOSUR It was assumed that EU companies would face fewer barriers to entering a market with more than 260 million consumers.

Several problems emerged that jeopardized the conclusion of this agreement. The most important factor in freezing the MERCOSUR–EU negotiation agreement was the crisis of globalization, the challenge to multilateralism and regionalism, and the rise of nationalist and far-right forces, which was further exacerbated by the global economic downturn (Sanahuja, 2019). During the beginning of the 2020s individual critical remarks regarding this agreement accompanied the negotiation process throughout the 20 years of its development, others were relatively new, driven by rising sentiments of economic nationalism and the emergence of new political forces opposed to free trade.

The most important factor in freezing the agreement was its non-acceptance by France, which was evident even when the document first began to be discussed, becoming more acute over the years. If the reasons for France's negative stance were initially quite vague, it was based on independent research, which argued that the agreement would increase the rate of deforestation and also increase greenhouse gas emissions in the MERCOSUR countries. In 2019, criticism of the pact focused on forest fires in the Amazon and protests by French farmers whose incomes were being hit by new trade terms. The French side insisted that the agreement would entail the gradual clearing of approximately 700,000 hectares of rainforest to create pastures, which would mean a 4% increase in beef sales. The result will be an increase in greenhouse gas emissions that would exceed the limits set by the Paris Agreement. All this led to other European countries beginning to share France's position, in particular Ireland, Austria, Belgium and Luxembourg, which were joined by a number of public organizations. EU countries have called for the agreement to be scrapped, insisting that MERCOSUR must be required to provide more guarantees to meet health and environmental requirements. Another negative factor that stalled the approval process was internal contradictions within MERCOSUR itself. In particular, Uruguay demanded flexibility for member countries to negotiate unilaterally with other markets, and Brazil began to push for the modernization of the Common External Tariff, calling for its significant reduction.

The result was that the historic EU–MERCOSUR agreement was left hanging, as the EU side insisted that its conclusion would create a negative precedent that could, over time, affect other agreements that the EU was developing. Critics have argued that the treaty would challenge EU leadership on environmental issues, especially after the announcement of the European Green Deal in 2019. Ratification of the EU–MERCOSUR agreement in its current form would symbolize that the EU is prioritizing economic interests over climate and social issues (Giles, 2021). The second victory in the French presidential elections of Emmanuel Macron (2017–present) in 2022 again suspended the ratification process of the agreement. at the time of writing, the text of the document is still subject to legal adaptation and purification and varying levels of ratification on both sides.

This position is actively resisted by a group of European countries, led by Spain, Portugal and the Northern European states, which advocate ratification of the treaty. This block of countries argues that the agreement, compared to previously signed EU agreements, includes a better version of the chapter on sustainable development, and its failure to conclude would entail a strengthening of China's position in LAC.

Despite the fact that negotiations on the agreement have reached a dead end, Brussels does not want to lose its position in this region and is trying to find solutions that can accelerate the development of relations along the MERCOSUR line. In 2021, the European Commission published a report on the impact of this agreement on three areas: socio-economic development, human rights, and the environment.[42] It was concluded that its launch would have positive

---

42   https://circabc.europa.eu/ui/group/09242a36-a438-40fd-a7af-fe32e36cbdoe/library/abfa1190-59d1-4f59-93a5-9b9810d2b744/details

consequences for both regions: the new terms of trade will not only help the economies affected by the COVID-19 pandemic recover from the crisis, but will also significantly strengthen the partnership between the regions based on common values. The report highlighted that the EU agricultural sector would benefit from this agreement by increasing its exports to South America, while sound policies would help avoid deforestation in MERCOSUR countries.

The lengthy process of agreeing on the document and its amendments led to the fact that the MERCOSUR countries were already beginning to lose patience. In particular, at the MERCOSUR Presidents' Summit, held in December 2022, Argentine President Alberto Fernandez (2019–2023) for the first time openly accused the EU of delaying the ratification of the EU–MERCOSUR agreement, noting that the EU is using the Amazon region only as an excuse, but, in reality, is afraid of competition with Latin American agricultural products in their market. He blamed the EU for the fact that it is thanks to EU politics that the agreement still remains paralyzed, adding the phrase "let's ask Europe to stop lying to us."[43] The head of the Uruguay Foreign Ministry noted that "a number of EU countries will not be able to meet environmental standards which Uruguay already fully meets."[44] In this regard, the President of the Assembly of the Republic of Portugal, warned that the impasse in the ratification process of this treaty jeopardizes Latin America's trust in the EU as a trading partner.

Thanks to the stalled agreement on treaties in three independent areas (EU–Mexico, EU–Chile and EU–MERCOSUR), LAC has already begun to form the opinion that the EU which is waving the flag of environmental protection are doing so primarily guided by the rise of protectionist sentiments rather than the need to protect nature.

∙ ∙ ∙

To summarize this section, it should be noted that in the 21st century trade became a priority for EU diplomacy in LAC (Table 7).

This confirms that economic cooperation was at the center of discussions at the II (2002), IV (2006) and V (2008) EU–LAC Summits. Since the mid-2010s the EU has not had a unified socio-political strategy for the LAC region. There are only a few unrelated initiatives, mainly related to the possibility of creating new cooperation programs with some individual countries. On the

---

43 https://elpais.com/argentina/2022-12-06/alberto-fernandez-sobre-la-demora-en-el-acuerdo-ue-mercosur-pidamos-a-europa-que-nos-deje-de-mentir.html.

44 https://www.valorcarne.com.ar/la-union-europea-habla-con-brasil-por-tratado-de-libre-comercio-con-el-mercosur/

TABLE 7   Volumes of mutual trade in 2021 within the framework of the main interregional agreements in the field of trade

	Agreement name	Date of signing	Volume of mutual trade for 2021 in euros
Mexico	Agreement on Economic Association, Political Coordination and Cooperation	2000	67 billion euros
Chile	Association Agreement	2002	18.2 billion euros
Colombia, Peru and Ecuador	Free Trade Agreement	2012	27.9 billion euros
Cariforum	Economic Partnership Agreement	2008	6.4 billion euros
Central America	Association Agreement	2012	15.1 billion euros
MERCOSUR	Free Trade Agreement	2019	97 billion euros

SOURCE: COMPILED BY THE AUTHOR BASED ON DATA FROM UNCTAD AND STATISTA

part of the EU, the emphasis on developing cooperation in the field of human rights, which has become an important issue in Latin America, has noticeably weakened.

Despite the fact that political dialogue was an important component of the system of interregional relations, it was extremely negatively affected by the lack of consensus in Latin America and in the EU. By the beginning of the 2020s, there was no longer agreement between the parties regarding such important issues as democratic principles, human rights, or possible solutions to the acute socio-political crises that erupted in Latin American countries. The crisis in Venezuela made a significant contribution to distancing the EU from the LAC: the strong political polarization on both sides, with populist governments, is significantly hindering the expansion of dialogue and the achievement of a common point of view regarding the mechanisms for resolving this crisis.

While the EU insists on trade agreements between the EU and LAC as the "core" of interregional relations, the pressing problems of the Latin American region, such as social inequality, poverty, crime caused by drug trafficking, which together destabilize states and societies, were excluded from the discourse of EU representatives. With such an economic-oriented policy, the EU is missing the opportunity to become a strategic partner for Latin America, helping to solve the main problems that currently plague the countries of the region.

The EU continues to consider trade agreements to be the core of its relationship with LAC. In an interview published in the December 2022 issue of the magazine *Pensamiento Latinoamericano,* representative of the EU for foreign affairs Josep Borrell mentioned trade agreements 12 times; human rights twice; and inequality once, while never mentioning the problems of poverty and rising crime.[45]

According to the EU approach, interregional relations are built based on the task of implementing "three transitions" (Spanish: "tres transiciones"), mentioned in order of their priority for the EU: digital, environmental, and socio-economic.[46] All of these are in line with the goals set out in global agreements such as the 2030 Agenda for Sustainable Development. It is the socio-economic transition which ranks last on this list of priorities, which is the top priority for LAC countries. All this confirms the low level of understanding of the real needs, requirements, and most pressing problems of Latin American societies. In addition, the EU's focus on trade agreements reflects the primacy of business interests, thereby ignoring the possibility of building interregional relations that go beyond the economic and trade aspects, where the political and social aspects of cooperation are at the center.

Free trade became one of the main drivers of interregional relations: the key partners of the EU in LAC were countries (Mexico and Brazil) that opened their economies, seeking to expand their trading presence in the EU and significantly increase FDI flows. Now LAC, whose countries are politically and ideologically divided, no longer has a consensus on the continuation of such a free trade policy, just as there is no common approach to the model of interaction with the EU.

The 2023 Summit demonstrated that the EU is seeking to take a leading role in implementing the energy and digital transition of the two regions, which could partially restore the EU's already shaky status as an important

---

45 https://dialnet.unirioja.es/servlet/articulo?codigo=8612856.
46 https://www.fundacioncarolina.es/visiones-cruzadas-desde-latinoamerica-y-la-union-europea-sobre-la-triple-transicion/

extra-regional actor in LAC. The position of Latin American countries regarding climate change is characterized by the concept of differentiated responsibilities: each individual country must solve its own problems and build national goals for nature conservation. This approach was also enshrined in the Belém Declaration, adopted as a result of the Amazon Summit 2023.[47] But not all LAC countries are ready to allow an expanded presence of the EU in LAC in the context of the initiative that developed, and therefore more actively polluting states should provide mechanisms for financing projects aimed at combating climate change in developing countries. The President of Bolivia sharply criticized any intervention by foreign actors in the Amazon, saying that if the US tries to influence LAC with military instruments, the EU will try to do this "through non-governmental organizations."[48]

As a result of the III EU–CELAC Summit, European investment in the region was 45 billion euros as part of the Global Gateway initiative, announced as a strategy to reduce the gap in the structure of capital investment. The Global Gateway will run until 2027 and will include more than 130 projects, most of which focus on areas such as mineral development (primarily lithium and copper), decarbonization of existing hydrogen production, and the development of green industry. For the EU, the Global Gateway has become a new tool to reduce China's economic expansion in LAC. Projects under the Global Gateway are designed to provide EU multinational corporations with access to the most important mineral resources in LAC, necessary for the implementation of the "green transition", even at the cost of environmental damage. Notable in this context is the signing in the summer of 2023 between the EU and Chile of a Memorandum of Understanding for the development of value-added lithium projects in Chile, which will create a strategic alliance to develop lithium and strengthen supply chains.[49] In addition, EU funding for new renewable hydrogen projects in Chile was also announced.

The conflict between Russia and Ukraine (2022) has become another issue that reflects the different approaches and priorities of the EU and Latin America. The EU views the situation around Ukraine as a global challenge to

---

47   La Declaración de Belém. Available at: https://otca.org/conozca-la-declaracion-de-belem-firmada-por-los-paises-amazonicos-en-la-cumbre/.
48   Deforestación y expectativas: el escenario de la Cumbre de Presidentes Amazónicos de Belém do Pará. Available at: https://elpais.com/america-futura/2023-08-08/deforestacion-y-expectativa-el-escenario-con-el-que-los-paises-de-la-amazonia-reciben-a-la-cumbre.html.
49   EU and Chile to develop lithium and green hydrogen projects. Available at: https://www.reuters.com/markets/commodities/eu-chile-sign-mou-value-added-lithium-projects-2023-06-14/

the system of international relations; LAC states perceive it as another conflict in the Old World. The wording enshrined in the final declaration of the EU–CELAC 2023 summit demonstrated a lack of agreement on this issue: despite pressure from the EU, there was no phrase condemning Russia's actions. Nicaragua refused to ratify the clause about Ukraine in the final text of the declaration.

The resumption of interregional Summits between Latin American and EU leaders has become an important event, facilitating the development of joint solutions to issues affecting the interests of both sides. First of all, such as the fight against climate change and the digital transition. The event confirmed that the EU and LAC have different foreign policy priorities. The lack of an updated network of agreements based on a model of horizontal relations continues to significantly weaken interregional cooperation. It should be noted that the text of the 2023 Declaration is very similar to the final document of the 2015 Summit: both documents contain similar plans for rapprochement and list the same unresolved issues and problems. Given the rapidly increasing influence of China in LAC, the EU again drew attention to the importance of ratifying trade agreements with countries in the region. One of the notable results of the EU–CELAC Summit 2023 was that the EU signed an association agreement with Chile and is partially closer to the beginning of the practical implementation of agreements with Mexico and MERCOSUR.

In terms of expanding interregional cooperation in the first quarter of the 21st century, where trade plays a special role, the EU and Latin America are experiencing a situation similar to the second half of the 1990s: the EU continues to follow the path of developing bilateral relations, rather than a unified regional strategy.

CHAPTER 5

Russia and LAC

1 The Place of Latin America in Russia's Foreign Policy Interests at the Beginning of the 21st Century

Compared to Soviet times, in the 1990s, Russia significantly reduced its participation in global politics and its weight in the world economy (Kosevich, 2023). The LAC direction in foreign policy was one of the most affected. The situation began to change noticeably in the early 2000s, mainly due to the rise in oil prices which led to the restoration of Russia's economic potential, resulting in the expansion of its foreign markets. President Putin's visit to Cuba in 2000, which the Russian Foreign Ministry called a "breakthrough", marked a new stage in the development of relations between Russia and LAC countries, characterized by the beginning of a more active policy in this region. It was based on the successful experience of building partnerships during the Soviet era. The development of cooperation with LAC took place in the context of three Russian foreign policy lines at the beginning of the 21st century: the formation of the image of a strong state with economic and political stability; strengthening its influence in the post-Soviet space, Eastern Europe, and the Baltic States; and an active search for partner countries contributing to the establishment of a multi-polar world (Ambrosio, 2005).

Russia's foreign policy acquired a multi-vector character in the late 1990s, becoming more focused on developing partnerships with both Western and non-Western countries. Russia emphasized that its policy would rely on Europe, China, and the Islamic world. Such a multi-vector policy could, with skillful diplomacy, make Russia a valuable, and possibly irreplaceable partner in the world community. From that moment on, foreign policy was targeted at the restoration of the "lost" partners of the Soviet Union, and the formation of its own course in world politics, expressly different from the course of the West. This was based on the idea of the need for a more active foreign policy to strengthen Russia's position as a great power in the emerging multipolar world.[1] Russia's approaches to solving the most acute problems of world politics could be completely different from the approaches of Western countries.

---

1 The National Security Concept of the Russian Federation. Moscow, the Kremlin on December 17, 1997. http://www.kremlin.ru/acts/bank/11782.

An important factor in Russia's return to LAC was the gradual withdrawal of the US from this region, which began under President George W. Bush (2001–2009), who, after 9/11, reoriented the country's foreign policy towards the Middle East and other regions (Scott, 2016). This policy partly continued during the Obama presidency.During the Trump presidency, inter-American relations entered a new phase, characterized by increased conflict and an even greater decline in Washington's interest in the region. Trump's policies and rhetoric have turned the border wall project into a kind of symbol that unites the conflicting issues of bilateral relations with Mexico, which caused a significant public outcry throughout Latin America and further intensified the conflict within the inter-American system (Kosevich, 2020). All this gave a new impetus to the diversification of extra regional ties of the states of LAC.

This section of the book is devoted to a comprehensive analysis of the main vectors of Russia's foreign policy strategy in Latin America in the 21st century: political, military, economic, and cultural relations between Russia and LAC.

1.1 *Political Dialogue*

In the late 1990s, the Russian Foreign Ministry developed a new foreign policy concept that formed the basis of Russian policy in developing countries in general, and in LAC, in particular. This concept was based on the thesis that Russia's policy in these regions is de-ideologized (unlike the USSR's) and does not pursue the goal of creating alliances directed against third countries.[2] The 2000 Russian Foreign Policy Concept reflected different priorities of Russian foreign policy in comparison with the 1993 Foreign Policy Concept of the previous President Boris Yeltsin (1991–1999). The main distinguishing feature of the 2000 Concept, approved by the Vladimir Putin (2000–2008, 2012–present) government was that Russia was no longer viewed in world politics as a successor state to the USSR, securing a complete rejection of ideological confrontation.[3] But, in reality, Moscow adhered to this concept only in the early 2000s. Beginning in 2005, the ideological component in the Russian strategy in LAC began to sharply strengthen again, and de-ideologization was present only declaratively (Jeifets, 2024).

Since the beginning of the 2000s, Russia began to actively develop political contacts and used financial resources in order to strengthen these contacts

---

2 Message from the President of the Russian Federation to the FEDERAL ASSEMBLY dated March 6, 1997. http://www.kremlin.ru/acts/bank/36355/page/1.
3 Russian Foreign Policy Concept. Moscow. Approved BY the President of the Russian Federation on June 28, 2000. https://docs.cntd.ru/document/901764263

over time. The second level was to be the expansion of Russia's economic presence in Latin America, focused primarily on establishing direct foreign economic ties with the largest regional markets. Such a two-step strategy should have brought a successful expansion in this region. However, Russia lacked the financial power to complete these plans. As a result, as in Soviet times, the priority of the political over the economic was entrenched, because this approach does not require financial investments. Beijing had been building its foreign policy line in Latin America according to a similar scenario and finally brought such a two-step strategy to a successful conclusion. China's economic growth, which began several decades ago, provided financial opportunities to increase China's presence in LAC (Harris, 2015).

There are three main groups of influence determining Russia's foreign policy at the beginning of the 21st century in relation to developing regions. The most important includes high-ranking officials. This group is headed by the President of Russia, who personally makes all decisions on all major issues of foreign policy based on information he receives mainly from high-ranking aides. The second group consists of circles related to security, defense, and industry, which also play a significant role in the elaboration and implementation of foreign policy. Their political influence is primarily determined by the high level of militarization of Russian society inherited from the former USSR. The third group of influence includes large financial and industrial structures, which look at Russia's relations with the outside world through the prism of their economic interests.

There are four conventional geopolitical directions around which Russia's contemporary policy in LAC was built. First, creating a counterbalance to US hegemony in the region and in the world. Here, special importance is attached to the concept of state sovereignty, which is a traditionally painful subject for LAC. The result of this approach is that for the region, accustomed to the interventionist ambitions and military actions of Washington, the Kremlin appears in a favorable light. Second, the diversification of foreign relations, which was dictated by Russia's need for access to markets for agricultural products and food, and the creation of new markets. This found the expected response in LAC, where a strengthening of the positions of extra regional actors with a gradual reduction in the dominant role of the US was taking place. Since the beginning of the 21st century, the extra regional directions of the foreign policy of LAC have become noticeably more active. Third, the formation of an allied bloc within major international forums and interstate associations was based on the anti-US turn in the LAC political mainstream and expanding the ideological spectrum of the region's public discourse. Fourth, the expansion of cooperation in the development of ICT, which has acquired particular relevance in the context of the need to exploit the scientific and technical potential of LAC.

The most favorable conditions for the development of relations with LAC appeared during the "Left Turn", which took place in the first decade of the 21st century. During the presidency of Néstor Kirchner (2003–2007) and Cristina Fernández de Kirchner (2007–2015) in Argentina, in just a few years, there was an unprecedented intensification of political and diplomatic contacts between Moscow and Buenos Aires. Cooperation with the countries of the Bolivarian Alliance for the Peoples of Our America (ALBA), which sought to reduce their dependence on the US, significantly strengthened and expanded. Some then-Latin American leaders felt a "natural sympathy" for Putin and Russia in general, among which Evo Morales (2006–2019) in Bolivia and Hugo Chávez (1999–2013) in Venezuela stood out. As president, Morales visited Moscow three times, repeatedly met with Putin on the sidelines of summits in Tehran and Brazil, and also publicly called the Russian leader a brother, and Russia a brotherly country. Chávez came to Russia on an official visit in May 2001 and became the first Latin American president to visit this country since Putin was elected president. During his entire presidency, Chávez visited Russia eight times. In addition, he publicly declared that Venezuela and Russia are very similar, and the countries are related by the fact that they are "being economically reborn".[4] The friendly relationship with Putin survived until the death of Chávez and the resignation of Morales.

Over time, the desire to create levers of retaliatory pressure on the US has become an important factor in the progressive development of Russia–LAC cooperation. A notable breakthrough for Russian foreign policy in LAC occurred during the presidencies of Luiz Inácio Lula da Silva (2003–2011) and Dilma Rousseff (2011–2016) in Brazil, who pursued limiting Washington's influence in the region, including by strengthening and expanding the presence of extra regional actors.[5] For Moscow, the intensification of dialogue with Brazil, which is pursuing the goal of becoming the regional leader and a notable player in international politics, has become an exceptional opportunity to strengthen its position in this direction.[6]

---

4 https://www.dw.com/es/hugo-ch%C3%A1vez-en-rusia-armas-hambre-y-amistades/a-3505324.
5 https://iz.ru/1098558/2020-12-11/lavrov-otmetil-nastroi-rossii-na-reguliarnye-kontakty-s-latinskoi-amerikoi.
6 https://www.mid.ru/problemy-vzaimootnosenij-so-stranami-latinskoj-ameriki-i-karibskogo-bassejna?p_p_id=56_INSTANCE_WWDp6t4OobgE&_56_INSTANCE_WWDp6t4OobgE_languageId=en_GB.

In Russia–LAC relations, one topic of great mutual interest can be distinguished: the formation of political synergy, which includes diplomatic interaction, political support within international organizations, and the consolidation of ties in the margins of regional forums.[7]

Diplomatic interaction, the development of which Russian political elites consider of great importance in the new millennium, has become a special platform for enhancing multilateral cooperation (primarily political) with LAC. 18 Russian presidential trips were made to LAC and over 30 ministerial meetings were organized during the 2000s and 2010s. In the same period, almost all Latin American presidents visited Russia at least once. During the Soviet era, there was no such active and multi-level political dialogue with the countries of Latin America. Of the Soviet leaders, only Leonid Brezhnev and Mikhail Gorbachev visited Latin America, and ministerial meetings were rare.

Concerning political support, the key role is assigned to the "triangle of direct influence in the Caribbean", which includes Venezuela, Nicaragua, and Cuba. The space of Russian geopolitical influence in LAC was created when anti-American sentiment dominated the political establishment of the region, and US interest in the region weakened. Russia embraced the moment and advanced its geopolitical interests, for which an important place was given to diplomatic rapprochement. In 2000–2019 Cuba, Venezuela, and Nicaragua became the most visited Russian official delegations in Latin America. The turning point in the establishment of the triangle of influence came in 2003, when post-Soviet Russia began to perceive LAC as a zone of its geopolitical interests. A year later, arms deliveries to the region resumed (Patiño Villa, 2014). The main priorities of cooperation with these three countries include the imposition of sanctions by the US when the Kremlin is counting on their support, and Moscow's reaction to any attempts at intervention in the internal affairs of LAC states. This was warranted more than once: in 2008 Nicaragua and Venezuela recognized the independence of Abkhazia and South Ossetia from Georgia, and Cuba expressed full support for Moscow's actions in the armed conflict in South Ossetia in 2008; in 2014, Cuba, Nicaragua, Venezuela, and Bolivia voted against a UN resolution condemning "the reunification of Crimea".[8] As a consequence, Moscow (along with Beijing) did not

---

7 The Ministry of Foreign Affairs of the Russian Federation. Open-access databases of international treaties. https://www.mid.ru/foreign_policy/international_contracts/international_contracts.

8 "The reunification of Crimea" is the official position of the Russian Government regarding the inclusion of the Crimean Peninsula into the Russian Federation in 2014.

condemn the Nicolás Maduro (2013–present) regime in Venezuela at the UN.[9]

The most promising platforms for the intensification of interstate dialogue through participation in international forums are the Group of Twenty (G20),[10] including Argentina, Mexico, and Brazil, and participation in the Asia-Pacific Economic Cooperation (APEC),[11] which includes Chile, Mexico, and Peru. Participation in G20 summits for the Kremlin acquired special significance after Russia was expelled from the Group of Eight (G8) in 2014 due to the events in Crimea. Therefore, Moscow views its membership in the G20 as a tool for dialogue with the leaders of countries of primary interest—the US, Germany, China, Turkey, and India. In general, Russia is trying to use its participation in this forum to gradually remove the risks associated with geopolitical tensions, and to conduct negotiations with EU partners, primarily to discuss such topics such as energy, adapting the role of international organizations to modern realities, and the transition to digital economy. The LAC bloc, marked by weak consolidation, is trying to use the G20 primarily to attract foreign investment. Until 2015, countries divided into separate groups, pursuing separate goals: Argentina and Brazil created a high-level bilateral committee to promote regional integration issues, and Mexico independently promoted its positions together with the US (Nahón, 2018). Argentina, Brazil, and Mexico have not been able to form a common agenda that they could promote within the forum. Their conjoint priorities within the forum are "labor flexibilization", "infrastructure for development", and "food security". This led to the fact that the G20 never turned into a platform for establishing a constructive dialogue between Russia and member countries representing Latin America.[12] In APEC, issues of bilateral relations and international cooperation, in general, are discussed. There is no high level cooperation between LAC and Russia within this

---

9 In 2019, Russia and China vetoed a US resolution in the UN Security Council on addressing the crisis in Venezuela, which called for new presidential elections in Venezuela and for admission of international electoral observers. https://www.un.org/press/en/2019/sc13725.doc.htm.

10 The Group of Twenty (G20)—is an intergovernmental forum, representing the world's major developed and emerging economies, founded in 1999. The G20 members are Argentina, Australia, Brazil, Canada, China, France, Germany, India, Indonesia, Italy, Japan, Mexico, Republic of Korea, Russia, Saudi Arabia, South Africa, Turkey, United Kingdom, United States, and European Union (EU).

11 The Asia-Pacific Economic Cooperation (APEC) is a forum of 21 economies of the Asia-Pacific region for cooperation in regional trade and investment facilitation and liberalization, established in 1989.

12 Group of Twenty. Open-access databases of official documents. https://www.g20.org/.

platform, despite the fact that the presidents of Russia and Latin American countries meet regularly at APEC summits. In BRICS,[13] Brazil is the weakest link in Russian policy. The role assigned to Brazil on the scale of Russian foreign policy priorities is several times lower than that designated to other BRICS countries, primarily China and India. The Large-Scale Russian-Brazilian Commission, created in the 1990s to expand bilateral cooperation, continues to be purely formal. Russia failed to achieve a strategic partnership with Brazil planned in 1997.

Russia maintains close ties with the regional forums ALBA, CELAC,[14] and UNASUR, which are used to strengthen its position in the region and increase trade. CELAC came up with an initiative in 2018 to expand its cooperation with BRICS. Compared to China, which created CELAC–China forums, aimed at expanding trade and economic partnership, Russia does not develop such multilateral negotiations. Undermining this strategy is the fact that the leading integration projects promoted by Cuba and Venezuela, and which are the political basis in LAC for Russia, are now in a shambles. In particular, CELAC and UNASUR are politically paralyzed, which was affected by the socio-economic crisis in Venezuela. Russia takes an interest in forging partnerships with sub-regional integration projects such as the Caribbean Community (CARICOM), but there have been no significant results achieved in this area. There is a relative activation of contacts through the Eurasian Economic Union (EAEU),[15] which, with a focus on expanding cooperation with the Pacific Alliance, signed a Memorandum of Understanding with Peru and Chile in 2015. In 2018, MERCOSUR[16] and the EAEU signed a Memorandum of Understanding to expand cooperation between the blocs, which prompted positive forecasts for the expansion of economic and trade ties. However, in general, the contractual base between LAC and pro-Russian integration associations and LAC is yet to materialize.

---

13   BRICS is an interstate association that includes Brazil, Russia, India, China, and South Africa, founded in 2006.
14   Community of Latin American and Caribbean States (CELAC) is a regional intergovernmental mechanism that includes 32 sovereign countries of LAC.
15   The Eurasian Economic Union (EAEU) is an international organization for regional economic integration, established in 2015. The member states are Armenia, Belarus, Kazakhstan, Kyrgyzstan, and Russia.
16   Southern Common Market (MERCOSUR) is an economic and political agreement between Argentina, Brazil, Uruguay, Paraguay, and Venezuela (membership was suspended since 2016), founded in 1991.

1.2 Defense and Security Cooperation

The sale of weapons, military diplomacy, and the exchange of experience and security technologies is an important instrument for enhancing Russia's influence in LAC (Ellis, 2015). By the beginning of the 2020s, Russia was able to "restart" relations with the regional allies of the USSR—Nicaragua and Cuba—and build a partnership dialogue with countries that bought Soviet weapons during the Cold War: Peru and, to a lesser extent, Argentina and Brazil. In 2005, a new direction began to develop—large-scale military-technical cooperation with Venezuela, the arms market of which was previously controlled by the US, a number of EU countries, and Israel. This was a consequence of Hugo Chavez's coming to power in 1999, whose foreign policy was aimed at weakening the country's economic and political dependence on the US.

In 2000–2017, Russian arms sales to LAC accounted for 4.5% of Russian arms exports, of which 80% went to Venezuela. In total, Russia sold $10 billion in weapons to Latin American partners (Connolly, 2017).[17] The demand for Russian weapons in LAC is fairly limited: Nicaragua and Venezuela purchase 60% of weapons from Russia, for other countries in the region this figure is less than 15%. In 2006–2014, Russia was the main supplier of arms to LAC, ahead of the US, which was ensured by Venezuela's multimillion-dollar purchases. Sales of Russian military equipment in LAC peaked in 2007 and 2013, after which a sharp decline began.[18] The most popular product sold by Russia to LAC is helicopters. Today, almost every major country in LAC has at least several Russian helicopters. In many ways, it was the interest of Mexico, Colombia, and Peru in the acquisition of helicopters that allowed Russia to establish a political dialogue with these countries, which have never been trading partners or ideological allies. Nevertheless, although Russian military equipment is still highly valued in LAC, the demand for it is still limited and unstable as the US already controls a large part of the arms market.

Within military diplomacy, educational exchanges along with visits by top leadership play an important role. The leading countries in terms of the number of military personnel sent for advanced training and the exchange of experience are Venezuela, Cuba, and Nicaragua.

Joint programs with LAC to combat drug trafficking have acquired a geopolitical dimension. Here security cooperation between Russia and Nicaragua stands out. Since 2012, special training courses for drug police officers from Central American countries have been held regularly in Managua, organized

---

17   Open access "Rostec" State Corporation Annual Reports (2015–2019).
18   Stockholm International Peace Research Institute. Open-access databases. https://www.sipri.org/databases.

jointly by the Russian Federal Drug Control Service and comparative power structures of Nicaragua. In 2017, the Training Center of the Russian Ministry of Internal Affairs in Nicaragua, specializing in conducting courses for Nicaraguan law enforcement agencies, opened. This initiative has had an important regional projection because it allowed the development of cooperation in this area with other countries of Central America—the traditional zone of influence of the US. In recent years, joint Russian-Nicaraguan anti-drug operations have been carried out on an ongoing basis. Bolivia, Argentina, and Colombia are other countries with which partnerships are developing in this sphere (Jost, 2012).

Cooperation between Russia and LAC in defense and security is primarily symbolic, not substantive. For Russia, that market plays a secondary role in the global context: 75% of Russian arms exports go to Asian countries.[19] Russia was an important supplier of weapons for the region only briefly and exclusively to countries experiencing a temporary aggravation in relations with the US. Russia is clearly not among those partners for whom the overwhelming majority of LAC countries are ready to risk their established ties with the US. An example is Mexico, which in February 2020, during the meeting the Russian and Mexican Foreign Ministers, decided to negotiate the purchase of Russian military helicopters. However, as soon as the US deputy assistant secretary for Central American bureau of Western Hemisphere Affairs threatened Mexico with sanctions in the event of a contract with Russia, the Mexican Ministry of Foreign Affairs immediately informed that the purchase of Russian helicopters was not being considered.[20] Since 2017 the sale of Russian arms to LAC has almost ceased, which indicates that even this traditional sphere does not have a solid basis for the development of long-term relations.

1.3   *Trade Relations*

Several specialized institutions have been established in Russia to develop trade cooperation with LAC. Since the beginning of the 21st century, the Russian Chamber of Commerce and Industry has begun to pay increased attention to the development of bilateral cooperation with LAC business circles. Business councils were formed in the 2000s with Argentina, Brazil, Cuba, Mexico, and Chile. The National Committee for the Promotion of Economic Cooperation with LAC, created in 1998, also assists in the implementation of joint projects. A similar system has formed in LAC, where the issues of enhancing trade

---

19   Open-access Rostec State Corporation Annual Reports (2015–2019).
20   https://www.abc.es/internacional/abci-mexico-enfrenta-sancion-estados-unidos-si-concreta-compra-helicopteros-rusia-202002150149_noticia.html.

relations and investments with Russia are also within the competence of special institutions that promote the development of economic cooperation in this area.

The volume of trade between LAC and Russia has increased markedly since 2000, from $3 billion to an estimated $15 billion in 2020.[21] Over those twenty years, two periods of sharp increases in trade volumes can be distinguished: in 2008 and 2014, which coincided with the stages of cooling of Russia's dialogue with Western countries.[22] In 2014, negotiations on expanding trade cooperation with LAC began the day after the official lists of goods exported from Western countries prohibited from being imported into Russia appeared. After the EU began to actively impose sanctions against the Kremlin in 2014, a number of LAC countries increased their food exports to Russia (Argentina, Ecuador, and Brazil) precisely by reducing supplies to the EU. Nevertheless, the fast growth of the trade interest in LAC, which arose as a result of the need to quickly fill large-scale gaps in the Russian market, did not produce the results that LAC expected. By 2019, the Russian market accounted for only 0.7% of the total volume of imported products from LAC (CEPAL, 2019). The example of food imports from LAC to Russia, the factor of the third group of influence in Russian foreign policy is most clearly manifested: large business clearly obstructed the expansion of contacts to protect their interests from Latin American competitors.

In the structure of Russia's foreign trade, the share of LAC is very modest: as of 2019, it was about 2.5%. Since 2006, Russia's trade with LAC has been conducted with a positive balance for the latter. In the structure of foreign trade with LAC, Russia also plays an insignificant role, accounting for just over 1% of the region's total foreign trade.

Within LAC, Brazil is Russia's main trading partner, accounting for about 40% of all trade with the region. This is followed by Mexico (14%), Ecuador (10%), Argentina (8%), Chile (7.6%), and Paraguay (5.3%). Russia's main political allies—Cuba, Nicaragua, and Venezuela—are not among Russia's leading trade partners in LAC. This confirms a strict division of Russian policy in LAC into two main lines: geopolitics—expanding political interaction with several countries, and economic diplomacy—dictated primarily by the demand of the Russian market for certain products (CEPAL, 2019). Since the beginning

---

21 The Ministry of Economic Development of the Russian Federation. Official Statistics of the Department of analytical support of foreign economic activity. https://economy.gov.ru/material/departments/d16/

22 Trade Map. Trade Statistics for International Business Development. https://trademap.org/.

of the 21st century, four groups of goods have dominated Russia's exports to this region: fertilizers, oil and petroleum products, iron, and equipment and vehicles. Latin America has become one of the priority areas for Russian producers of mineral fertilizers, which is due to the absence of protective duties in Latin American markets, and fairly stable demand. The main buyer is Brazil, which is due to the relative cheapness of Russian fertilizers and the large share of the agricultural sector in Brazil's economy. Since 2010, the share of supplies of metals and metal products from Russia to a number of Latin American countries, in particular to Mexico, has noticeably increased (Kosevich, 2021). This was caused by the revitalization of the mechanical engineering and automotive industries in Mexico. Almost one-fourth of all power plants in Argentina operate using Soviet equipment, which predetermined the country's stable demand for Russian industrial and power equipment. Some Latin American countries use Russian-made agricultural machinery. The interest in these goods is explained by the traditions of cooperation in this area that were formed during the Soviet era, and the need for technological modernization of national agricultural production. Exports from Latin America to Russia mainly consist of agricultural and food products (primarily fruits and nuts; meat and meat products; fish and seafood; coffee and cocoa).[23]

The level of investment interaction remains low, demonstrating a high degree of continuity with the past century. In 2007–2015, when, due to the "Left Turn", there was a certain rapprochement with Russia, the total volume of Russian investments in this region amounted to between $6 and $10 billion.[24] The main recipients of Russian FDI were Brazil, Venezuela, and Panama. Some countries became popular offshore for Russian investors. By 2019, the main recipients of Russian FDI were the Caribbean offshore: the British Virgin Islands, and the Bahamas.[25] These island offshores are used by Russian businesses for two purposes: for round-tripping FDI (making pseudo-foreign investments when registering Russian enterprises offshore), or for transshipping FDI (performing as "terminal stations" in order to provide a more convenient control over subsidiaries through holdings located in third countries). The 2000s, the total amount of Russian FDI in LAC, excluding offshore operations, slightly exceeded $3 billion, which is less than 1% of the country's FDI.[26] There

---

23   Federal State Statistics Service of the Russian Federation. Official Statistics of External Economic Activities. https://rosstat.gov.ru/
24   Open-access External Sector Statistics. https://www.cbr.ru/eng/statistics/macro_itm/svs/.
25   Bank of Russia. Open-access databases of Statistical materials. https://www.cbr.ru/statistics/.
26   https://eng.gks.ru/figures/activities.

is practically zero investment activity of Russian small and medium-sized businesses in LAC (Artner, 2020; Milosevich-Juaristi, 2019).

The most notable activities of large Russian corporations are based on agreements reached at the highest level. This was a legacy of the USSR. First of all, the investment projects of Gazprom,Rosneft, Lukoil, Rostec, and Power Machines are distinguished. In this context, the concept of "corrosive capital" is partly confirmed. This approach is based on the thesis that money flows from authoritarian countries (Russia, China, Turkey, Iran) to Latin America successfully taking advantage of the weaknesses of the authorities at national and regional levels: primarily the lack of transparency in financing, the failings of state responsibility to its citizens, and socio-political tension. Gradually, the political elites of these countries are getting preferential access to the strategic sectors of the economy of the Latin American region, such as energy, telecommunications, banking and transportation. As big business, controlled by oligarchic clans, plays a significant role in Russian foreign policy in developing regions, this predetermined that the main instrument of the Kremlin's influence in Latin America is large-scale projects that act as a means of political pressure on their Latin American partners. Stephanov and Vladimirov argue that the penetration of "corrosive capital" into the main sectors of the Latin American economies leads to the rapprochement of Russian big business with Latin American oligarchic groups, which results in a restriction of competition in the markets and an increase in shadow cash flows, rather than contributing to the sustainable development of the region.

In the 21st century, trade and investment cooperation between Russia and this region have been developing at an extremely slow pace, for several reasons. First, the traditions and positive experiences of Russian–LAC interregional cooperation in the trade sphere are either absent or episodic. Secondly, there is no developed legal framework, nor a network of trade agreements with LAC. Thirdly, there is a low level of awareness of export and import opportunities, an undeveloped transport and logistics network and no stable supply chains. Tariffs on Russian goods are also a serious negative factor. At the turn of the century, the main economies of the region were not interested in recognizing Russia as a country with a market economy, which resulted in the application, by several LAC countries, of trade policies of protection against Russian exports, which included a large number of prohibitive anti-dumping measures (in Argentina, Brazil, Mexico, Peru).[27] These anti-dumping measures, which were almost all introduced in the early 2000s (in Peru they were introduced

---

27   The Ministry of Economic Development of the Russian Federation. Registry of restrictive measures. Official information as of August 1, 2021. https://www.economy.gov.ru/material/directions/vneshneekonomicheskaya_deyatelnost/dostup_na_vneshnie_rynki_i_zashchitnye_mery/reestr_ogranich_mer/

in the late 1990s), are aimed at such goods as hot-rolled and cold-rolled steel products, metallic magnesium in ingots, and tires for buses and trucks.

In 2021, large-scale deliveries of the Russian Sputnik V vaccine against COVID-19 to Latin America took place, which was regarded by the Kremlin as a new mechanism for Russia's foreign economic activity in developing regions.[28] Argentina was the second country after Belarus to officially allow the use of the Sputnik V vaccine. Within a few months, Argentina became the first country in its region to launch the production of the Russian vaccine. In the first months of 2021, the use of the vaccine was immediately approved in 12 countries of Latin America, the first of which were Paraguay, Bolivia, Venezuela and Mexico. Even Colombia, a traditional US ally in the region, initiated negotiations with Sputnik V manufacturers about a possible purchase of a Russian vaccine. The main reasons for the increased interest of Latin American countries in the Russian vaccine were the lower price compared to its Western counterparts and the simple conditions for its transportation and storage (from +2°C to +8°C), which make it suitable for use in countries with a low or medium level of development. The new circumstances only slightly expanded the space for dialogue between Russia and the countries of Latin America. Nonetheless, despite the fact that the pandemic has completely changed the agenda for the governments of the region, putting the protection of its population at the forefront, it is unlikely that Russia will be able to significantly change the quality of trade relations with the countries of Latin America because of the COVID-19 pandemic.

1.4   Cultural and Humanistic Cooperation

Since the 2010s, Russia has been steadily expanding its cultural and humanistic presence LAC. Three tools of soft power can be distinguished which contribute to its ideological, cultural, and political presence. The first is the promotion of the Russian language. Here, the activities of the Pushkin Institute, founded in 1966, and the "Russkiy Mir" Foundation, created in 2007, which are the main structures for promoting the Russian language and culture in LAC, stand out. To date, the Pushkin Institute offices operate in Brazil, Mexico, Peru, Bolivia, Colombia, and Ecuador. The institute, whose mission is to spread and support

---

28   Sputnik V is the first Russian vaccine against COVID-19, created at the Gamalei Institute of Epidemiology and Microbiology, which was registered on August 11, 2020. In 2021, the majority of Russian citizens were vaccinated against COVID-19 with the Sputnik V vaccine.

Russian around the world, is working to expand cooperation with Latin American universities. The range of tasks of the "Russkiy Mir" Foundation is much wider, including cooperation development with scientific, commercial, and charitable organizations, interaction with the Russian Orthodox Church and the support of foreign Russian-speakers and Russian media. There are eight centers of the "Russkiy Mir" in the region, operating at universities.[29]

Cooperation in the field of culture continues to be one of the weakest instruments of Russia's soft power, because the interest of the local audience in the Russian language, culture, and art, in general, is low. The main reasons for that are the ideological perception of Russia as a successor to the USSR among Latin Americans, and the lack of a far-sighted Russian strategy for promoting cooperation in the cultural field. The majority of Latin Americans associate modern Russia mainly with weapons and war, and not with culture. Despite the fact that in all LAC countries, without exception, the best works of Russian classical literature are included in the basic school curriculum.

The second tool of soft power is the promotion of educational programs. To this end, the Federal agency "Rossotrudnichestvo" was created in 2008, whose activities are focused on humanistic cooperation and the formation of a positive image of post-Soviet Russia. Three offices operate in Chile, Peru, and Argentina. The agency's employees work as part of Russian embassies in five other countries. The results of the agency's work, focused on the promotion of educational programs in Russia, are on average 4,000 applications from Latin American students to study at Russian universities. Most of the students come to Russia from Ecuador, Colombia, and Brazil. In LAC, about 30,000 people annually register for Russian language courses, allowing them to study without leaving their home country. However, these numbers are still insignificant compared to the traditional partner countries of LAC in the field of educational and scientific mobility: 80,000 Latin Americans study annually in the US,[30] and 19,000 in Spain.[31]

The third and most effective instrument of the Kremlin's soft power in the region is the Russian media, broadcasting in both Spanish and Russian. Moscow began to apply the strategy of information influence offensively in the early 2000s. In LAC, Russian media appeared at the end of the 2000s. In 2009, the Russian-language television channel "ITR TV", began satellite broadcasting

---

29 In Cuba, Costa Rica, Nicaragua, Ecuador, Argentina, Paraguay, Brazil, and Peru.
30 https://www.bbc.com/mundo/noticias-40649093.
31 https://alnavio.es/se-dispara-el-numero-de-estudiantes-de-master-latinoamericanos-en-espana.

in LAC.³² Since 2010, the channel Russia Today (RT), has become the one of the most popular foreign TV channels, broadcasting in Spanish in almost all countries of the region.³³ RT is planning to start broadcasting in Portuguese in 2024. The expansion of the RT network in Latin America is planned through the creation of a large country hub in Rio de Janeiro.

The channel management succeeded in establishing close cooperation with the Venezuelan channel TeleSUR, and with many independent media in South America. The success of RT, in becoming an alternative source of information in the region, lies in many programs that discuss topics of interest to Latin American audiences: corruption, human rights, and crimes with criticism of the US and EU policies.

The popularity of Russian channels in this region is explained, among other things, by the use of a flexible communication strategy (Gil de Zúñiga, 2019). Firstly, over the decade of its existence, the programs produced by the Russian media adapted to the preferences of the local audience, and Latin American journalists were the presenters. Due to this, the "one of our own" effect was successfully achieved. Secondly, the Russian channels were included in the basic cable and satellite TV packages offered by more than 350 regional providers. This has led to the fact that most Latin American viewers do not even realize that these channels are foreign media. For example, more than 5.2 million people have already subscribed to the "RT en Español" channel on YouTube and 3.4 million on Twitter. Russia's main tool is a set of measures to improve the position of Russian media sites in the results of search engines for certain user searches and active promotion of their content in social networks. Together with fast reactions to key events in the world, which presents them from a pro-Russian perspective, the visibility of the popularity of these resources is created and a "presence effect" is achieved. The activity of the news agencies "Sputnik" and "Russia Beyond" is also successful in the region, attracting new readers through their alternative points of view on a wide range of issues, invariably characterized by a critical view of US and European policies. The central task of information support for Russia's foreign policy, designed to influence the audience in line with foreign policy interests, is the prompt selection and dissemination of information to bring the Russian point of view on international processes to the wider world community. Taking into account

---

32   Inter Russia TV Channel (ITR TV) was the first independent Russian-language channel to start broadcasting to Latin America in 2009, when ITR included 12 TV channels, among them was RT. Due to the increased popularity of RT, ITR TV was closed after a few years.

33   https://www.lavanguardia.com/vida/20180403/442164333823/la-cadena-rusa-rt-tripl ica-su-audiencia-en-america-latina-segun-estudio.html.

the rapid development of ICT at the global level, it can be predicted that in the near future Russia will use new information resources in foreign policy more actively.

In the information space Russia was able to secure a truly impressive presence in the region, noticeably ahead of the EU and China and coming very close to the US, partly compensating for the small volume of investment and trade. The entire information strategy of Russian media in the region is based on a special type of meta-narrative strategy, which is based on the confrontation between "us" and "them", presented as overcoming an unfair asymmetric world order. The Russian information strategy in this part of the world is represented through the implicit media discourse of the category of the new "world power" and the category of a multipolar world, the construction of which is possible through the activation of "anti-imperialism" and "anti-hegemonism" in non-Western regions. This metanarrative and its categories, thanks to which Russia seeks to strengthen in the information sphere the contradictions between LAC on the one hand, and the Global West on the other, resonate with the broad masses of the LAC population.

Russia's information influence strategy in LAC actively uses various methods, where the key role is played by the media system and Spanish-language social networks, as well as new AI mechanisms, which have already become an important weapon for increasing Moscow's influence in this part of the world.

Four stages can be distinguished in the intensifying Russian actions in the LAC information field, covering 2008, 2014, 2016 and 2022, were caused by the growing influence of Western media in the post-Soviet states and the expansion of the anti-Russian information agenda.

Russia's technologies of information influence in relation to the LAC countries have been transformed in accordance with the logic of the "mirroring"—a special policy that includes mechanisms of behavioral struggle against elite structures, inciting regional conflicts, suppressing the national will to resist, combined with offensive actions in cyberspace. The logic of this strategy is based on the importance of imitating and simulating the enemy's behavior as accurately as possible.

Russia, which is actively increasing the use of AI technologies that falsely inflate the real interest of the LAC audience in Russian media, itself risks falling into its own trap of the "system of illusions of influence". Effectively building Russia's presence in the virtual environment of Latin America, which is an integral part of the Russian strategy to counter Western influence and promote its image as a world power, cannot in itself replace practical cooperation with the countries of this region, which is now at a low level.

1.5 Russia–Latin America Relations in the Context of the Ongoing Global Systemic Transition

Russia's so-called "special military operation" in Ukraine, which began on February 24, 2022, led to another wave of confrontation with the West, portrayed as a struggle between the value systems of the West and non-West, covering all aspects of international life. The Russia–Ukraine conflict demonstrated that most Latin American countries, in particular Brazil, Argentina, Nicaragua, Cuba, and Venezuela, which are included in the conditional "first level" priority groups for the Kremlin in the context of the entire LAC, are not following the policy of Western sanctions on Russia (Kosevich, 2022). Despite the fact that throughout its history, LAC has repeatedly faced international interventions and all kinds of external interference, most LAC governments have not condemned the Kremlin for the invasion, have not justified Russian policies, and have not supported Ukrainian President Volodymyr Zelensky, diligently maintaining a position of neutrality. Kyiv's attempts to change this approach did not find a wide response in Latin America.

This was confirmed by the rejection by MERCOSUR of the request of the President of Ukraine to speak at the summit of its leaders, which took place in July 2022 in Paraguay, despite the fact that since the outbreak of hostilities in Ukraine, Zelensky has spoken at various international forums, in including at NATO, the G7, UN, and World Economic Forum. In the context of this indifference, a video conference was held in Chile in August 2022, at which Zelensky spoke. This event was the first address of the Ukrainian president to LAC after the start of the Russia-Ukraine conflict,[34] in which Zelensky called on the entire region to provide humanitarian and security assistance to Ukraine, as well as to isolate the Russian economy. Notably, the organizer was not a government, as is the case in most such events, but the Pontifical Catholic University of Chile. The absence of Chilean President Gabriel Boric and Foreign Minister Antonia Urrejola at the conference, citing busy work schedules, and questions to Zelensky from conference participants representing various LAC countries, confirmed that this region chose to remain indifferent to the conflict.

The only Latin American president to have visited Ukraine and offered token support, at the time of writing, is Guatemalan President Alejandro Giammattei, who met with Zelensky in the summer of 2022. A manifestation

---

34   The Russian authorities define the Russia-Ukraine conflict, which began on February 24, 2022, as a "special military operation." The Russian government has introduced a ban on the use of the words "war" and "invasion" in publicly published materials concerning this crisis, which is assessed as an unreliable presentation of the essence of the ongoing military operation and discrediting the actions of the Russian government abroad.

of support for Kyiv was the regional initiative 'Aguanta Ucrania', led by former High Commissioner of Peace, Sergio Jaramillo, which aims to assist the Ukrainian people throughout LAC. The ideologies of this project appeal to the fact that it is precisely the struggle against attacks by a stronger power against a weaker one that is an idea that traditionally unites the LAC population.

The division of LAC countries into several groups that hold different positions on this crisis was manifested at the first regional reaction to the Kremlin's actions on the territory of Ukraine: on February 25 the OAS approved a declaration in which it "strongly condemned the illegal, unjustified, and unprovoked invasion of the Russian Federation into Ukraine", as well as Russia's recognition of the separatist territories of the Donetsk and Luhansk regions.[35] The declaration "The situation in Ukraine", supported by most LAC, was never signed by the delegations of Argentina, Brazil, or Bolivia, despite the fact that their representatives expressed an absolute rejection of aggression and violence. CELAC, whose relations with Russia are developing in the context of the idea of building a multipolar and multilateral world, only adopted an initiative to create a Regional Advisory Assistance Network to coordinate the repatriation of citizens of LAC countries from Ukraine, given that not all the countries of the region have diplomatic missions there.

With the escalation of the Russian-Ukrainian conflict, and the strengthening of Western sanctions and pressure on Russia, a group of countries has formed within LAC that have taken a position of "active neutrality". Cuba, Bolivia, Nicaragua, Venezuela, and El Salvador abstained from voting on the most important resolutions concerning the Russia–Ukraine conflict at the UN.[36]

Bolivia, Cuba, Nicaragua, and Venezuela became conditional "allies" of the Kremlin in LAC with the isolation of Russia, which was facilitated by the transition to a new level of their bilateral relations with Moscow, which took place at the beginning of the 21st century. Several Latin American governments are trying to adhere to the policy of omnibalancing in terms of the Ukrainian crisis. In particular, Mexican President López Obrador openly calls Washington's support for the Ukrainian government a big mistake, while avoiding criticism of the Kremlin's actions, which ensures him the Kremlin's sympathy. Obrador, on occasion, condemns the US for providing military funding to Kyiv faster than

---

35 Declaración "Situación en Urania". OAE/Ser G. CP/INF.9293/22 rev. 31/ 27 de Febrero 2022.
36 https://www.ohchr.org/en/press-releases/2022/03/human-rights-council-establis hes-independent-international-commission; https://digitallibrary.un.org/record/3990 673; https://digitallibrary.un.org/record/3966630?ln=en; https://news.un.org/en/story /2023/02/1133847.

economic assistance to the countries of Central America.[37] Brazilian President Luiz Inacio Lula da Silva said in an interview that Putin and Zelensky share equal responsibility for this conflict.[38] Emphasizing the maintenance of international peace, as a traditional priority of Brazilian foreign policy, Lula da Silva declared that he would create a special international mechanism consisting of states which are influential but not involved in the conflict in Ukraine, such as Brazil, which have the best chance of becoming mediators and concluding a peace agreement. The Paraguayan authorities called on Kyiv to meet Russia, carry out demilitarization, and abandon plans to join NATO.[39]

The governments of Argentina, Colombia, Brazil and Mexico refused to send military equipment to Ukraine, explaining their position by the fact that this would lead to an even greater escalation of the conflict. The head of Colombia, Gustavo Petro, explained his decision by recourse to the Colombian constitution, which stipulates that "peace is order in the international arena".[40] Recall that Bogota regarding the US invasion of Iraq in 2003 supported Washington without hesitation, despite the fairly strong opposition that had developed throughout the LAC. In 2023, LAC did not support the economic sanctions that the US and the EU imposed on Russia: the countries of the region continue their trade relations with Moscow, albeit at a very modest level.

∙ ∙ ∙

All this suggests that LAC, seeking to move out of the category of secondary actors in world politics, is trying to form a more pragmatic approach to the system of international relations formed in the 21st century, including its relations with Russia. Despite the fact that the Russian leadership has already recognized Latin America as an important player on the world stage, one of the centers of power in the new multipolar world, and represents a profitable market, Russian policy in LAC has not become more intelligible or consistent.

---

37   https://www.telemundo52.com/noticias/mexico/amlo-lopez-obrador-eeuu-ayuda-ucrania-centroamerica/2291733/.
38   https://www.latribuna.hn/2023/03/20/el-arsenal/.
39   https://www.adndigital.com.py/canciller-sobre-invasion-a-ucrania-paraguay-debe-defender-principios/?amp.
40   https://www.infobae.com/colombia/2023/01/25/el-presidente-petro-no-le-jalo-al-llamado-de-estados-unidos-para-enviar-armamento-de-fabricacion-rusa-a-ucrania/.

2 Russia's Zones of Political and Economic Activity in LAC

In Russia, neither in scientific discussions, nor in expert-analytical activities and diplomatic practice, has the question of making the countries of LAC a priority of foreign policy ever been raised (Kosevich, 2022). The Russian Foreign Ministry has always proceeded from the conviction that the Latin American region is an important foreign policy area, but far from being the main one for Moscow. LAC has traditionally entrenched itself in the "triad of developing regions", which also includes Asia and Africa. Neither in the Soviet nor in the post-Soviet period could LAC's place in the Kremlin's priority scale be changed, first of all, by the political and economic conditions. The only exception to this "rule of indifference" was Cuba, which has held the title of Moscow's strategic partner in the region since the times of the USSR.

In the 1960–1990s, building bilateral relations with LAC countries, the Russian Foreign Ministry divided the states of this region into three blocks: "priority partners", which included Cuba as the main regional ally, standing apart, and Nicaragua; the "trinity" of the region's leading economies—Brazil, Mexico, and Argentina; and states of the "second row", which included all the rest of states, characterized by a low priority for the Kremlin. Venezuela belonged to the last bloc.

At the beginning of the new millennium, Kremlin changed its "map of priorities" in LAC, which was facilitated by the "left turn" of the region in the late 1990s, marked by the coming to power in several countries of regimes that sharply criticized the neoliberal model of development (Kosevich 2020). An important prerequisite for the formation of a new geopolitical reality of the LAC was a sharp drop in US attention to the Western Hemisphere. Washington began to prioritize relations with other regions, which led to the fact that LAC countries, for the first time in many decades, had a taste of more autonomous foreign policy, which was built primarily based on their own national interests. Attempts by the US to return to a model of relations with "hegemonic-subordinate communities" was strongly rejected by the LAC states. In the speeches of Hugo Chavez, as one of the most prominent representatives of the "Socialism of the 21st century", the anti-American ideological platform was manifested more clearly. During the "left turn", the Russian Foreign Ministry divided LAC into different groups, starting from the degree of friendliness of their political regimes and the level of anti-American discourse: countries of "active left drift"—Venezuela, Cuba, Nicaragua, Bolivia, Ecuador; states of "moderate left drift"—Argentina, Brazil, Uruguay; conservative regimes—the rest of LAC.

Since 2008, which was marked for Russia by the events in South Ossetia and Abkhazia, the Kremlin began to develop a so-called proactive foreign policy focused on preventing Western actions and tracing Western mechanisms of influence. From this moment the appeal to the regional sentiments of confrontational autonomy, implied the creation of military-political alliances, and the intensification of work on the development of bilateral relations with new partners. Together this would allow the "dependent" country to ignore the strategic interests of the "center", gradually becoming more independent (Puig, 1979; Salazar, 2008). This began to be clearly manifest, and on the basis of which Latin America was divided into groups of countries, and the foreign policy dialogue with each was built in different ways.

Thus, in Latin America, the Kremlin began to pursue a proactive foreign policy, which was based on the idea of ensuring the sustainable manageability of world development. Since 2008, the anti-American ideological component has become more active, significantly influencing the model of interstate dialogue.

Russian foreign policy in the 21st century divides all the states of Latin America into four groups. Traditional partners include countries, relations with which were built in Soviet times, characterized by relative resilience against the changing environment in world politics: Cuba and Nicaragua. Ideological allies include countries whose governments pursue anti-American policies: Venezuela and Bolivia. Relations with Trade partners are built on commercial goals: Brazil, Mexico, Ecuador, and Argentina. The low priority group includes all the other states of Latin America, which are viewed by Moscow as unpromising areas. This division can explain the differences in the dialogues between Moscow and different Latin American countries, and the possibilities and limits of interstate and interregional cooperation (Kosevich, 2022).

Russia's cooperation with LAC countries continues to be characterized by instability. The COVID-19 pandemic led to an improvement in Moscow's negotiating position with the leading states of LAC. In 2021, about 70 million vaccines were sent to the region. The Russian vaccine was one of the main vaccinations to prevent the spread of coronavirus infection in Latin America. Production of Sputnik V was launched in Argentina and bottling and packaging was organized in Mexico. Sputnik V was registered by regulatory authorities in 15 Latin American countries. Sales of vaccines to other regions helped temporarily restore Moscow's positive image of a "savior" given that Western countries concentrated mostly on vaccinating their own populations. On the other hand, Russia's "military special operation" in Ukraine, which began on February 24, 2022, caused a sharp reaction throughout LAC. Officials of LAC countries reacted with lightning speed to the events unfolding in Ukraine. The region actually divided into several camps, which confirmed the author's hypothesis about the existence of four models of interstate interaction between LAC countries and Russia.

2.1 Traditional Partners

For many decades, the traditional partners have been headed by Cuba, which since Soviet times has firmly held the title of Moscow's main strategic partner in LAC (Harris, 2015). Cuba is important for Russia primarily due to its geographical proximity to the US and its opposition to US hegemony, in terms of diplomatic support within major international organizations and in terms of funding (Bain, 2005). At the end of the 20th century, bilateral relations cooled after Russia drastically reduced its investment in Cuba. More than 500 projects were unfinished and trade turnover fell by 95%. In addition, at the 1992 UN General Assembly session, Russia abstained from voting on a resolution condemning the US economic and trade blockade of Cuba.

In the 2000s, Russian presidents visited Cuba five times and noticeable progress was made in several areas of cooperation. This was primarily due to the strategic decision of the Kremlin to cancel the Cuban debt to the former USSR (over $32 billion) in 2014. 90% of the Cuban debt was written off, and the remaining amount was used to finance the island's economy. Gradually, military-technical cooperation regained its status as the basis for the geostrategic partnership between Russia and Cuba. In 2015, the countries announced another expansion of cooperation in this area, which led to Russia becoming the main source of financing for the modernization of the Cuban military-industrial complex. Agreements on the Russia use of the Lourdes radio-electronic center were reached. At the beginning of 2019, Russia issued a new large loan to Cuba (€38 million). By 2020, Cuba had become the largest importer of Russian civil aircraft in Latin America.

Notable successes were observed in the participation of Russian businesses in energy cooperation. In 2011, the Russian oil company "Zarubezhneft" and the Cuban "Cupet" signed an agreement on pilot operations and the introduction of modern oil recovery methods at the Boca de Jaruco field. In Cuba, methods of enhanced oil recovery began to be introduced, developed jointly with Russian research institutes. Since 2017, the Russian oil corporation "Rosneft" has been modernizing the Cuban "Cienfuegos" refinery and supplying petroleum products. In 2018, a roadmap was approved for modernizing the Cuban fuel and energy complex. The visit of then-Prime Minister Dmitry Medvedev in 2019 to Cuba received wide publicity. The visit resulted in the signing of an agreement on the modernization of local railways (€2 billion) and the approval of a project to create an irradiation center in Cuba.[41]

In 2013, Russia and Cuba signed an agreement on cooperation in the space sector. In 2018, as part of these agreements, a station for the GLONASS satellite navigation system was placed in Cuba, considered as a new stage in increasing Russia's influence in the Latin American region. In the same year, "Roscosmos" agreed on a contract for the installation of a complex for receiving information from satellites for the remote sensing of the Earth in Cuba.[42] Since the 2010s, the level of interaction in the field of healthcare has grown between the two countries, implementing several joint high-tech projects For instance, the drug "Eberprot-P" for the treatment of diabetic ulcers has been produced by the Russo-Cuban Medical Center in Nizhny Novgorod.

In the 2020s, Russian-Cuban relations developed steadily and positively. It was significant that in November 2019, a delegation of the Federation Council of the Russian Federation, headed by Matvienko, participated in the Cuban capital in ceremonial events dedicated to the 500th anniversary of the city of Havana. The head of the Russian delegation met with Raul Castro and Miguel Diaz-Canel, who had just become the new Cuban leader, and was also present at the opening of the dome of the National Capitol building, restored with the assistance of Russian specialists. Just a few weeks later, Diaz-Canel arrived in Moscow for an official visit.

In October 2019, an Agreement was signed between the Russian and Cuban governments on scientific, technical and innovative cooperation, according to which the parties will contribute to the development of scientific, technical, and innovative cooperation by stimulating joint activities. In November 2022, an official visit of Cuban President Diaz-Canel to Moscow took place, which was a clear demonstration of the support provided by Havana to the Kremlin in the context of the introduction of large-scale anti-Russian sanctions by Western countries. During his stay in Russia, the Cuban held detailed negotiations with Putin, and also spoke during a plenary session of the State Duma. The head of Cuba, Miguel Diaz-Canel, became one of the nine presidents who came to Moscow in May 2014 to participate in the military parade in honor of the 79th anniversary of the victory of the USSR in the Second World War, being the only representative of the LAC region. Taking into account the increasing isolation of the Russian regime from Western countries, the visit of the head of Cuba to Moscow became a gesture of solidarity with the policies Russia

---

41 The Ministry of Foreign Affairs of the Russian Federation. Database.
42 https://ria.ru/20160526/1439314685.html.

pursues around the world. The arrival of the head of Cuba in Moscow in May 2024 was timed not only to coincide with the military parade, but, above all, to events in honor of the tenth anniversary of the signing of the treaty on the Eurasian Economic Union (EAEU),[43] which had taken place on May 29, 2014, in Astana. Cuba is an observer country of the EAEU, which allowed Diaz-Canel to agree on new formats of cooperation with a number of representatives of the countries of the post-Soviet space such as Armenia, Belarus, Kazakhstan, the Kyrgyz Republic, and Uzbekistan.[44] As part of the negotiations, Diaz-Canel expressed interest in expanding Cuba's participation in the mechanisms of the EAEU to achieve deeper integration.

In 2019, Russo-Cuban bilateral trade was $387.9 million, an increase of more than 50% compared to 2010. In 2022, trade turnover was $452 million.[45] Cuba is 90th in terms of its share in Russian trade: Cuba's share in Russian foreign trade is 0.05%.[46] Although the level of Russia's economic presence in Cuba has been steadily growing since the 2010s, China, Canada, and Spain are still the main trading partners of Havana. One of the problems of modern Russian-Cuban relations is the extremely weak economic basis, if we compare the volume of Russian-Cuban cooperation with the trade turnover of Cuba and its main trading partners. Complications in the development of a bilateral dialogue have also been created by the supply of Russian oil to Cuba, which is very unstable and has an extremely unsystematic nature, contrasting with Soviet times.

Despite some progress in the development of bilateral cooperation, Russo-Cuban relations have not been able to reach the level of partnership, unanimity, and mutual understanding as during the 1970s. Several factors influence this situation: the memory of the difficult economic situation and Russia's rapid flight from Cuba in the 1990s; the repeated sharp turns in Russian foreign policy; and the transition to the normalization of US-Cuban relations, which began during the Obama administration. The fact that there is still a "coldness" in bilateral relations is evidenced by the fact that Cuba, unlike Venezuela and Nicaragua, did not recognize the independence of Abkhazia and South

---

43 The Eurasian Economic Union (EAEU) is an international organization for regional economic integration which includes Armenia, Belarus, Kazakhstan, the Kyrgyz Republic and Russia.
44 https://cubaminrex.cu/es/discurso-pronunciado-por-el-presidente-miguel-diaz-canel-bermudez-en-la-reunion-del-consejo-supremo.
45 http://government.ru/news/48518/.
46 The Ministry of Economic Development of Russia Statistics.

Ossetia, despite the fact that the Kremlin has repeatedly expressed its hope for this.

Moscow's second traditional outpost in Latin America is Nicaragua. In the 1980s, the USSR supported the Sandinista Revolution, one of the leaders of which was the now President Daniel Ortega, and relations with this state became a strategic partnership for Moscow (Varas, 1981). Having survived a short period of "freezing" at the turn of the century, the bilateral dialogue intensified with renewed vigor, the impetus for which was the Ortega's return to power in 2007.

Although Russian-Nicaraguan relations have enjoyed the status of a strategic partnership for a shorter period of time compared to Russo-Cuban relations, by and large, they have developed in a similar way. Nicaragua's debt to Russia under Soviet loans ($3.4 billion) was settled in 2004. Russia forgave Nicaragua this debt, including accrued interest. As a result, Russia became the largest creditor state in terms of the volume of debts forgiven to Nicaragua. Another similarity with the Cuban scenario is that Russia has become the main supplier of vehicles to Nicaragua. Similarly to Cuba, Nicaragua has become dependent on Russia for military hardware. After the signing of an agreement in 2013, according to which the Kremlin financed the modernization of the Nicaraguan armed forces, Russia began equipping Nicaragua with modern weapons and began training military personnel in Russian military universities. In 2015, an intergovernmental agreement was signed on a simplified procedure for the entry of the Russian Navy into Nicaraguan ports.[47]

Close interaction between Russia and Nicaragua stands out in various international platforms. Nicaragua's representatives have consistently voted for draft resolutions submitted by the Kremlin to the UN and other multilateral forums, unconditionally supporting the Russian leadership in recent conflict situations. In 2008, Nicaragua was the first foreign country to recognize the independence of South Ossetia and Abkhazia. In 2014, it voted against the draft resolution of the UN General Assembly, which did not recognize the results of the Crimean referendum. Russia also became an ally of the Ortega government in the international arena. After the deployment of Russian warships in Managua in 2013, the Russian authorities announced that they would support Nicaragua in any armed conflict, indirectly hinting at the Nicaraguan-Colombian dispute over the ownership of the islands of San Andres and Providencia.

---

47   The Ministry of Foreign Affairs of the Russian Federation. Database.

In the 21st century, Russia launched several joint projects with Nicaragua aiming at influencing all of South America. Among them is the construction of a joint venture for the production of vaccines called "Mechnikov" against influenza and the ground station for collecting GLONASS data. In 2009, the IT company "Yota de Nicaragua S.A." was launched. Russia controls 75% of the joint venture. In 2020, the company became the second most popular Internet operator in Nicaragua. Cooperation between law enforcement agencies occupies a special place in the bilateral dialogue. In 2017, the Training Center of the Ministry of Internal Affairs of Russia was opened in Managua. This project involved expanding security cooperation with Central American countries. The volume of bilateral trade, excluding armaments, remains rather modest at $53 million in 2019.[48]

For Moscow, the construction of the Nicaraguan Canal, connecting the Caribbean Sea and the Pacific Ocean, is of particular strategic and geopolitical importance, allowing Russia to compete with the Panama Canal. Nevertheless, the ambitious construction of the "project of the century" has been frozen since 2015 due to the cessation of financing from China. The visit of Russia's Defense Minister to Cuba, Venezuela, and Nicaragua in 2015 was devoted to discussing Russia's participation in this project, along with the signing of a number of new military contracts, becoming another "response" to the alleged US involvement in the conflict in Ukraine.

Meanwhile, repeated mass protests against the Ortega government and the brutal methods used by the authorities to quell demonstrations, turned the overwhelming majority of the population, including political allies, against the leader of Nicaragua. That gave rise to Russia's fears about the imminent "loss" of another friendly regime in Latin America. In the current dialogue with Cuba and Nicaragua, Moscow has embarked on a course of catching up, primarily through large-scale investments. However, in the short term, due to the global financial crisis caused by the COVID-19 pandemic, this course of action changed markedly (Kosevich, 2020). It may nullify all the advances of Russian foreign policy achieved in the second decade of the 21st century with Moscow's traditional partners in Latin America.

It was significant that the governments of Cuba and Nicaragua, carefully avoiding the term "invasion" in relation to the special military operation of Russia in Ukraine strongly criticized the US policy, which ultimately led to the gradual approach of NATO to the borders of Russia.

---

48   Bank of Russia. Databases.

Thus, in the 21st century interaction between Russia and its traditional allies copies the successful Soviet partnership model. Cooperation is developing only in some areas, the main engines of which are large state-owned enterprises, whose activities are based on the contractual and legal framework mainly formed in the last century. The changing conditions for foreign capital in Cuba and Nicaragua led to a sharp increase in investment interest from different countries, compared to which Russian businesses were uncompetitive. The internal political situation in both Cuba and Nicaragua is losing its stability, becoming less controlled by the authorities, and they are losing their allies in LAC, which negatively affects the development of bilateral dialogue. The Miguel Díaz-Canel and Daniel Ortega regimes, based on a rigid political monopoly, which are regional symbols of "a crisis of democracy", consider their relations with the Kremlin as an important tool in the geopolitical game, both in domestic and foreign policy, in the absence of stable and diversified partnerships.

2.2 *Ideological Allies*

The second group of "ideological allies" united by anti-American sentiments is led by Venezuela (Kosevich, 2023). Unlike Cuba and Nicaragua, Russian-Venezuelan relations cannot boast the same high level of partnership as with the USSR. In contrast to these countries, Venezuela is an "oil" power, which, since the beginning of the 20th century, made a bet on this particular industry to the detriment of other areas of domestic and foreign policy. The significant participation of foreign investors in the oil industry, mainly from the US, did not contribute to the rapprochement between the USSR and Venezuela. During the second half of the 20th century, Venezuela was the richest and most stable democratic country in Latin America. This lasted until the moment when Hugo Chavez entered politics, completely changing Caracas' political course. The personal meeting between Putin and Chavez at the UN Millennium Summit in 2000 became an important step in promoting cooperation between Russia and the "new" Venezuela transforming towards the Socialism of the 21st Century. The formation of the contractual framework governing bilateral trade cooperation began from this meeting, resulting in a constellation of agreements.[49]

The US decision to impose an embargo on the replacement of obsolete American-made Venezuelan military equipment was a powerful impetus for the Chavez government, which was characterized by a populist and anti-American orientation, to "strengthen friendship" with Moscow. According to

---

[49] The Ministry of Foreign Affairs of the Russian Federation. Database.

Russian political analysts, "Washington itself pushed Venezuela into the arms of Russia" (Sudarev, 2015). During his presidency, Chavez made eight visits to Russia, which resulted in a rapid intensification of ties, in which military-technical and energy cooperation dominated. In 2004, Caracas began large-scale purchases of Russian weapons, which were facilitated by Venezuelan oil. The construction of a facility for the production of Kalashnikov assault rifles and a plant for the production of cartridges, agreed to in 2006, received a strong response in Latin America. However, none of these projects were completed.

Cooperation between Moscow and Caracas gained a strategic scope in 2008, assisted by the visit of Russia's then President Medvedev to Venezuela and joint naval exercises. The diplomatic crisis that broke out between Colombia on the one hand, and Ecuador and Venezuela on the other hand, after the death of one of the leaders of the Revolutionary Armed Forces of Colombia (FARC) in Ecuador, only reinforced Caracas' loyalty to Moscow.

In August 2011, Moscow provided Venezuela with a $5 billion loan, and hundreds of Russian military specialists on temporary contracts flooded the country. Eventually, Moscow's interest in selling weapons to Venezuela, whose debts were rapidly growing accompanied by dim prospects of their repayment, began to fade in 2012, which China successfully took advantage of. In 2012, the Chinese company "Norinco" signed a major deal for the sale of Chinese-made ground weapons for more than $500 million. After the final plunge of Venezuela into the socioeconomic crisis in 2014, Russia stopped supplying military equipment (Cavanagh, 2020). Between 2005 and 2015, Venezuela had bought $15 billion worth of Russian military equipment.[50]

With the end of the Kremlin's interest in developing military-technical cooperation, Russia focused on strengthening its presence in Venezuela's energy sector. The largest oil companies Rosneft, Lukoil and Gazprom launched a number of oil and gas exploration and production projects. Since the beginning of the 21st century, the volume of investments in this area has amounted to more than $20 billion.[51]

Despite the complete outfitting of the Venezuelan army with Russian equipment, non-military trade between the countries has not grown. In 2019, the trade turnover was $85 million, 99% of which consisted of Russian exports,[52] confirming the temporary nature of the Russian-Venezuelan partnership.

In 2010–2019, Russia issued loans worth $17 billion to Venezuela. This debt has been restructured many times since, due to the fact that Caracas has not

---

50 Rosoboronexport Annual Report.
51 The Ministry of Foreign Affairs of the Russian Federation. Database.
52 Bank of Russia. Databases.

been able to fulfill its debt obligations. Caracas is paying off loans issued by Moscow in two ways: by delivering oil, and by transferring its energy assets to Russian companies. Rosneft, which has gained control of Venezuela's oil and gas sector, ended up on the top of the pyramid built by Russia's largest oil companies in Venezuela. Rosneft and Petróleos de Venezuela, Sociedad Anonima (PDVSA) have established five oil production joint ventures. The Trump administration's sanctions against Caracas have provided Russia with exclusive access to oil fields, which has strengthened its capacity to influence global oil prices. The fact that bilateral cooperation in the energy sector continues to evolve is also evidenced by the decision of the Venezuelan government to move the European office of PDVSA from Lisbon to Moscow in 2019. By 2020, most of the largest oil projects in Venezuela were transferred to Rosneft. A noticeable increase in Rosneft's activities over the past ten years has resulted in it becoming the major foreign player in Venezuela's oil sector.

The coup attempt in Venezuela in 2019 raised even more fears about the debt repayment. Realizing the hopelessness of the debt situation, the Russian government decided to classify Venezuela's debt to Russia. Such steps confirm that bilateral Russian-Venezuelan relations, despite the massive financial injections, do not have either a legal or institutional framework.

Internationally, Russia and China became the main supporters of Maduro's government. The main driving force behind this stance was the desire to strike a blow at the US regional hegemony. Russia's positions in Venezuela, gained over the past decades, are weakening every year due to the fact that Venezuela's closest neighbors openly support US foreign policy. By 2021, the main driving force behind Russian foreign policy in Venezuela was the desire to gain more control over oil supplies, which could increase Russia's geopolitical influence.

Bolivia is Russia's second most important regional ideological ally after Venezuela. Russian-Bolivian relations received a new impetus in 2006, when Evo Morales became president. In 2009, Morales became the first-ever Bolivian leader to pay an official visit to Russia. The result of that meeting was the conclusion of an agreement on military-technical cooperation and the creation of an intergovernmental commission on trade and economic cooperation, intensifying bilateral dialogue. A bilateral visa-free travel regime was introduced in 2016.

Both countries held similar positions on most key international issues, and in the first decade of the 21st century, political contacts noticeably intensified. The leftist Morales adhered to an anti-American position, which became a point of contact with the Kremlin. This was especially evident after 2008, when a wave of civil unrest swept across the country, for which Morales blamed Washington, eventually expelling US diplomats. In 2017–2018, when

Bolivia was elected a non-permanent member at the UN Security Council, it repeatedly expressed support for the Russian involvement in Syria, criticizing the US position. In 2018, Bolivia supported Russia in the "Skripal case". Morales also came to Moscow on the eve of the 2019 Bolivian presidential elections, in which he ran for his fourth term. During this visit, the Bolivian leader emphasized his intention to further strengthen political and military ties with Russia. Despite the intensification of the bilateral diplomatic dialogue, mutual trade remained insignificant: in 2019, it was $16.7 million (1% of Russia's foreign trade).[53]

As in the Venezuelan case, fuel and energy sector cooperation between Russia and Bolivia has become the main area of economic activity, demonstrating noticeable progress over the past decade. The Kremlin's interest in expanding cooperation in this area is centered around the fact that Bolivia ranks third in South America in terms of hydrocarbon production. The Memorandum of Understanding between Gazprom and the Bolivian state oil and gas company YPFB, signed in 2007, became the basis for bilateral cooperation in the electric power industry. Gazprom, in partnership with Bolivian companies, took part in a number of projects to develop promising oil, gas, and hydrocarbon fields. A representative office of Gazprom International B.V. was opened in Santa Cruz to oversee the implementation of joint projects.[54]

A new impulse for bilateral cooperation in nuclear energy was given by the signing of an intergovernmental agreement on cooperation in the use of atomic energy for peaceful purposes and mutual approval of the construction of a Nuclear Research and Technology Center in Bolivia in 2016. In 2017, a contract between the Atomic Energy Agency of Bolivia and Russia's Rosatom for the construction of the Nuclear Research and Technology Center in El Alto was signed. For Russia, this project had a special symbolic meaning, since this was Rosatom's first project in Latin America. However, so far these expectations have not materialized. In 2020, the new Bolivian authorities decided to freeze the construction of this facility. In 2018, the Russian company Akron agreed on the construction of two fertilizer plants in Bolivia, which have not come to fruition. Since 2015, Russian companies have been trying to develop Bolivia's lithium deposits, centered on the Uyuni salt flats. However, Russian companies failed to obtain permission from the Bolivian authorities for exploration, despite the fact that the bilateral Memorandum of Understanding on cooperation in the field of geology was signed in 2018.

---

53   Bank of Russia. Databases.
54   "Gazprom International B.V." is a specialized enterprise for the implementation of Gazprom's foreign projects.

An intergovernmental agreement on military-technical cooperation was signed in 2009, under which Russia granted Bolivia a loan for the purchase of military equipment and a new agreement on military cooperation was signed in 2016. As a part of the latter, Bolivia bought Russian helicopters to fight drug cartels inside the country, and not for external threats as in the case of Venezuela and Nicaragua. In humanitarian cooperation, Russia provides annual state scholarships for training Bolivian engineers.

In the 21st century, Russian-Bolivian relations were based mainly on anti-American sentiments that characterized the course of the Morales government. However, Bolivia never turned into a full political partner of Russia. Over the past decade, Moscow has repeatedly announced large-scale investment projects in the energy sector, but most of them remain unfulfilled. All this can be explained by the fact that Morales, positioning himself as a left-wing radical, in reality, pursued cautious foreign and domestic policies. His economic policy was quite liberal, attracting both regional and non-regional investors. In this context, his resignation in 2019 was viewed by Russia primarily as an expected transformation of the Latin American political map, entailing dubious prospects and a revision of agreements, but not as a "tangible loss".

Regarding Russia's "special military operation" the Venezuelan Foreign Ministry expressed its support for the struggle of the Kremlin against "NATO aggression." Venezuela received a US delegation just two weeks after the start of Russia's "special military operation" with the main goal of finding new oil suppliers in view of Washington's sanctions on Moscow. The negotiations between Venezuela and the US, which broke off diplomatic relations in 2019, were recognized by both sides as the beginning of the restoration of interstate dialogue. The President of Bolivia expressed regret that the crisis could not be resolved by peaceful means, calling on the parties to peace, while avoiding criticism of the Kremlin's actions. Bolivia has increased supplies of its own liquefied natural gas to countries of the Western Hemisphere, the demand for which has risen after the increase in gas prices after the outbreak of hostilities in Ukraine, also indicating its interest in expanding trade cooperation with the US. A little later, these three LAC countries—Cuba, Bolivia, Nicaragua—were among the 35 abstaining countries in the voting on UN General Assembly Resolution ES-11/1, condemning Russia's military actions in Ukraine, confirming their status as "traditional partners" and "ideological allies" of Russia.[55] Venezuela could not join them, due to the fact that the country was temporarily

---

55   Resolution adopted by the General Assembly on 2 March 2022, *UN General Assembly*, 18 March 2022, https://digitallibrary.un.org/record/3965290?ln=ru#record-files-collapse-header.

deprived of the right to vote in the UN General Assembly due to non-payment of UN contributions.

Instability is the main distinguishing feature of interstate interaction between Russia and the "ideologically allied" Venezuela and Bolivia in comparison with the "traditional partners" Cuba and Nicaragua. Unlike traditional partners, the formation of bilateral partnerships with Caracas and La Paz took place against the background of a radical restructuring of the models of political and socio-economic development of these countries. The gains occurred in the context of a new course towards building socialism, and were accompanied by the aggravation of disagreements with the US. All this ultimately predetermined their instability, intensified by the lack of a legal and institutional basis. Instability is the main distinguishing feature of the model of interstate interaction between Russia and "ideological allies" in comparison with "traditional partners".

2.3 Trade Partners

Brazil is at the head of the "trade partners" group, which views commerce as the basis of cooperation. The Kremlin perceives Brazil as the most important potential partner in Latin America, both economically and strategically. Brazil is the largest Latin American country and, playing a significant regional role, aspires to become a noticeable actor in world politics.

Russian-Brazilian relations are based on trade and cooperation in international forums, due to which their bilateral dialogue has acquired a global character, unlike with other countries in Latin America. This is confirmed by the creation of a Russian-Brazilian strategic alliance in 2005 and regular contacts between the leaders of Russia and Brazil over the last decade. The Russian president visited Brazil in 2004, 2008, 2010, and 2014. In the last decade, the presidents of Brazil have also regularly visited Russia.

The political nature of the Russian-Brazilian dialogue is especially evident in the UN. In 2014, Brazil abstained from voting on the General Assembly Resolution on the territorial integrity of Ukraine. Russia continuously supports Brazil's bid for a permanent seat on the UN Security Council.

However, within BRICS, Brazil found itself out of the focus of Russia's interest. The large Russian-Brazilian commission, created at the end of the 20th century to expand bilateral cooperation, continues to be only formal in nature. The strategic partnership originally planned in 1997 has never been achieved.

There is virtually no bilateral military-technical cooperation. In 2000–2020, Brazil made only single purchases of Russian weapons. Almost all the announced large-scale contracts in this area were eventually suspended by the Brazilian government. Russian companies are also not represented in the

Brazilian oil and gas sector. The only exception is Rosneft, which started a joint project with Brazilian partners HRT Participacoes em Petroleo and Petrobras in the Solimoes Basin in 2019. In 2007, Gazprom and Petrobras signed a Memorandum of Understanding providing for cooperation in the exploration, production, and sale of hydrocarbons. Gazprom opened a representative office in Rio de Janeiro in 2012. However, all joint projects remain at the negotiating level.

In the energy sector, Rosatom concluded an agreement on the construction of a nuclear power plant in Brazil in 2014, and a memorandum of understanding to develop cooperation in the peaceful use of atomic energy was signed in 2017.

In 2010, the Kremlin announced the expansion of scientific and technical cooperation in economic interaction with Latin America. Despite this, trade continued to be the main engine of the Russian-Brazilian dialogue. In general, Russian-Brazilian relations are built on a solid international legal basis: more than 60 intergovernmental and interdepartmental documents have been signed, and more than two dozen are under development.

Brazil is Russia's largest trading partner in LAC and an important supplier of agricultural products to the Russian market. Russian-Brazilian trade turnover in 2021 was $7.5 billion and continued the upward trend in 2022. There are Russia-Brazil and Brazil-Russia entrepreneurial councils, which include representatives of large Russian and Brazilian companies. In terms of its share in Russian trade, Brazil occupied 30th place in 2019 ($5 billion), and 10th place in 2022 ($10 billion).[56] Almost 45% of all imports from Latin America are from Brazil, which is also the main recipient of Russian products in the regional context: almost 37% of all Russian exports to LAC go to Brazil. Russia ranks 20th in the list of Brazil's main business partners. Russia accounts for 3% of Brazilian imports, which is the sixth highest among Brazil's foreign partners.[57]

Jair Bolsonaro's victory in the 2018 presidential elections in Brazil meant a significant loss for Russia in this region. The new president was known for his pro-American views, which meant closing the doors for Moscow in this strategically important country. Bolsonaro has repeatedly stated that he is ready to deploy a US military base in Brazil to counter the Russian influence in the region (Malamud, 2018). Meanwhile, Russia's negative expectations only partially materialized.

---

56   Trade Map. Trade Statistics for International Business Development.
57   https://santandertrade.com/en/portal/analyse-markets/brazil/foreign-trade-in-figures#-classification_by_country.

The coming to power in Brazil in 2023 of the classic left-wing politician Lula da Silva, who expectedly took the side of US opponents in the struggle to establish a new world order, returned a positive tone to relations between Russia and Brazil. In light of the sanctions imposed by Western countries against Russia, Russian-Brazilian cooperation has once again begun to be built on a common vision of the need to reform the outdated international financial and economic architecture, which does not take into account the increased economic weight of emerging market economies and developing countries.

A number of bilateral initiatives have been frozen, despite the fact that the volume of trade at the level of public and private companies has not changed greatly since 2015. Cultural, educational, and humanitarian cooperation are developing at a slow pace. For example, in 2017, an Agreement between Russia and Brazil on the establishment and conditions of operation of cultural centers was signed but has not yet entered into force.

This was largely due to the fact that during the reign of leftist governments in Brazil, a fairly solid legal and regulatory framework was created, covering almost all areas of bilateral cooperation.[58] However, Russia failed to bring bilateral relations to a higher level, even during favorable times.

Mexico is Russia's second largest trade partner in Latin America after Brazil. Historically, Russian-Mexican relations were characterized by a fairly high degree of mutual understanding in the absence of significant political and economic achievements (Kosevich, 2019). Mexico has always been quite careful in its relations with Russia. The Kremlin considered Mexico as Washington's natural sphere of influence with limited opportunities to increase the Russian presence (Kosevich, 2021).

In politics, bilateral relations were quite friendly. The beginning of the century was marked by a noticeable diplomatic rapprochement, manifested in frequent high-level meetings, held mainly at international forums such as APEC, UN, and G-20 summits. The approaches of both countries to major international problems were similar, but there were exceptions. Mexico, along with other Latin American countries, voted in support of the UN General Assembly resolution on the territorial integrity of Ukraine, which recognized the Crimean referendum as invalid, and also supported the West's position on the "Skripal case".

The period 2009–2019 was characterized by an increase in bilateral trade (from $600 million to $3 billion). Mexico emerged as an important destination for Russian wheat exporters as Mexico's consumption increased sharply over

---

58 The Ministry of Foreign Affairs of the Russian Federation. Database.

the previous decade. Meanwhile, the practically zero level of mutual investment confirms a low level of business awareness about each other's market environment. Only a few major investment projects were realized. In 2007, the Russian company Power Machines took part in the equipping of one of the world's highest ground hydroelectric power plants, La Yesca. In 2016, Russia invested $1.7 million in pipe production for the transportation and storage of natural gas in 12 Mexican states. Two tenders for exploration in the Gulf of Mexico were won by Lukoil. In 2020, the joint venture Eni, created by Lukoil and the UK's Capricorn, discovered a new oil field offshore from Mexico.

Bilateral cooperation is developing most actively in aviation and road transport, energy, and mechanical engineering. Mexico purchased 22 "Sukhoi Superjet 100" aircraft. However, in 2019, Mexico announced its intention to resell these aircraft to third countries, citing the fact that it was not satisfied with the after-sales service. Helicopters "Mi-17", Russian cars "Ural", off-road vehicles "UAZ Hunter" and motorcycles "Ural" were delivered to Mexico in the 2010s. There was a deepening of Russian-Mexican cultural ties, which manifested in a number of art exhibitions, and fairs of national crafts and traditions. Since 2010, Mexico has introduced an "electronic permit system", which has allowed Russian citizens to get online visas, which led to about 50,000 Russian tourists visiting Mexico annually.[59]

Bilateral political dialogue at the highest level is not developing. Despite the considerable efforts made by the then Ambassador of Mexico, Ruben Beltran, during his time in Russia (2013–2017) to organize a presidential meeting, all his attempts met with indifference on the part of the Russian Foreign Ministry. The diplomat also failed to achieve the expansion of economic and investment cooperation, although these were the main tasks assigned to Beltran by the then President of Mexico, Peña Nieto. This confirms that Russia continues to be an unpredictable destination for Mexico Rouvinski 2022. In Russian-Mexican dialogue, the "Washington factor" is invisibly present, which noticeably limits the development of bilateral cooperation. The Mexican government is forced to reckon with the opinion of the White House on any Russian-Mexican projects, given that the US has effective leverage over its southern neighbor. For example, in 2020, Mexico's attempt to buy Russian military helicopters was canceled after threats of sanctions by the US.[60]

---

59 Federal Agency for Tourism Statistics.
60 https://www.abc.es/internacional/abci-mexico-enfrenta-sancion-estados-unidos-si
    -concreta-compra-helicopteros-rusia-202002150149_noticia.html?ref=
    https%3A%2F%2Fwww.google.com%2F.

The coming to power in Mexico of Andrés López Obrador in 2018, who outlined his intention to diversify foreign economic relations, and the ongoing decline in the US interest in Latin America in general, opened the door to new geopolitical opportunities for Russia. Obrador has already accepted an invitation to visit Moscow someday. This gave rise to a new hope for rapprochement, given that the last official visit of a Mexican leader took place in 2005 when President Vicente Fox visited Moscow. The central tasks of the Obrador government are the solution of internal social problems and the implementation of programs to support the population during the pandemic. In this context, in 2021, a working visit of the head of the Mexican Foreign Ministry to Russia took place, aimed at expanding cooperation on the "Sputnik V" vaccine. Unlike other LAC countries, a bilateral mixed commission on cultural cooperation was formed with Mexico. In addition, Mexico is very popular among Russian tourists: the country is among the top twenty in terms of tourist flow from Russia.

Although the potential for interaction in a number of spheres is being partially realized, Russia continues to be on the periphery of Mexico's foreign policy interests and Mexico is still insignificant on the Kremlin's priority list. Russian politicians and businesses have not yet been able to abandon the stereotype of Mexico as the "backyard" of the US, where any Russian initiative invariably runs into a wall.

In contrast to Mexico, Russia-Ecuador relations can be characterized as stable and predictable, in the center of which is economic cooperation, while political interaction is of secondary importance. The intensification of political and diplomatic contacts was largely due to the ideology of the Rafael Correa government, in which the development of relations with the member countries of the socialist alliance ALBA was given special importance. The then Russian President Medvedev first met with the Ecuadorian leader in 2008 at the ALBA summit in Caracas (Puyosa, 2019).

In 2009, Correa made the first official visit to Russia of an Ecuadorian president, followed by a second, in 2013. The result of these meetings was the signing of the Declaration on Strategic Partnership, and a number of cooperation agreements, which gave a new impetus to bilateral dialogue. However, neither the Russian president nor the prime minister have paid a return visit to Ecuador. The progressive development of Russian-Ecuadorian cooperation was largely due to the idea of reducing its dependence on the US, which was given special importance in the foreign policy of the Correa presidency. Over time, this projected onto the trade sphere, where several areas sharply intensified: military cooperation, energy, infrastructure construction, and the banking sector.

Ecuador became the third largest trading partner of Russia in Latin America. The most favored nation treatment in trade had been enshrined in a special agreement (1969), which continues to be the main one for the development of bilateral cooperation in this area. Since 2014, the volume of bilateral trade has been $1.6 billion annually: imports from Ecuador are almost 4.5 times higher than Russian exports to Ecuador. More than 90% of bananas sold in Russia come from Ecuador.[61]

One of the main areas of cooperation is in the energy sector, at the level of large and medium-sized businesses. In 2009, the Russian company Premium Engineering and the Ecuadorian Petroecuador agreed on a plan of cooperation in the production and processing of gas in Sucumbíos Province. In 2010, Tyazhmash and Rao Ues signed a contract to supply electromechanical equipment for the Ecuadorian Toachi Pilatón hydropower station. Since 2013, a joint project has been implemented to build a gas turbine and a steam turbine at Termogas Machala. In addition, a number of agreements were signed on the construction of the hydroelectric power stations Cardenillo and Chonta, and two hydro-technical facilities.[62]

However, in the modernization of the power generating and power grid infrastructure of Ecuador, Russia is significantly behind China, which participates in 10 large projects through Chinese banks and companies. The most expensive Russian initiative is the Gazprom project for the production of gas on the continental shelf of Ecuador, which is estimated at $1.5 billion.[63] In 2008, an Intergovernmental Agreement on Military-Technical Cooperation was signed, under which Ecuador purchased helicopters and anti-aircraft missile systems.[64] In 2017, Russia delivered 100 Uaz vehicles. Cooperation in education and culture is developing. In terms of the number of students studying in Russia, Ecuador is among the leaders from Latin America.[65]

The coming to power in Ecuador of Lenin Moreno led to a sharp turn in foreign policy, together with a radical change in the country's economic strategy. Moreno attached particular importance to the development of an open trade policy and attracting foreign investment. In 2018, Ecuador announced its withdrawal from the ALBA alliance, confirming the ideological, regional, and global change in its orientation. However, the political turn in Ecuador did not affect the character of the relationship with Russia. This was primarily due to

---

61 Bank of Russia. Databases.
62 https://tass.ru/info/3331430.
63 https://www.kommersant.ru/doc/1991131.
64 Rosoboronexport Annual Report.
65 Ministry of Science and Higher Education of the Russian Federation Statistics.

Ecuador's interest in the Russian market, where food products and agricultural raw materials are supplied in large volumes, the demand for which was growing annually. In 2018, the Russia-Ecuador Entrepreneurial union was formed, and negotiations on the creation of a Russian-Ecuadorian bank began. It is symptomatic that Ecuador has officially confirmed its interest in concluding a free trade agreement with the Eurasian Economic Union. Given the new tensions in relations between Russia and the West, mutual trade progressively expanded, even after the coming to power in Ecuador in 2021 of Guillermo Lasso, a representative of the center-right party.

By 2023, Russia had become the second main buyer of Ecuadorian bananas with 1.37 million tons per year, which is equivalent to 23% of Ecuador's total banana exports, second only to the EU, and more than 90% of bananas arriving on the shelves in Russia come from Ecuador. This alone is enough to understand that modern trade relations between Russia and Ecuador have become very interdependent. Under the administration of the representative of the National Democratic Action party, Daniel Noboa, who came to power in 2023, relations between Russia and Ecuador cooled sharply. At the beginning of 2024, Russian authorities decided to suspend the activities of five Ecuadorian banana companies exporting bananas to Russia, which was announced almost immediately after it became known that the Ecuadorian government was going to supply Soviet military equipment to the US, who said they intended to send it to Ukraine. In exchange for these weapons, the US intended to supply Ecuador with modern American equipment worth $200 million. The exchange of "unused Soviet equipment" for the latest US weapons had been actively promoted by Washington to Latin American countries since 2022. The White House called this proposal an "ideal deal." However, all Latin American countries invariably refused this "tempting offer," thereby continuing their line of neutrality regarding the Russia-Ukraine conflict, which escalated in February 2022. Thus, Ecuador became the first Latin American country to decide on a "perfect deal" with the US, thanks to which the country could become involved in a geopolitical conflict involving Russia, Ukraine and the US. The restrictions imposed on the supply of Ecuadorian bananas to Russia were lifted after a meeting took place between the Russian Ambassador to Ecuador and President Daniel Noboa, who confirmed that he had refused to supply weapons to the US.

Argentina is Russia's fourth most important economic partner in Latin America. In some years, the USSR was the world's largest importer of Argentine goods, which laid the foundation for effective trade and economic cooperation. Although since the days of the Soviet Union, bilateral relations have been built around commercial activities, regular contacts in the humanitarian sphere were established. The largest number of Russian immigrants to Latin America live in Argentina.

The intensification of bilateral economic ties began at the end of 1998, leading to the fact that by 2008 the volume of trade increased from $55 million to $2 billion, which was due to the accumulated experience of economic cooperation. For the first decade of the 21st century, Russia became one of the main importers of Argentinean products, which the devaluation of the peso in 2002 made competitive and extremely attractive for the Russian market. The main share of supplies from Argentina was food products and agricultural raw materials. Bilateral trade in the last decade has averaged $1 billion annually with a negative trade balance for Russia.[66] Almost one-fourth of all Argentinian power plants still run on Soviet equipment, which predetermined that the main goods supplied from Russia to Argentina are industrial, power, and construction equipment.[67]

Such successful economic cooperation gave impetus to the intensification of political and diplomatic contacts. In 2008, the countries agreed on a strategic partnership initiative, where an important role was given to the expansion of the presence of new actors in bilateral relations: private firms, banking structures, associations of entrepreneurs, consulting organizations, and law firms. This favorably distinguished Argentina from other Latin American countries. The Intergovernmental Russian—Argentine Commission on Trade, Economic, Scientific, and Technical Cooperation opened in 1996, and the Russia-Argentina Council of Entrepreneurs was established in 2003. In 2009, an agreement on visa-free travel was signed.

A new incentive to bilateral cooperation was given in 2010, when, for the first time in the history of Argentina–Russia relations, a Russian president visited Argentina, as a result of which agreements were reached on Russia's billion-dollar investments in advanced branches of Argentinean industry. In 2014, the Russian president again paid an official visit to Argentina. Less than a year later, Argentine President Cristina Fernandez paid a return visit to Moscow. All this led to the fact that bilateral relations moved to the level of a comprehensive strategic partnership, which meant mutual support on key international issues: Russia supported Argentina's position as in the Argentine-British conflict over the Malvinas (Falkland) Islands, and in negotiations with "vulture funds"; Argentina abstained from voting on the UN Resolution on the territorial integrity of Ukraine.

---

66   http://www.cear.org/es/estadistica-comercial/.
67   The Ministry of Economic Development of the Russian Federation Statistics.

During the Fernandez presidency, a record number of bilateral agreements were signed (more than 60). The coming to power in Argentina in 2015 of opposition candidate Mauricio Macri marked the beginning of large-scale transformations in the domestic and foreign policies of the country. However, negative assumptions about the possible closure of bilateral projects were mostly not fulfilled. Two factors contributed to this: the protectionist trade policy of the Trump administration, which revealed Argentina's foreign trade vulnerability; increasing trade and attracting foreign direct investment became one of the main tasks of the Macri government.

In 2017, the first joint business forum "Russia-Argentina" took place, resulting in the signing of an agreement on cooperation between the councils of entrepreneurs. In the same year, a delegation of the Security Council of Russia arrived in Argentina on an official visit to discuss issues of military-technical cooperation, at the end of which a Memorandum on cooperation in security matters was signed. A year later, Macri arrived in Moscow on an official visit, confirming Argentina's intention to fill bilateral cooperation with new content. During the visit, the Argentine leader and the heads of 18 of the largest Russian companies discussed opportunities for cooperation, among which was the initiative of Rosatom to build a Russian nuclear power plant in Argentina. Putin even announced that "Argentina for Russia is a priority partner in Latin America."[68] Eleven months later, Putin met again with Macri in Buenos Aires to discuss opportunities for increasing cooperation. His visit finished with the opening of the branch of the Russkiy Mir Foundation in Argentina.

As for specific projects, in 2018, Gazprom announced its intention to participate in a project for the exploration and production of fuel at the Estación Fernández Oro hydrocarbon field together with the Argentine company YPF. The Russian company Power Machines, whose equipment had already been supplied to five Argentine hydro power plants, has also shown interest in participating in investment projects. In 2010, Argentina signed an agreement with Russia on the use of the GLONASS satellite system, and in 2018, the Mechita railway technology center, created with Russian participation, started operations.

Significant progress was archived in energy cooperation. New opportunities for Russia in this area were opened after the re-nationalization in 2012 of the largest national energy company YPF, which was previously owned by the Spanish company Repsol. In 2012, on the sidelines of the G-20 summit, as part of a meeting between the Russian and Argentinian presidents, an agreement was reached to develop cooperation with Gazprom. A year later, Gazprom

---

68   https://www.ng.ru/world/2018-01-24/6_7157_argentina.html.

won a tender for the supply of ten shipments of liquefied natural gas for the Argentinean companies YPF and Enarsa. Nevertheless, the Argentine government still preferred cooperation with the American company Chevron, with which YPF signed an agreement in 2013 on the joint exploitation of the Vaca Muerta shale formation, which is important for the oil and gas sector of the Argentine economy.[69]

Under the embargo on imports from Western countries in response to anti-Russian sanctions, Argentina, like Brazil and other South American countries, began to gradually increase the supply of meat, dairy products, and fruits to Russia. In September 2014, Argentina even sent a special delegation to negotiate the expansion of meat exports to Russia. As a result, by 2018, Russia ranked second in the world in terms of purchases of Argentine beef, behind only China.[70]

In 2019, Alberto Fernandez became the new president of Argentina, which marked the return of the foreign policy course to that of the Christina Fernandez government, and new prospects for developing cooperation for Russia. However, in its desire to expand its presence in Argentina through participation in large investment projects, Russia has been forced to compete with strong rivals: China and the EU.

It is noteworthy that on the eve of the start of Russia's "special military operation" on the territory of Ukraine in February 2022, the President of Argentina Alberto Fernandez and the President of Brazil Bolsonaro visited Russia (with the latter, negotiations were held in the 2+2 format between the Ministry of Foreign Affairs and the Ministry of Defense of both countries). The main topic of the negotiations was new and potential opportunities for expanding interaction between countries. At the end of August 2023, Fernandez officially announced that his country would join the BRICS bloc, an interstate association that has previously included only five countries. It should be noted that in four provinces of Argentina, Brazil is the main trading partner and destination of Argentine exports, and for another eight Argentine provinces, China is now the main trading partner. India is an important buyer of Argentine corn and the main importer of Argentine-produced wheat and barley. According to the Argentine Foreign Ministry, the five current members of the BRICS group account for 30% of Argentina's total national exports. In this regard, President Alberto Fernandez emphasized that Argentina's entry into BRICS "will open up new business opportunities."

---

69 https://www.vedomosti.ru/business/news/2013/07/17/chevron-vlozhit-12-mlrd-v-razrabotku-slancevogo.
70 https://rosng.ru/post/rossiya-zanyala-vtoroe-mesto-po-importu-govyadiny-iz-argentiny.

The new Argentinian president, Javier Milei, abandoned plans for Argentina to join BRICS. According to the foreign policy goals of the Milei administration, Argentina's geopolitical allies should be exclusively the US, Israel, and the EU. This led to Buenos Aires's relations with Moscow and Beijing cooling. Javier Milei's Argentina withdrew its application to join the BRICS bloc, submitted under the previous president and requested to be a "global partner" of NATO in April 2024. Argentina's approach to NATO is linked to the new foreign policy developed by the ultra-liberal government of Javier Milei, which has the US and Israel as priorities. In addition to the recent visit to Argentina of the commander of the United States Southern Command, Army General Laura Richardson, with the aim of expanding defense collaboration, the South American country is clearly aligned with Israel both in the war in the Gaza Strip against the armed wing of Hamas and in the recent crisis with Iran. The Ministry of Defense of Argentina also signed an agreement for the purchase of 24 used US F-16 fighter jets from the Danish Army.

The foreign policy of the Latin American countries of the "trade partners" group towards Russia is distinguished by a purely pragmatic character, meaning that their dialogue relies on economic cooperation, and not on political partnership (Scott, 2016). This confirms the fact that all four "trade partners" Brazil, Mexico, Argentina, and Ecuador took a position of neutrality regarding the Russia-Ukraine conflict. Brazilian President Bolsonaro, who personally met with Putin in Moscow a week before the start of the special military operation", tried not to mention the Ukrainian crisis at all in his public speeches. The strong dependence of the Brazilian agricultural sector on foreign-imported fertilizers has led the Brazilian government to insist on the exclusion of Russian fertilizers from the list of sanctioned goods. Mexican President Andrés Manuel López Obrador confirmed that his country would not join the sanctions against Russia. A position of "sympathy" and "without criticism" was taken by Argentine President Alberto Fernandez, who also met with Putin in Moscow on the eve of the "special military operation". The President of Ecuador, whose agricultural export sector immediately began to suffer losses due to Western sanctions imposed against Russia, also spoke from a reserved position. Nevertheless, all four countries voted in favor of supporting UN GA Resolution ES-11/1. Brazil and Mexico were among the 58 states that abstained from voting on the Resolution on the suspension of the rights of Russia's membership in the UN Human Rights Council. The two main economies of LAC, Brazil and Mexico, took a double position regarding the Russian-Ukrainian conflict: on the one hand, measured condemnation of Russia's armed operation in Ukraine; on the other hand, they ruled out economic sanctions against the Kremlin and defense assistance to Ukraine, despite the fact that these measures were actively promoted by the US and the EU. It is noteworthy that Argentina, Bolivia, Brazil, and Mexico did not join the joint statement condemning Russia's actions in Ukraine, which was adopted at the 52nd OAS General Assembly, held in October 2022 in Peru.

It is in "trade partners" group of countries that "limited rapprochement" is most clearly manifested. A system of agreements on the absence of double taxation and the protection of capital investments has already been formed between Russia and the leading industrial-agrarian Latin American countries, while there are no multilateral or bilateral agreements on free trade. This is due to the fact that Latin America is very strong in the export of agricultural products, and if free trade agreements were signed with Russia, then Russian agriculture will not be able to compete with Latin American goods, which are noticeably superior in quality. Russia is openly afraid of transferring trade relations with this region to the level of free trade, despite the fact that this would provide a new impulse for the development of relations.

2.4   Low Priority Countries

The "low priority" group includes all other Latin American countries. In this article, the author analyzes the relations with Chile, Colombia, and the countries of North Triangle of Central America, with which Russia has not established stable ties. This is primarily due to the economic dependence of these Latin American states on the US and as a result, Russia perceives the chances of significant relations as "hopeless".

Chile has traditionally been one of Washington's closest allies in the Southern Cone. Last century, Chilean conservative military governments viewed Russia with suspicion, accusing the Kremlin of supporting leftist political organizations in the region. Notable changes in bilateral dialogue took place during the presidencies of Michelle Bachelet. Despite the fact that the focus of the Bachelet government was internal problems, Chile-Russia cooperation was finally given a new impetus. This was facilitated by the fact that Bachelet spoke some Russian. The Chilean leader first met with the then Russian President in 2008 at the APEC summit in Peru, and in 2009 Bachelet paid an official visit to Russia.

Vladimir Putin visited Santiago in 2004 to meet with the then President of Chile, Ricardo Lagos, who, like Bachelet, was a representative of the Socialist Party of Chile. The noticeable rapprochement between the two countries began in 2014 during Bachelet's second presidential term. In those presidential elections, she was nominated by the New Majority coalition, which also includes the Communist Party, which was assessed by the Kremlin as a harbinger of a new stage in the development of bilateral relations. Just months after

Bachelet's inauguration in 2014, the Russian Foreign Minister paid an official visit to Santiago, where he met with the Chilean foreign minister and the president. In the same year, the heads of Russia and Chile met again on the sidelines of the APEC summit in Beijing. During this period, inter-parliamentary ties also intensified: in 2016, Santiago held a meeting of the delegation of the Russian Federation Council with the chairman of the Chilean Senate, and Russia-Chile friendship groups were created in both countries.

Bilateral military-technical cooperation continued to remain minimal. Chile traditionally purchases weapons from the US and Europe. Russian helicopters are the only exception.[71] In the space sector, Russia resumed the operation of the Pulkovo Astronomical Observatory, located in Chile. There is practically no cooperation in the energy sector. Only a few minor projects have been launched. In particular, in 2012 the Russian company RusHydro took part in the construction of a power plant in Chile that converts the energy of sea waves into electricity.

Economic cooperation is developing very slowly. Despite the fact that Chile is one of the regional leaders in the agricultural sector, which plays a crucial role in the country's economy, in 2019 bilateral trade was over $900 million, which remained unchanged in 2022. In terms of share in Russian trade turnover, Chile ranks 73rd. The main share of supplies from Chile to Russia are food products and agricultural raw materials. Chile understands that it has not taken advantage of the sanctions against Russia and the Chilean Embassy in Moscow organizes an annual presentation of products from Chilean suppliers, aimed at winning the confidence of Russian consumers. The coming to power in Chile of Sebastian Piñera in 2018 marked another shift to the right. However, it has not led to significant changes in political and trade interaction between the two countries, which continue to remain extremely limited. Gabriel Boric, a representative of the new left forces who came to power in Chile in 2022, took the toughest position among Latin American politicians regarding the Russia-Ukraine conflict. The Chilean president has repeatedly spoken critically of Russian President Vladimir Putin.[72] Moreover, at the Belt and Road summit held in China in 2023, Borich and the head of the Chilean Foreign Ministry assured that there would be no contacts with Russia.[73] Skepticism towards interaction with the current Chilean leadership can also be seen on

---

71 Rostec State Corporation Annual Reports (2015–2019).
72 https://www.infobae.com/america/america-latina/2022/04/06/gabriel-boric-con-infobae-putin-es-un-autocrata-que-esta-realizando-una-guerra-de-agresion-inaceptable/.
73 https://www.gob.cl/en/news/president-boric-at-eu-celac-summit-2023-what-is-happening-in-ukraine-is-an-unacceptable-war-of-imperial-aggression/.

the Russian side. The Kremlin denies the importance of intensifying cooperation with Chile.

Relations with Colombia, which is Washington's traditional outpost in the region, follow a similar scenario. The main obstacle to the development of cooperation with Russia is the high level of US-Colombian cooperation. Trade and political bilateral interactions continue to be at an extremely low level, despite the fact that there have never been conflicts between Bogota and Moscow in the international arena. For the first two decades of the 21st century neither the president of Colombia nor the president of Russia have not paid each other an official visit. The most significant event of recent years was the trip of the then Defense Minister of Colombia Juan Manuel Santos to Moscow to participate in the Interpol meeting in 2008. However, Santos did not pay a second visit to Russia as President of Colombia (2010–2018). In the last decade, the meetings were held mainly at the level of heads of ministries and departments.

The legal and regulatory framework for bilateral relations is underdeveloped, within which the most important documents are an agreement on military-technical cooperation (1996), a trade agreement (2000) and an agreement on cultural and scientific cooperation (2000). In 1986, an agreement was signed on the mutual recognition and equivalence of educational documents and academic degrees, becoming one of the first such agreements, agreed between the USSR and a Latin American country. In 2009, the Colombian government decided to abolish visas for Russians.

Both sides have repeatedly expressed interest in developing bilateral ties in trade. This is facilitated by the Russian-Colombian intergovernmental commission, created in 1979, and the Colombian-Russian Chamber of Commerce, formed in 2008. A notable event was the cancellation of anti-dumping duties on Russian goods in 2004–2005, providing favorable conditions for their access to Colombia. A similar regime applies to Colombian products in Russia. However, the annual volume of trade reached a record low $400 million in 2019. In 2022, trade turnover was $530 million.[74]

The largest Russian oil companies are represented in Colombia, but no large-scale projects in this area have been implemented. The most significant joint project in recent years was the overhaul of the hydroelectric unit of the Colombian hydro power plant, conducted by Power Machines in 2015.

The visit of the Russian Minister of Industry and Trade to Colombia in 2017, despite the wide range of issues raised, did not become an impetus for the

---

74 Bank of Russia. Databases.

development of trade relations. Although, due to a favorable investment climate, Colombia ranks third in Latin America in terms of foreign direct investment after Mexico and Brazil, the share of Russian investments is almost zero.[75] Most of the Russian-Colombian projects are concentrated in the hydropower sector. The only exception to this indifference is military-technical cooperation. In 2006, Russian vehicle kits were delivered to Colombia, which at various times bought Russian ships, missiles, engines, and artillery in small quantities. Colombia gave priority to the procurement of Russian helicopters which began back in 1997. The only service center in Latin America for MI helicopters, which have demonstrated their efficiency in operations to combat drug trafficking, was opened in Colombia. Difficulties with servicing Russian aircraft delivered to Colombia sharply worsened after the start of Russia's "special military operation" in Ukraine in 2022. This has led to the fact that since 2022, the Russian helicopter service center has been virtually paralyzed, despite the fact that the Russian authorities deny this.

One of the truly unique joint initiatives was the opening of Corrida, the Russian-Colombian Center for the Exchange of Technologies and Innovations in Bucaramanga, in which scientific organizations are involved. The large-scale purchase of Russian arms by Venezuela and the length of its border with Colombia (more than 2,000 km), have become a new obstacle to the development of bilateral relations. The negative reaction of the Colombian government is also caused by Russia's support for the Maduro regime. This was especially evident after the 2019 crisis when Juan Guaidó declared himself acting president. Colombia, more than other Latin American states suffers from the influx of Venezuelan migrants and their involvement in drug trafficking, is an active ally of the Venezuelan opposition. The Colombian government is concerned about Russia's plans to rebuild military facilities in Cuba and Nicaragua. Moscow and Bogota agree on the inadmissibility of a military solution to the Venezuelan crisis, but their points of view on the legitimacy of the Maduro government are diametrically opposed. After the leftist government of Gustavo Petro came to power in Colombia, bilateral relations remained steady, even taking into account the escalation of the Russia-Ukraine conflict.

Despite the persistent security challenges that have made the North Triangle of Central America one of the most dangerous regions on the planet, it occupies an important place as a bridge between the two parts of the American continent (Ungar, 2020). This subregion has acquired special geo-economic importance, which is confirmed by its participation in a number of important

---

75 Rosstat. Federal State Statistics Service.

projects.[76] Guatemala, Honduras, and El Salvador are a hotbed of instability for the entire region, while the US traditional zone of influence, which is the most important source of funding for those countries, together with the EU. This led to the fact that the leaderships of these countries have been "spoiled" by financial support for development projects, invariably considering any joint projects as charitable aid, and not as bilateral initiatives. Russia, which is accustomed to give-and-take, is not satisfied with this approach. All these factors significantly influence the formation of Russian policy in this direction, characterized by a lack of ambition, presence, and cooperation.

The only Russian embassy in the whole Northern Triangle is in Guatemala (which opened in 2007). The diplomatic staff numbers fewer than ten, in contrast to the US embassy, which is represented by dozens of employees. Bilateral political dialogue is not developing. Guatemalan presidents have never visited Russia in the new century, and the Russian leader has visited this country only once, in 2007.

In 2022, trade turnover between Russia and Guatemala amounted to $230 million, having quadrupled compared to 2017. Trade is conducted with a positive balance for Russia, while Russian exports to Guatemala are 80% metals and mineral products. The Russian-Guatemalan Center for the Study of the History and Culture of the Maya and the Orthodox Monastery of the Holy Trinity "Lavra Mambre" were opened for the development of cooperation of intercultural communications. In 2010, bilateral agreements on cooperation between law enforcement agencies were signed, but no noticeable results having been achieved. Relations between Russia and Guatemala during the presidency of the representative of the center-right political party Vamos Alejandro Giammattei (2020–2024) began to experience a period of sharp cooling. Giammattei became the only Latin American president to visit Ukraine since the outbreak of war. Almost immediately after the start of Russia's "special military operation" in Ukraine, Guatemala recalled its ambassador from Russia. In addition, in 2022, the US Treasury imposed sanctions on Russian citizens doing business in the Guatemalan mining sector for alleged bribes to the Giammattei government. This led to the fact that all joint commercial projects with Russia in this industry in Guatemala were temporarily suspended.

There are no Russian embassies in Honduras and El Salvador—the Russian ambassador to Nicaragua serves as the ambassador to these countries. The Honduran President has visited Russia only once, in 1999. Russian presidents have never paid a visit to this country. In 1994, two countries signed an

---

76   Bank of Russia. Databases.

agreement on cultural, scientific, and technical cooperation, which resulted in the creation of a joint Honduran-Russian company Innotex-Honduras SA, which is engaged in the development of the mining sector.[77]

During the 2009 political crisis in Honduras, caused by the organization of an illegal referendum by then-President Manuel Zelaya to amend the constitution and ending with his arrest by the Supreme Court, Russia supported the ousted president. This contributed to the formation of a negative image of Moscow among the population and the political elites of Honduras, which affected all areas of cooperation. In 2022, trade turnover between Russia and Honduras was $165 million, an increase of 127% ($91 million) compared to 2020.

Russia's relations with Honduras, which has been headed by the left-wing politician Xiomara Castro since 2022, have developed in a relatively positive manner. In particular, Russia supported the initiative of Honduras to conclude an intergovernmental agreement on the mutual recognition of documents on higher education. It is noteworthy that similar agreements are currently being worked out with several LAC countries, including Guatemala. In addition, Honduran Foreign Minister Eduardo Enrique Reina publicly spoke positively about BRICS, noting that the bloc is "a hope for developing countries" and, also, represents an alternative for global development.[78] In particular, he added that Honduras is interested in access to the BRICS Development Bank.

The level of political dialogue within Russia-El Salvador relations is the lowest of the entire group of countries in the Northern Triangle. It is significant that this country did not maintain diplomatic relations with the USSR. The most significant events on the bilateral agenda over the past decades were the official visits of the Minister of Foreign Affairs of Salvador in 2010 and 2017, and the visit of the Russian Foreign Minister to El Salvador in 2011. The countries signed a number of agreements on cooperation in the fight against drug trafficking (2012) and crime (2019).[79]

In order to develop mutual trade, delegations of Russian entrepreneurs went to El Salvador in 2014–2015, which did not give an impulse to the development of economic cooperation. In 2022, Russia's trade turnover with El Salvador was estimated at $90 million. The most notable project was the supply of equipment by the Russian company Tyazhmash and the construction of a substation for the hydro power plant in Chaparral in 2016. In 2015, the head of the Ministry of Foreign Affairs of El Salvador came on a working visit to Moscow in

---

77   The Ministry of Foreign Affairs of the Russian Federation. Database.
78   https://latamnews.lat/20230922/honduras-ve-a-rusia-como-un-mercado-importante-y-resalta-su-avance-en-ciencia-y-energia-1143997977.html.
79   The Ministry of Foreign Affairs of the Russian Federation. Database.

order to discuss issues of developing bilateral cooperation. The Salvadoran and Russian Ministers for Foreign Affairs noted the similarity of the approaches of both countries on key issues of world politics, expressing hope for expanding bilateral dialogue in such areas as the fight against terrorism, drug trafficking, transnational organized crime, and other new security threats. However, it did not help to take bilateral relations to a new level. The populist President of El Salvador, Nayib Bukele (2019—present), who did not publicly condemn Russia for the outbreak of hostilities in Ukraine, planned to make a trip to Russia in 2022, but in the end, it never took place. Bukele's government has pursued a highly repressive crime-fighting strategy in the country, including a series of punitive initiatives against criminal gangs and the use of mass incarceration. While this approach ultimately led to a significant drop in homicide rates across the country, thereby removing El Salvador from the list of the most dangerous countries in Latin America, it also led to accusations of unprecedented human rights abuses from Washington. The beginning of distancing between El Salvador and the US contributed to the expansion of the Salvadoran-Russian dialogue. In particular, in 2024, President Putin announced the friendly nature of relations between Russia and El Salvador,[80] and as part of the inter-Ministry of Foreign Affairs political consultations, both sides expressed their readiness to expand the entire range of ties between the states.[81]

The relations between Russia and the "low priority" group are characterized by a lack of achievements in political and economic cooperation, and some successful cooperation in the field of training law enforcement. With this group of countries, Russia has never been able to form a system of bilateral and multilateral partnerships, which is characterized by the lack of mutual interest.

In this connection, it is not surprising that countries representing the vast majority of the LAC and the "low priority" group sharply condemned Russia's actions in Ukraine. Chile and Colombia were among those LAC countries that took a sharply negative stance: they confirmed they would join the West's sanctions on Russia. The only exception to this list of countries, unexpectedly, was El Salvador, which became the fourth LAC country to abstain from voting on the UN GA resolution "Aggression against Ukraine", and the third LAC country to abstain from voting a resolution to suspend Russia from the UN Human Rights Council. This position was primarily due to a temporary increase in tension in the bilateral dialogue between El Salvador and the US, which arose

---

80   https://tass.ru/politika/19966677.
81   https://tass.ru/politika/20002675.

in the wake of a report by the US Department of the Treasury, published in December 2021, which stated that the government of Nayib Bukele secretly negotiated a truce with the leaders of criminal gangs.

Honduras and El Salvador did not support US pressure on Latin American states within OAS in April 2022, where a decision was made to suspend Russia's permanent observer status with the organization. However, this did not mean the transfer the relations of Russian with Salvador and Honduras to a new level, given that the countries of the Northern triangle of Central America—Guatemala, Honduras and El Salvador—are the main source of instability for the entire region and are also a traditional zone of influence of US, which acts as the most important source of funding and where constant financial injections from the EU also play an important role.

• • •

Russia, in comparison with the USSR, has noticeably increased its presence in Latin America. The model of cooperation that emerged at the beginning of the 21st century is characterized by a rigid "mapping" of the region into certain groups, and instrumental and institutional disorganization. Moscow's real interest in Latin America has remained low, and the geography of Russia's political and economic presence is limited. Only a few countries have formed stable cooperation, in the majority this partnership is only declared. The Kremlin's foreign policy priority in this region continues to be resistance to Washington's hegemony, viewing Latin America as the US "living space". This confirms the strong ideological component of Russian foreign policy in this region. At the beginning of the 21st century, the central role in building a foreign policy course in this direction was played only by the Russian leadership and large businesses. The ideologeme of Russia's "special path", based on the rejection of the Western system of values, has turned into an aggressive ideological platform of the Kremlin's foreign policy in the 21st century. Russia's policy in Latin America is filled with momentary actions based on this ideologeme, marked in accordance with the system of short-term priorities of the power vertical.

CHAPTER 6

Where Are the Extra-regional Powers in Latin America Going?

At the beginning of the 21st century, we witnessed a sharp increase in interest in LAC on the part of extra-regional powers, which, due to historical, cultural, and geographical factors, traditionally did not have stable and diverse ties with the countries of this region. All this happened against the backdrop of the new millennium seeing a transformation in the US foreign policy approach towards its LAC neighbors. Washington abandoned the use of harsh "unilateral invasion" measures that were traditional for it during the Cold War. This led to the development of a unique situation within the inter-American system of relations. Conditions were formed that reduced LAC's dependence on the US, and increased its autonomy in world politics and economics, despite the fact that at the beginning of the 21st century no other extra-regional power had a military deployment in LAC on the scale of the US.

Despite the fact that the geopolitical situation in the Western Hemisphere has become noticeably more complicated due to the multidirectional foreign policy strategies of the leading LAC countries, as well as new integration schemes, which not only failed to unite the continent, but led to its further fragmentation. Attempts to divide the Americas into North and South, and division into Pacific and Atlantic America, have led to the fact that some trends directly collide with others, leading to crisis situations. The US, which is losing its influence in the LAC in the 21st century, does not intend to exclude this region from the orbit of its geopolitical claims, especially since Washington and the countries of the region are linked by a whole chain of free trade agreements, and joint initiatives and projects.

By the beginning of the 2020s, LAC countries have managed to significantly diversify their international relations, which has allowed them to develop a foreign policy that is much more autonomous and resistant to new global challenges. To traditional relations with the US, which invariably permeated the entire Latin American foreign policy agenda, while being characterized by asymmetry and dependence, new extra-regional areas of cooperation were added, primarily with the Asia-Pacific region, Africa, and Russia.

The 2020s has become an era of systemic rivalry and global competition, when the value of each individual partnership, union or alliance has increased sharply. This emerging wave of extra-regional interest in the LAC is not caused by a desire to expand trade and investment presence, but by the desire of actors new to the Americas to use LAC to gain greater geopolitical influence. In this regard, the expansion of their presence and influence in LAC countries is considered by actors in international relations from the point of view of providing strategic resources in order to secure the necessary advantages in the growing confrontation between the non-West and the West.

By the 2020s China has radically changed its approaches to LAC. Large investment projects have replaced billion-dollar purchases of raw materials. Beijing has begun to rely on its long-term presence in this area of the world, the consequence of which is a gradual reduction in the influence of the US and the EU. Using niches created by American trade protectionism, the general decline in US investment in LAC and the cooling of relations that has occurred, China is laying a solid foundation for the further advancement of its interests.

China has maintained and successfully applied different strategies towards individual LAC countries that have distinctive characteristics. While China's overall investment flow under BRI has slowed by 2024, Beijing continues to strengthen its ties with LAC to gain access to raw materials to fuel its economy and help realize its vision of a green version of the Belt and Road project.

China's military-technical cooperation with the LAC countries faces objective limiting factors, such as close ties between LAC armed forces in the US, China's limited ability to project power in the region, and differences in the approaches to methods and tools for ensuring internal security.

Despite the fact that China's growing activity and diversification of activities along all the LAC confirms Beijing's unchanged intentions in this part of the world, LAC needs China to a much greater extent than China needs LAC. It was thanks to LAC's cooperation with China that in a number of LAC countries it was possible to significantly expand the middle class, reduce poverty, and develop targeted programs aimed at reducing the gap between social strata.

For China, LAC is seen as increasing its geopolitical influence and a resource-rich region, which is important from the point of view of China's long-term development prospects. The attractiveness of the LAC region for Beijing will increase due to growing restrictions on Chinese capital in North America and the EU and the gradual exhaustion of attractive investment opportunities for Chinese companies in Southeast Asia. Without a doubt, in light of the ongoing changes in the geopolitical world map, by the beginning of the 2020s, it will be possible to observe the consolidation of even more diverse relations between China and LAC. This creates even more opportunities for China to expand its influence in LAC, as more LAC countries are willing to ride the "China Express" in their quest to achieve national development goals.

Russia's relations with the countries of Latin America are developing according to a completely different scenario, within the framework of which Moscow has relied on political interaction to the detriment of trade and economic partnership.

Post-Soviet Russia's foreign policy in LAC is characterized by, first, the fact that geopolitics, not economics, is the basis of Moscow's foreign policy in LAC, which remains an important obstacle to Russian expansion in this direction. The Russian elites focus on what is common in the political mainstream of LAC (anti-US sentiment), rather than on how they differ from each other. The bet is on the "allied triangle", which includes the authoritarian left regimes of Cuba, Venezuela, Nicaragua, and Bolivia. The inflexible orientation towards a narrow circle of ideological partner countries, unable to go beyond the usual rhetoric, has led to the fact that the vacuum of US leadership in recent years has been successfully used by other non-Western powers. Second, Russia's foreign economic policy in LAC is based on a unidirectional strategy, within which the main efforts of public and private companies are aimed at a few countries and market segments. Third, it was in the information space that Russia was able to secure a truly impressive presence in the region, noticeably ahead of the EU and China and coming very close to the US, partly compensating for the small volume of investment and trade. A special type of meta-narrative strategy on which the entire information technology of Russian media in the region is based, is founded on the confrontation between "us" and "them", presented as overcoming an unfair asymmetric world order. Russia's information influence strategy in the LAC actively uses various methods of waging information wars, where the key role is played by the media, Spanish-language social networks, and new AI mechanisms, which have already become an important weapon for increasing Moscow's influence in this part of the world.

All this allows us to conclude that the LAC direction in the Kremlin's foreign policy is characterized as symbolic and reactive. A clear confirmation of this thesis was the tours of the Russian Foreign Minister to Latin American, which has already become an annual event. The main task of such visits became to convey the Kremlin's position on the Russia-Ukraine conflict to all LAC countries, most of which support, albeit implicitly, Kyiv. In the new Foreign Policy Concept of the Russian Federation, it was stated that the Kremlin's special interest is in deepening its multifaceted partnership with Brazil, Cuba, Nicaragua, and Venezuela. In this regard, just a month after the announcement, a large Latin American tour of the Minister of Foreign Affairs took place to all the listed LAC countries. Less than a year later, in February 2024, the Russian Foreign Minister again visited Cuba, Venezuela and Brazil.

An important diplomatic achievement of Russia in the Latin American direction was the support for Brazil, taking into account the influence that it has in LAC. Given the adage "where Brazil looks, all of Latin America will follow," Russia is seeking to further deepen its engagement with the left-wing government of Luiz Inacio Lula da Silva, which has openly stated that "Kyiv is partly responsible for the war being waged on its territory." The President of Brazil expressed interest in helping to resolve the Russia-Ukraine conflict through negotiations, which he views as part of a strategy for promoting the "Global South" as a new actor in world politics.

This position of Brazilian President Lula da Silva was completely in keeping with the updated foreign policy course taken by Brasilia during Lula da Silva's first presidential term. This strategy was aimed at ensuring maximum coverage of Brazilian foreign policy. Latin America was considered as an important destination for the export of industrial products of Brazil and a platform for the projection of its global influence; from a global perspective, the main goal was to obtain the status of an actor capable of changing the system of geopolitical coordinates of world politics and economics. In this context, the promotion of the doctrinal foundations of the principle of non-intervention was given particular importance, taking as a basis the main regional doctrines, in particular the doctrines of Calvo,[1] Drago,[2] Bello,[3] Carranza[4] and Estrada.[5] Great

---

1 The Calvo Doctrine is a Pan-American doctrine of international law formed in 1889–1890 by Argentine lawyer Carlos Calvo. The doctrine stipulates that foreigners must present their demands, claims, and complaints subject to the jurisdiction of local courts, avoiding diplomatic pressure or armed intervention from their own state or government.
2 The Drago Doctrine was proclaimed on December 29, 1902 by Argentine Foreign Minister Luis Maria Drago. This doctrine establishes that no foreign state may use force against any country within the Americas to collect a financial debt.
3 The Bellista Doctrine of International Law has become the collective name for the enormous contribution of the works of the Venezuelan thinker Andres Bello, who became the first Latin American author to use the term "international law" in Spanish, marking the beginning of the "American point of view" on international law. The Bello doctrine is associated with the thoughtful legal language that became part of the general sphere of activity of the enlightened people of Latin America.
4 The Carranza Doctrine is the principles of foreign policy formed in 1918 by Mexican President Venustiano Carranza. Key ideas of the doctrine are that all countries are equal; no country shall interfere in any way or for any reason in the foreign affairs of others; citizens and foreigners must be equal before the sovereignty of the country in which they are located; legislation should be uniform and equal as far as possible, without distinction based on nationality.
5 Created in the 1930s, the Estrada Doctrine, put forward by Mexican Foreign Minister Genaro Estrada, enshrined the idea that recognition by the government of any country does not require a special act of foreign states, and the emergence of a new government poses before participants in international communication only the question of whether to enter into diplomatic relations with it.

importance was attached to the development of clear restrictions in order not to unilaterally or collectively generate tension between countries. All this had the broader goal of painlessly adapting LAC countries to a regional scenario where internal factors led to fragmentation of the region and external factors plunged it into a state of uncertainty.

In any case, the historical and cultural ties of both China and Russia with LAC countries are much less stable and traditional than the ties of the LAC with the member states of the EU. In his landmark study, The Clash of Civilizations, Samuel P. Huntington described LAC as a "branch" of the West and even an offshoot of Western Europe. While Latin Americans themselves are divided in what degree their region belongs to the Western world, there is no doubt that LAC countries are eminently "Euro-compatible." Compared to LAC's relations with China and Russia, the EU-LAC relationship is truly "special", primarily due to the presence of shared values and a long history of close cooperation in various fields. They are, however, complex and dual in nature.

On the one hand, when it comes to international cooperation, LAC gives clear preference to EU member states over other potential partners. This suggests that most LAC countries still view themselves as part of the Euro-Atlantic region, interpreting the mission of the LAC and the goals of the development strategy in a Western manner. Interregional relations are based on the idea of dialogue, which emphasizes the equal position of the parties. The EU is the largest investor, largest source of development finance, and LAC's third largest trading partner.

On the other hand, LAC remains a low priority region for EU foreign policy, just as the European Community is outside the foreign policy priorities of LAC states. In addition, there is no single strategy in the EU's foreign policy regarding LAC. It is characterized by inertia, reactivity and trend chasing. This has led to very low expectations in LAC that the EU will be able to significantly increase its presence in key areas in the near future in terms of addressing the region's most pressing problems. Here, the US and China are already playing major roles, thereby confirming that the EU–LAC interregional ties will continue to be viewed by Latin Americans as of secondary importance.

This allows us to conclude that the hopes placed by both sides in a sharp expansion of interregional cooperation, voiced after the first EU–LAC summit in 1999, remained largely unjustified. In the 2000s, the EU neglected its relations with LAC and focused on other foreign policy areas, which led to a decrease in the intensity of contacts with the region. The exception was Spain, which, even before its accession to the EU, played and continues to play a very important role in the development and deepening of interregional dialogue, especially in terms of the formation of a common EU policy regarding LAC. As for expanding interregional partnership, the EU has obviously chosen the path of developing bilateral relations rather than forming a comprehensive regional strategy. It is obvious that the EU is not yet ready to recognize LAC as a significant actor in international relations, which ultimately led to a decline in the EU influence in this region by the 2020s.

The military operation Iron Swords, launched by Israel in the Gaza Strip in the fall of 2023, revealed the acute polarization that now exists in the political establishment of LAC countries, which, because of oscillations of the political pendulum, has undergone noticeable transformations of left and right forces towards the center. While some LAC governments have expressed their strong opposition to Israeli actions against Hamas (the Palestinian Islamist political and military organization that has controlled the Gaza Strip since 2007), other Latin American governments have demonstrated their unconditional support for the Jewish state. Brazil under Lula da Silva has become the main Latin American critic of Israel; Chile under Gabriel Borich is a defender of the Palestinian population; Colombia, led by Gustavo Petro, seeks to mediate peace talks; Mexico, led by Andrés López Obrador, is trying to pursue a policy of equidistance regarding the conflict between Palestine and Israel, maneuvering between the parties and avoiding open support for either country, which Mexico City began in the late 1920s. The rise of far-right politician Javier Milei in Argentina in December 2023 marked a huge change not only for the foreign and domestic policies of this country, but also for LAC's relations with Israel as a whole. Under Milei, Argentina not only officially refused to join BRICS, but also became Israel's main ally in all of Latin America.

In the 2020s, there was a sharp change in the ideological map of LAC, which began to be dominated by the so-called "new left" governments. In this new political reality, which still recognizes the importance of the world moving towards multipolarity, there is no longer sharp anti-Americanism or the pursuit of a radical transformation of the inter-American system, but there is a clear focus on solving pressing practical problems such as regional and national development and rapprochement with international monetary and financial organizations. The modern bloc of the LAC left is in completely different conditions than the one that emerged in the early 2000s, and the distinctive feature of this new trend is its heterogeneity.

LAC's new left turn is pushing governments to gradually "shift their focus" from security issues to addressing pressing issues that are now triggering protests, such as public health, crime, and poverty. One of the results of such a policy will be that the distance of LAC from the US will increase, given that the fierce fight against drug trafficking continues to act as an "irritant" in relations between LAC and Washington. This trend cannot be changed even by the fact that, unlike Donald Trump, Joe Biden's strategy towards LAC was based on a liberal-internationalist approach, where the protection of democracy, human rights, and minorities became a priority. An important characteristic of the new LAC governments is that their foreign policy is much more open to extra-regional alternative cooperation to the detriment of the traditional Atlantic direction. All this creates serious obstacles to the interests of the US and the EU in this region, and creates new opportunities for China and Russia. Given that the COVID-19 pandemic, the Russia-Ukraine conflict (2022), the war in Gaza (2023), and their negative consequences, have already exposed all the weaknesses of the existing global governance architecture, led by Western countries, which has proven unable to respond to these new challenges, we can predict an even greater strengthening of the positions of extra-regional actors in LAC, which will gradually change the established paradigm of relations in the Americas.

References

Abdenur, A. and De Sousa Neto, D. (2013) La creciente influencia de China en el Atlántico Sur. *Revista CIDOB d'Afers Internacionais*, 102/103: 169–197.

Actis, E. and Malacalza, B. (2021) Las Políticas Exteriores de América Latina en Tiempos de Autonomía Líquida. Nueva Sociedad. Available (consulted 23 August 2022) at: https://nuso.org/articulo/las-politicas-exteriores-de-america-latina-en-tiempos-de-autonomia-liquida/#footnote-17.

Acuña Ortigoza, M., Aguirre Saavedra, E., Ávila Ramírez, P., and Mendoza Vera, A., (2018) Ruta de la seda. Nuevas alianzas para la participación de América Latina. *Revista Venezolana de Gerencia* 23 (83): 530–540.

Agramont, D. L. (2021) China's security and military cooperation in Latin America and the Caribbean: Implications for Europe. *Konrad-Adenauer-Stiftung* (76): 6–34.

Aguinaga Morínigo, M. A. (2016) América Latina en el contexto de Multipolaridad y Globalización. Available (consulted 21 May 2024) at: https://www.researchgate.net/publication/319008291_America_Latina_en_el_contexto_de_Multipolaridad_y_Globalizacion.

Alarcón, R. D. (1990) *Identidad de la psiquiatría latinoamericana: voces y exploraciones en torno a una ciencia solidaria*. Madrid: Siglo XXI de España Editores, S.A.

Ambrosio, T. (2005) *Challenging America Global Preeminence: Russian Quest for Multipolarity*. Chippenheim: Anthony Rose.

América Latina y el Caribe Poder, globalización y respuestas regionales frente a un Nuevo Orden Mundial. CRIES. Icaria Editorial.

An, J. (2013). Mao Zedong's "Three Worlds" Theory: Political Considerations and Value for the Times. *Social Sciences in China*, 34(1), 35–57.

Aranda, G. and Morandé, J. (2011) Los Derechos Humanos en la Política Exterior de Chile. Pragmatismo y Énfasis multilateral. In: Saltalamacchia N., Covarrubias A. (eds). *Derechos Humanos en Política Exterior. Seis Casos Latinoamericanos*. México: Editorial Porrúa.

Arenal, C. (2009) Las relaciones entre la UE y América Latina: ¿abandono del regionalismo y apuesta por una nueva estrategia de carácter bilateralista? *Documento de Trabajo 36/2009*. Madrid, Real Instituto Elcano: 3–4.

Arenal, C. (2010) Balance de la asociación estratégica entre la Unión Europea (UE) y los países de ALC. *Foro eurolatinoamericano de centros de análisis. Diálogo UE-ALC. Debate y conclusiones*. Madrid, Fundación Carolina: 25–55.

Arenal, C. (2015) Americanocentrismo y relaciones internacionales: la seguridad nacional como referente. In: Arenal, C. del-Sanahuja, J.A. *Teorías de relaciones internacionales*. Madrid: Tecnos.

Artner, A. (2020) Can China lead the change of the world?. *Third World Quarterly* 41(11): 1881–1899.

Auchter, J. (2013) Border monuments: Memory, counter-memory, and (b)ordering practices along the US-Mexico border. *Review of International Studies* 39(2): 291–311.

Ayuso, A. (2021) Keys to reactivating the EU–CELAC partnership and channelling the globalisation of the future. *CIDOB—Barcelona Centre for International Affairs*. Available (consulted 21 May 2024) at: https://www.cidob.org/en/publications/publication_series/notes_internacionals/247/keys_to_reactivating_the_eu_celac_partnership_and_channelling_the_globalisation_of_the_future.

Bain, M. (2005) Cuba–Soviet Relations in the Gorbachev Era. *Journal of Latin American Studies* 37(4): 769–791.

Beaumont, N. (2020) EU-Latin American Relations: A Return to Multilateralism. *IED Institute of European Democrats*. Available (consulted 21 May 2024) at: https://www.iedonline.eu/download/geopolitics-values/31-Beaumont-Latin_American_relations_-_A_Return_to_Multilateralism_-_FINAL.pdf.

Bernal-Meza, R. (2005) *América Latina en el Mundo. El Pensamiento Latinoamericano y la Teoría de las Relaciones Internacionales*. Buenos Aires: Nuevo hacer.

Bernal-Meza, R. (2013) Heterodox Autonomy Doctrine: Realism and Purposes, and its Relevance. *Revista Brasileira de Política Internacional* (56): 45–62.

Bizzozero, L. (2001) El acuerdo marco interregional UE-MERCOSUR: dificultades y perspectivas de una asociación estratégica. Los rostros del MERCOSUR. Un difícil camino de lo comercial a lo social. *CLACSO*: 373–390.

Bonfili, C. (2010) The United States and Venezuela: The Social Construction of Interdependent Rivalry. *Security Dialogue* 41(6): 669–90.

Bonilla, A., and A. Páez. 2006. Estados Unidos y la región andina: distancia y diversidad. *Nueva sociedad* (206): 126–139.

Borón, A. (2013) *América Latina en la geopolítica del imperialismo*. Gipuzkoa: Hiru Argitaletxea.

Borón, A. (2009) *Socialismo Siglo XXI: ¿Hay Vida después del Neoliberalismo?*. Buenos Aires: Luxemburg.

Boza, S., Núñez, A. and Molina, M. (2022). Agricultural Trade and Investments between Latin America and China: Development, Implications, and Challenges. In: López, D., Song, G., Bórquez, A., Muñoz, F. (eds) *China's Trade Policy in Latin America. Contributions to International Relations*. Springer.

Briceño Ruiz J., Simonoff A. (2017). La Escuela de la Autonomía, América Latina y la teoría de las relaciones internacionales. // Estudios internacionales (Santiago). No. 49(186). P. 39–89.

Brun, E. (2015) Un mundo sin definición. *Foreign Affairs Latinoamérica*. Available (consulted 21 May 2024) at: https://revistafal.com/un-mundo-sin-definicion/.

Buzan, B., and Hansen, L. (2009) *The Evolution of International Security*. Cambridge: Cambridge University Press.

Calduch, R. (1981). Las relaciones internacionales en la obra de los dirigentes soviéticos: Una reflexión teórica // Revista de Estudios Internacionales. Vol. 2. No. 3. P. 543–597.

Calle, F., and DerGhoukassian, K. (2003) El guardián del mundo unipolar y sus críticos. La estrategia de Seguridad Nacional de Estados Unidos y la construcción del espacio alternativo. *Colección.* (14): 65–97.

Cardoso, F. (1973) *Problemas del Subdesarrollo Latinoamericano.* México: Nuestro Tiempo.

Cardoso, F. (1977) La originalidad de la copia: la CEPAL y la idea de desarrollo. *Revista de la CEPAL* (4): 7–40.

Cavanagh, P. (2020) Russia became an important arms supplier for Latin America, but its sales have dropped. *Global Affairs.* Available (consulted 21 May 2024) at: https://www.unav.edu/web/global-affairs/detalle/-/blogs/russia-became-an-important-arms-supplier-for-latin-america-but-its-sales-have-dropped.

Ceceña, A. (2008). El Posneoliberalismo y sus Bifurcaciones. *Observatorio Latinoamericano de Geopolítica* (10): 1–12.

Celi, P. (2015) La seguridad multifuncional en la región. In: Alda Mejías, S., and S. Ferreira. *La multidimensionalidad de la seguridad nacional: retos y desafíos de la región para su implementación.* Madrid: Instituto Universitario General Gutiérrez Mellado.

CEPAL (1951) *Estudio económico de América Latina,* Nueva -York, Naciones Unidas. Publicación de las Naciones Unidas, N' de venta: 195 1.II.G. 1.

CEPAL (1966) *Estudio económico de América Latina,* Documento E/CN. 12/752/Rev. I Nueva York: ONU.

CEPAL (2013) *Foreign Direct Investment in Latin America and the Caribbean 2012.* NU. CEPAL. Unidad de Inversiones y Estrategias Empresariales.

CEPAL (2019) *Perspectivas del Comercio Internacional de América Latina y el Caribe.* Santiago.

CEPAL. (1985) *Panorama Económico de América Latina.* Santiago de Chile.

CEPAL. (1990) *Panorama económico de América Latina 1990.* LC/G.1638. NU. CEPAL. División de Desarrollo Económico.

Cervo, A. (2010) Brazil's Rise on the International Scene: Brazil and the World. *Revista Brasileira de Política Internacional* (53): 7–32.

Colacrai, M. and Lorenzini, M.E. (2005) La Política Exterior de Chile: ¿Excepcionalidad o Continuidad? Una Lectura Combinada de 'Fuerzas Profundas' y 'Tendencias'. *Confines* (2): 45–63.

Connolly, R. and Sendstad, C. (2017) *Russia's Role as an Arms Exporter. The Strategic and Economic Importance of Arms Exports for Russia.* Chatham House.

Coral, M. (2007) El diálogo político como pilar de las relaciones entre la Unión Europea y América Latina: reflexiones sobre su desarrollo y contenido. *Oasis* (12): 483–493.

Correa Serrano, M.A. and Salgado, E.C. (2016) La Alianza del Pacífico: Entre la Geopolítica de China y de Estados Unidos. *México y la Cuenca del Pacífico* (14): 19–52.

Cruz, J. M. (2011) Criminal Violence and Democratization in Central America: The Survival of the Violent State. *Latin American Politics and Society* 53(4): 1–33.

Cueva Perús, M. (2010). India y China en las relaciones económicas internacionales. *Revista De Relaciones Internacionales De La UNAM* (103): 135–154.

Delgado, G.R. (2010) Neoliberalismo y Convergencia Contable. Orígenes, Características y Propuestas. *Lúmina* (11): 264–278.

Delgado-Ramos, G. C., and S. M. Romano. (2011) Political-Economic Factors in US Foreign Policy: the Colombian Plan, the Mérida Initiative, and the Obama Administration. *Latin American Perspectives* 38(4): 93–108.

Domínguez, R. (2022) EU-Mexican Relations: Adaptation to global trade relations. *Latin America-European Union relations in the twenty-first century* (eds. García M., Gómez A.). Manchester: Manchester University Press.

Dussel, E. (2007) *Política de la liberación. Historia mundial y crítica.* Madrid: Editorial Trotto, S.A.

Ellis, E. (2015) *The New Russian Engagement with Latin America: Strategic Position, Commerce, and Dreams of the Past.* U.S.: Army War College.

Ellner, S. (2008) *Rethinking Venezuelan politics: Class, conflict, and the Chávez phenomenon.* Lynne Rienner Publishers.

Ellner, S. (2009) La Política Exterior del Gobierno de Chávez: La Retórica Chavista y los Asuntos Sustanciales. *Revista Venezolana de Economía y Ciencias Sociales* (15): 115–132.

Ellner, S. (2012) The distinguishing features of Latin America's new left in power: The Chávez, Morales, and Correa governments. *Latin American Perspectives* 39 (1): 96–114.

Escudé, C. (1992) *Realismo Periférico.* Buenos Aires.

Estudio Económico de América Latina y el Caribe 2013: tres décadas de crecimiento económico desigual e inestable. CEPAL. Available (consulted 21 May 2024) at: https://www.cepal.org/es/publicaciones/1085-estudio-economico-america-latina-caribe-2013-tres-decadas-crecimiento-economico.

European Commission. (2021) *European Commission publishes final Sustainability Impact Assessment and Position Paper on the EU-MERCOSUR Trade Agreement.* Available at: https://policy.trade.ec.europa.eu/news/commission-publishes-final-sia-and-position-paper-eu-MERCOSUR-trade-agreement-2021-03-29_en.

Fajnzylber, F. (1988) Competitividad Internacional: Evolución y Lecciones. *Revista de la CEPAL* (36): 7–24.

Faller, C. (2021) Statement of Admiral Craig S. Faller Commander, United States Southern Command Before the 117th Congress Senate Armed Services Committee. Available (consulted 21 May 2024) at: https://www.southcom.mil/Media/Special-Coverage/SOUTHCOMs-2021-Posture-Statement-to-Congress/.

Fonseca, J. G., de Aguiar Patriota A, Milani, C., and Valls Pereira L. (2022) *Multilateralismo e Multipolaridade.* Rio de Janeiro, Brazil: CEBRI.

Freres Ch., Gratius S., Mallo T., Pellicer A. and Sanahuja J.A. eds. (2007) ¿Sirve el diálogo político entre la Unión Europea y América Latina?, Madrid, Fundación Carolina

Available (consulted 21 May 2024) at: http://aei.pitt.edu/9891/1/Carolina-ICEI_DT15.pdf.

Gálvez, A. S. (2010) Orden multipolar en el siglo XXI: efectos globales y regionales. *Encrucijada Americana* 4 (1): 19–41.

Giacalone, R. (2016) Conceptualización y marco analítico explicativo del multilateralismo latinoamericano. *OASIS* (24): 7–25.

Gil de Zúñiga, H. (2019) Digital Media and Politics: Effects of the Great Information and Communication Divides. *Journal of Broadcasting & Electronic Media* 63(3): 365–373.

Giles Carnero, R.G. (2021) La oportunidad de una cláusula ambiental de elementos esenciales en acuerdos comerciales de la Unión Europea con Estados terceros: a propósito del Acuerdo Unión Europea-MERCOSUR. *Documentos de Trabajo*. Fundación Carolina. (44): 1–23.

Gooch, E. and Gale, F. (2018) China's Foreign Agriculture Investments. *U.S. Department of Agriculture, Economic Research Service*. Available (consulted 21 May 2024) at: https://www.ers.usda.gov/webdocs/publications/88572/eib-192.pdf?v=9495.

Harris, R. L. (2015) Understanding China's Relations with the Latin American and Caribbean Countries: Research Notes. *Latin American Perspectives* 42(6): 27–41.

Hellinger, D. (2021) *Comparative Politics of Latin America Democracy at Last?* Routledge.

Hofman, A.A. (2000). *The economic development of Latin America in the twentieth century*. ECLAC: Edward Elgar Publishing. 322 p.

Hongbo, S. (2012) A Model for Energy Cooperations between China and Latin America. *Revista Latinoamericana de Economía. Problemas de Desarrollo* 176 (45): 9–30.

Ikenberry, D. L. (2002) La ambición imperial de Estados Unidos. *Foreign Affairs Latinoamérica* 2(3): 2–21.

Jaguaribe, H. (1969). Dependencia y Autonomía en América Latina. In: Jaguaribe H. (ed). *La Dependencia Político-económica de América Latina*. México: CLASCO.

Jaguaribe, H. (1979). Hegemonía Céntrica y Autonomía Periférica. *Estudios Internacionales* (46): 91–180.

Jeifets, V. Rusia en América Latina: los nuevos retos y viejos problemas (2014) Rangel Delgado, Jose Ernesto y Furlong y Zacaula, Aurora (eds.). Rusia en el scenario internacional del Siglo XXI. Gobierno del Estado de Puebla-Secretaria de Educacion-Concytep. pp.199–238.

Jenkins, R. (2022) China's Belt and Road Initiative in Latin America: What has Changed? *Journal of Current Chinese Affairs* 51(1): 13–39.

Jiménez, M. and Raúl, M. (2015) La educación popular en el siglo XXI. Una resistencia intercultural desde el sur y desde abajo. *Praxis & Saber* 6 (12): 97–128.

Jost, S. (Ed.) (2012) *Colombia: ¿una potencia en desarrollo? Escenarios y desafíos para su política exterior*. Bogotá: Konrad Adenauer.

Kaplan, M. (1983) Aspectos Políticos del Dialogo Norte-Sur. *Revista de estudios políticos* (33): 187–206.

Kashin V. Presencia china en América Latina: objetivos y motivos. *Iberoamérica*, 2023 (2): 167–194.

Kashin, V.B. and Kosevich, E. (2024) China's Defense Cooperation with Latin America and Caribbean: Trends and Limitations. *Vestnik Volgogradskogo gosudarstvennogo universiteta. Seriya 4. Istoriya. Regionovedenie. Mezhdunarodnye otnosheniya* 29 (1): 203–213.

Katz, M. N. (2006) The Putin-Chavez Partnership. *Problems of Post-Communism* 53(4): 3–9.

Kosevich E. (2023) EU—Latin America: Institutions for Cooperation and Latin Americans' Trust in Them. // *World Economy and International Relations*, vol. 67, No 2, pp. 114–129.

Kosevich E. (2024) Cybersecurity, cyberspace and cyberthreats at the beginning of the 21st century: a Latin America typology and review, *Area Development and Policy*, 9:1, 86–107.

Kosevich E. (2024). European Union—Latin America: Arrangements and Competition. *World Economy and International Relations*, 2024, vol. 68, no. 4, pp. 87–97.

Kosevich, E. (2019) New orientations of Mexico's foreign policy. *Latin America* (9): 23–37.

Kosevich, E. (2019). China's place in priorities of Mexico's foreign economic policy. *Vostok. Afro-Aziatskie obshchestva: istoriia i sovremennost* (1): 167–179.

Kosevich, E. (2020) Latin America: the coronavirus and the new political landscape. *Latin America* (10): 39–53.

Kosevich, E. (2020) *Mexico in the system of geopolitical coordinates of the beginning of the 21st century*. Moscow; Saint Petersburg: Nestor-Historia.

Kosevich, E. (2020) Hierarchy of Motives for Latin American Protest. *International processes* 18 (2): 92–109.

Kosevich, E. (2021) Historia de la cooperación política y económica entre Rusia y México a principios del siglo XXI (2000–2019). *America Latina en la Historia Económica* 28 (3): 1–21.

Kosevich, E. (2021) Social Protests in Latin America in the Focus of Regional Internet Media and Social Networks. *World Economy and International Relations* 65 (5): 107–116.

Kosevich, E. (2022) Russia's Relations with the Countries of Latin America at the beginning of the 21st Century: Four Levels of Interstate Interaction. *Russian Politics* 7(3): 450–484.

Kosevich, E. (2023) Russian Foreign Policy in Latin America and the Caribbean in the Twenty-first Century. *Latin American Perspectives*: 50(5), 238–254.

Kosevich, E. (2023) Russia-Venezuela Relations (and US Interests): A Fully-Fledged and Long-Term Strategic Partnership? *Russian Politics* 8(4): 493–518.

Kosevich, E. (2023). Theoretical foundations of the foreign policy of Latin American nations. *International Trends* Vol. 21. No. 1 (72), pp. 162–188.

Landa, R and Roger, A. (2022) Los desafíos del multilateralismo en un mundo multipolar y tiempos de crisis. ¿Avanzamos hacia un mundo multipolar? *CLASCO*. Available (consulted 21 May 2024) at: https://www.clacso.org/wp-content/uploads/2022/02/V1-Conv04-Los-desafios-del-multilateralismo-09-Landa-Reyes-VENEZUELA.pdf.

Lechini, G. (2009) La Cooperación Sur-Sur y la Búsqueda de Autonomía en América Latina: ¿Mito o Realidad? *Relaciones Internacionales* (12): 55–81.

Le-Fort, M. P. (2006) China y América Latina: estrategias bajo una hegemonía transitoria. *NUSO*. Available (consulted 21 May 2024) at: https://nuso.org/articulo/china-y-america-latina-estrategias-bajo-una-hegemonia-transitoria/.

LeoGrande, W. M. (2007) A Poverty of Imagination: George W. Bush's Policy in Latin America. *Journal of Latin American Studies* 39(2): 355–385.

León J. L. (coord.) (1999). *El nuevo sistema internacional. Una visión desde México*. México, Secretaría de Relaciones Exteriores-Fondo de Cultura Económica, 416 pp.

León-Manríquez, J. L. (2016) Power Vacuum or Hegemonic Continuity?: The United States, Latin America, and the 'Chinese Factor' After the Cold War. *World Affairs* 179(3): 59–81.

Llenderrozas, E. (2015) América Latina frente a las transformaciones globales. *Revista Escuela de Historia* 14 (1): 1–17.

Lo Brutto, G. and González Gutiérrez, C. (2014) El Papel de La Cooperación Sur/Sur en América Latina y el Caribe como Alternativa al Sistema Tradicional de Ayuda en la Primera Década del Siglo XXI. *Revista del CESLA* 17: 119–149.

Long, T. (2017) *Latin America Confronts the United States: Asymmetry and Influence*. Cambridge University Press.

Loveman, B. (2004) *Strategy for Empire: U.S. Regional Security Policy in the Post-Cold War Era*. Oxford: SR Books.

Lowenthal, A. F. (1987) *Partners in Conflict: The United States and Latin America*. Baltimore: The Johns Hopkins University Press.

Luis León, J. (1999) *El nuevo sistema internacional. Una visión desde México*. Secretaría de Relaciones Exteriores-Fondo de Cultura Económica.

Magnotta, F. P. (2011) Multipolaridade e multilateralismo: o G20 e a relação entre poder e governança no século XXI In: 3° ENCONTRO NACIONAL ABRI 2011, 3. São Paulo.

Malamud, C. (2018) ¿Qué le espera a Brasil con Bolsonaro como presidente? *Real Instituto Elcano*. Available (consulted 21 May 2024) at: https://www.realinstitutoelcano.org/comentarios/que-le-espera-a-brasil-con-bolsonaro-presidente/.

Mantilla Baca, S. (2015) La expansión de China en América Latina. *Centro Latinoamericano de Estudios Políticos*. Quito, Ecuador.

Manwaring, M. G. (2001) *US Security Policy in the Western Hemisphere: Why Colombia, why Now, and what is to be Done?* Carlisle, PA: Strategic Studies Institute, US Army War College.

Marini, R.M. (1973). *Dialéctica de la dependencia. En: América Latina, dependencia y globalización. Fundamentos conceptuales Ruy Mauro Marini*. Antología y presentación Carlos Eduardo Martins. Bogotá: Siglo del Hombre – CLACSO,. P. 9–77.

Martí, J. (1894) *El Tercer Año del Partido Revolucionario Cubano*. La Habana.

Martín-Carrillo, S., Lajtman, T. and Romano, S. (2019) Bolivia en la nueva geopolítica mundial. *Centro Estratégico Latinoamericano de Geopolítica—CELAG*. Available (consulted 21 May 2024) at: https://www.celag.org/bolivia-en-la-nueva-geopolitica-mundial/.

Merino, G. E. (2016) Tensiones mundiales, multipolaridad relativa y bloques de poder en una nueva fase de la crisis del orden mundial. Perspectivas para América Latina. *Memoria Académica* 7 (2): 201–225.

Mijares, V. M. (2017) Soft Balancing the Titans: Venezuelan Foreign-Policy Strategy Toward the United States, China, and Russia. *Latin American Policy* 8(2):201–231.

Milani, L. P. (2021) US Foreign Policy to South America since 9/11: Neglect or Militarisation? *Contexto Internacional* (43): 121–146.

Milosevich-Juaristi, M. (2019) *Rusia en América Latina: repercusiones para España*. El Real Instituto Elcano.

Mosquera, M. and Morales Ruvalcaba, D. (2018) La estrategia institucional de China hacia América Latina. Análisis comparado entre los foros Celac-China y Celac-Unión Europea. *OASIS*. (28): 123–149.

Myers, M. and Jie, G. (2015) China's agricultural investment in Latin America: A critical assessment. *The Dialogue*. Available (consulted 21 May 2024) at: https://www.thedialogue.org/analysis/chinas-agricultural-investment-in-latin-america/.

Nahón, C. (2018) Latin America in the G20: Continuities and Ruptures of the Regional Agenda (2008–2018). *International Organisations Research Journal* 13(4): 39–54.

Neoliberalismo en América Latina. Crisis, tendencias y Alternativas (2015). Ed. by L.R. Villagra. Asunción: CLACSO. 316 p

Nieto, J. Z. (2007) U.S. Security Policies and United States-Colombia Relations. *Latin American Perspective* 34(1): 112–119.

Noya, J. (2005) La imagen de Europa. *Real Instituto Elcano*. Available (consulted 21 May 2024) at: https://www.realinstitutoelcano.org/analisis/la-imagen-de-europa-2/.

O'Donnel, G. (1972) *Modernización y Autoritarismo*. Buenos Aires: Paidós.

O'Donnel, G. (1982) *El Estado Burocrático Autoritario*. Buenos Aires: Prometeo libros.

Palma, D. A. (2009) Civilizaciones, multipolaridad y confederaciones en el nuevo orden mundial. *XXVII Congreso de la Asociación Latinoamericana de Sociología. VIII Jornadas de Sociología*. Asociación Latinoamericana de Sociología.

Partiño, R. (2015) *CELAC-UE: Una asociación birregional que se fortalece para el desarrollo de nuestros pueblos*. Available (consulted 21 May 2024) at: https://eulacfoundation.org/es/system/files/CELAC_UE_Pati%C3%B10_Ecuador.pdf.

Pasternak, B. (1957). *Doctor Zhivago*. Moscow: Edition Azbuka, 349 p.

Pastrana, E. and Sánchez, A. (2014) Retos de la Gobernanza Global frente a una Multipolaridad Creciente. In: Pastrana, E. and Gehring, H. *Suramérica en el escenario global: Gobernanza multinivel y birregionalismo*. Bogotá: Editorial Pontifica Universidad Javeriana.

Patiño, V. and Carlos, A. (2014) EE.UU.-Rusia: ¿hacia una reconfiguración geopolítica de América latina y el gran Caribe? *Análisis Político* (82): 196–211.

Peña, F. (2000) *Multilateralismo, regionalismo y las negociaciones MERCOSUR-Unión Europea* Available at: http://www.felixpena.com.ar/index.php?contenido=wpapers&wpagno=documentos/2000-07.

Pietikäinen, D. (2020) EU-Latin America: reviving the 'other' transatlantic relationship. *Friends of Europe*. Available (consulted 21 May 2024) at: https://www.friendsofeurope.org/insights/eu-latin-america-reviving-the-other-transatlantic-relationship/.

Portes A., L. Guarnizo y P. Landlot. (1999). "The Study of Transnationalism: Pitfalls and Promise of an Emergent Research Field" // Ethnic and Racial Studies. 40(9). P. 1486–1491.

Portillo, A. (2013) La dinámica geopolítica de América Latina y el Caribe en el contexto de la globalización. *Revista geográfica venezolana*, 54 (2): 317–328.

Prebisch, R. (1970) Las Fuerzas Espontáneas y la Estrategia del Desarrollo en el Sistema Económico. In: Iglesias E.V. (ed). *Transformaciones y Desarrollo. La Gran Tarea de América Latina*. México: Fondo de Cultura Económica.

Prebisch, R. (1981) *Capitalismo periférico: Crisis y Transformación*. Santiago: Fondo de cultura económica.

Prevost G., Vanden H. E., Oliva C., and Ayerbe L.F., eds. (2014). *U.S. National Security Concerns in Latin America and the Caribbean: the Concept of Ungoverned Spaces and Sovereignty*, New York: Palgrave Macmillan.

Puig, J. C. (1979) *Doctrinas internacionales y autonomía latinoamericana*. Caracas: Universidad Simón Bolívar.

Puig, J. C. (1986) Integración y Autonomía en América Latina en las Postrimerías Siglo XX. *Integración Latinoamericana* 11 (109): 40–62.

Puig, J.C. (1984) *América Latina: Políticas Exteriores Comparadas*. Buenos Aires.

Puyosa, I. (2019) Rusia, Venezuela y el ALBA In: Gisela K. R. (ed.) *La Izquierda Como Autoritarismo En El Siglo XXI*. Buenos Aires.

Quiliconi, C. and Salgado Espinoza, R. (2017) Latin American Integration: Regionalism àla Carte in a Multipolar World? *Colombia Internacional* 92: 15–41.

Ramírez Montañez, J. C. (2017). "Balance de los quince años del Plan Colombia (2001-2016): recuperación de la institucionalidad colombiana y consolidación de la presencia del Estado en el territorio nacional." *Estudios internacionales (Santiago)* 49 (186): 187–206.

Ramos, M. (2015) "Nuevos" modelos de guerra y potenciales amenazas al Estado ecuatoriano. *Revista de Estudios Estratégicos* (5): 209–28.

Rocha, A. (2019) América Latina en las aguas agitadas de la multipolaridad del orden mundial emergente.: Política y geopolítica regional (2000–2018). *Revista de Sociología* 29: 127–157.

Rochlin, J. (2011). Plan Colombia and the revolution in military affairs: The demise of the FARC. *Review of International Studies* 37(2): 715–740.

Rodríguez Hernández, L. E. (2014) De la unipolaridad a la multipolaridad del Sistema Internacional del siglo XXI. *Revista de Estudios Estratégicos* 1: 57–83.

Rodríguez Hernández, L. E. (2022) Configuración multipolar del sistema internacional del siglo XXI. *Política Internacional* 4 (1): 108–124.

Romero, V., B. Magaloni, and A. Díaz-Cayeros. (2016) "Presidential Approval and Public Security in Mexico's War on Crime." *Latin American Politics and Society* 58 (2), 100–123.

Rouvinski, V., & Jeifets, V. (Eds.). (2022). *Rethinking Post-Cold War Russian–Latin American Relations* (1st ed.). Routledge. https://doi.org/10.4324/9781003183372.

Ruano, L. (2018) La Unión Europea y América Latina: Breve historia de la relación birregional. *Revista Mexicana de Política Exterior*. Available (consulted 21 May 2024) at: https://revistadigital.sre.gob.mx/index.php/rmpe/article/view/261/241.

Salazar, R. (2008) La política exterior de Hugo Chávez. *Revista Mexicana de Política Exterior* (83): 221–254.

Sanahuja, J. A. (2016) "Regionalismo e integración en América Latina: de la fractura Atlántico-Pacífico a los retos de una globalización en crisis". *Pensamiento Propio* 21 (44): 29–76.

Sanahuja, J.A. (2011) Multilateralismo y regionalismo en clave suramericana: el caso de Unasur *Pensamiento propio* 33 (16): 115–158.

Sanahuja, J.A. and Rodríguez J.D. (2019) Veinte años de negociaciones Unión Europea MERCOSUR: Del interregionalismo a la crisis de la globalización. *Documentos de Trabajo no. 13 (2ª época)*. Madrid, Fundación Carolina. Available (consulted 21 May 2024) at: https://www.fundacioncarolina.es/catalogo/veinte-anos-de-negociaciones-union-europea-mercosur-del-interregionalismo-a-la-crisis-a-la-crisis-de-la-globalizacion/.

Sánchez, G. (2011) "La política de defensa y seguridad de Estados Unidos a principios del siglo XXI." In: Benítez, R.. *El Salvador. Seguridad y defensa en América del Norte: Nuevos dilemas geopolíticos*. Washington, D.C.: Woodrow Wilson International Center for Scholars.

Santana, C.O. and Bustamante, G.A. (2013) La Autonomía en la Política Exterior Latinoamericana: Evolución y Debates Actuales. *Papel político* (2): 719–742.

Schoultz, L. (1999). *Beneath the United States*. Harvard University Press.

Scott, J. M. and Carter, R. G. (2016) Promoting democracy in Latin America: foreign policy change and US democracy assistance, 1975–2010. *Third World Quarterly* 37(2): 299–320.

Scott, J. M. and Ralph C. G. (2016) Promoting democracy in Latin America: foreign policy change and US democracy assistance, 1975–2010. *Third World Quarterly* 37(2): 299–320.

Senra, R. (2017) Los ejercicios militares "inéditos" que tendrán lugar en la triple frontera entre Brasil, Colombia y Perú con la participación de Estados Unidos. *BBC Mundo*. Available (consulted 21 May 2024) at: https://www.bbc.com/mundo/noticias-amer ica-latina-39826017.

Serbin, A. (2012) *América Latina: ¿un multilateralismo sui-generis?* Available (consulted 21 May 2024) at: https://www.academia.edu/1771665/Am%C3%A9rica_Latina_un _multilateralismo_sui_generis.

Serbin, A. (2019) *Eurasia y América Latina en un mundo multipolar*. Barcelona-Buenos Aires: Editorial Icaria-CRIES.

Simonoff A.C. and Lorenzini M.E. (2019). Autonomía e Integración en las Teorías del Sur: Desentrañando el Pensamiento de Hélio Jaguaribe y Juan Carlos Puig. *Iberoamericana* (48): 96–106.

Stoessel, S. (2014) Giro a la izquierda en la América Latina del siglo XXI. Revisitando los debates académicos. *Polis Revista Latinoamericana* Available (consulted 21 May 2024) at: https://journals.openedition.org/polis/10453?lang=en.

Stuenkel, O. (2019) The Trouble Ahead for Argentina-Brazil Ties. *Americas Quaterly*. Available (consulted 21 May 2024) at: https://americasquarterly.org/article/the-trou ble-ahead-for-argentina-brazil-ties/.

Sudarev, V. (2015) Litigios territoriales en Latinoamérica y Rusia. *Iberoamérica* (3): 56–64.

Sunkel, O. (1987). Las Relaciones Centro-periferia y la Transnacionalización. *Pensamiento Iberoamericano* (11): 31–52.

Sunkel, O. (1991) *El Desarrollo desde adentro: Un Enfoque Neoestructuralista para la América Latina*. México.

Tokatlian J. and Russel R. (2002) De la Autonomía Antagónica a la Autonomía Relacional: Una Mirada Teórica desde el Cono Sur. *Perfiles Latinoamericanos*. 10 (21): 159–194.

Tokatlian, J. G. (2012) Crisis y redistribución del poder mundial. *Revista CIDOB d'Afers Internacionals* (100): 25–41.

Tokatlian, J. G. (2015) The War on Drugs and the Role of SOUTHCOM. In: Bagley B. and Rosen J. D (eds) *Drug Trafficking, Organized Crime, and Violence in the Americas Today*. Miami: University Press of Florida.

Tomassini, L. (1989) *Teoría y Práctica de la Política Internacional*. Santiago: Universidad Católica de Chile.

Torrent, R. (2005) Las relaciones Unión Europea-América Latina en los últimos diez años: el resultado de la inexistencia de una política. Un análisis empírico y esperanzado. *UNU-CRIS Occasional Papers o-2005/10*. Barcelona, EULARO/OBREAL: 38–39.

Tulchin, J. S. (2010) *La política y los intereses de seguridad de Estados Unidos en América Latina*. Friedrich Ebert Stiftung. Available (consulted 21 May 2024) at: https://library.fes.de/pdf-files/bueros/la-seguridad/07423.pdf.

Turzi, M. (2011) ¿Qué importancia tiene el BRIC? *Estudios Internacionales* 43 (168): 87–111.

Ugarte, J. C. (2015) Una visión geopolítica en favor del respeto entre naciones, la integración económica mundial y la armonía con el medioambiente. *Javier Colomo Ugarte*. Available (consulted 21 May 2024) at: https://www.javiercolomo.com/index_archivos/Nueva_multip.htm.

Ungar, A. (2020) The Armed Arena: Arms Trafficking in Central America. *Latin American Research Review* 55(3): 445–460.

United States—Latin America and the Caribbean Trade Developments (2023) CEPAL. Available (consulted 21 May 2024) at: https://www.cepal.org/en/notes/latin-america-and-caribbean-accounted-nearly-fifth-us-foreign-trade-during-first-six-months.

Vadell, J.A. (2018) El Foro China-CELAC y el nuevo regionalismo para un mundo multipolar: desafíos para la Cooperación 'Sur-Sur. *Revista Carta Internacional, Belo Horizonte* 13 (1): 6–37.

Vaicius, I., and Isacson, A. (2003) *The "War on Drugs" meets the "War on Terror": The United States' military involvement in Colombia climbs to the next level*. Washington, D.C.: Center for International Policy.

Varas, A. (1981) *America Latina y la Union Sovietica: relaciones interestatales y vinculos politicos*. FLACSO.

Vasquez, P. I. (2018) China, Oil, and Latin America: Myth vs Reality. *The Atlantic Council* Available (consulted 21 May 2024) at: https://www.researchgate.net/publication/323768185_China_Oil_and_Latin_America_MYTH_VS_REALITY_Atlantic_Council.

Vigevani, T. and Cepaluni, G. (2007) A Política Externa de Lula da Silva: A Estratégia da Autonomia pela Diversificação. *Contexto Internacional*. 29(2): 273–335.

Vitelli, M. (2016) "América del Sur: de la seguridad cooperativa a la cooperación disuasoria." *Foro Internacional* 56(3): 724–755.

Weeks, G. (2024) *Embracing Autonomy: Latin American–US Relations in the Twenty-First Century*. University of New Mexico Press.

Zapata, S. and Martínez-Hernández A.A. (2020) "La política exterior latinoamericana ante la potencia hegemónica de Estados Unidos y la potencia emergente de China". *Colombia Internacional* (104): 63–93.

Zevallos, N. (2014) La hoja de coca y la ENLCD 2007–2011: el problema público en el control de cultivos. *Revista de Ciencia Política y Gobierno*. Available (consulted 21 May 2024) at: https://revistas.pucp.edu.pe/index.php/cienciapolitica/login.

Zhang, H. and Cheng, G. (2016) China's Food Security Strategy Reform: An emerging global agricultural policy. In: F. Wu y H. Zhang (Eds) *China's Global Quest for Resources. Energy, Food and Water*. London: Routledge.

Zhang, Y. (2019) *Development Trends in Sino-Latin American Agricultural Trade and Investment. In Sino-Latin American Economic and Trade Relations*. Springer: 147–163.

Index

ACP   70, 146, 166–67
Africa   9, 55, 89, 92–93, 115, 118, 150, 199, 230
agenda   57, 62, 82, 144, 154, 156, 177, 192
agreements   97, 104–7, 120, 122, 142, 144, 147–48, 161–67, 169–70, 172–76, 179, 201–2, 212
agreements on cooperation   97, 142, 202, 219, 227
ALBA   25, 27, 29, 161, 183
Alliance   16, 43, 53, 78, 98, 230
allies   23, 33, 44, 93, 142, 197, 204, 206, 222
Americas   4–5, 25, 47–48, 56, 60, 65–66, 68, 70, 72, 79–80, 85, 87–88, 230–31, 236–37, 247–48
APEC   100, 164, 185, 213
Argentina   2, 19–21, 50–51, 55–56, 61–62, 68, 73, 75, 97–103, 112–19, 122, 126–27, 131–33, 135, 138–40, 172–73, 185–86, 188–93, 199–200, 217–22
armed forces   72, 79, 83, 100, 113, 115, 123, 204, 231
Asia   9, 44, 82, 92–93, 97, 101, 128, 133, 150, 153
Asia-Pacific region   52–53, 97–98, 118–19, 185, 230
assistance   57, 78, 87, 113, 115, 117, 143–44, 148–50, 154–55, 162–63, 169
  economic   33, 46, 87, 198
association agreements   145, 147–48, 151, 162–64, 169, 179
  comprehensive   169
Australia   92, 123, 185
autonomy   7–16, 19–20, 22–24, 27–28, 30–31, 34–35, 38, 41, 90, 144, 161

balance   4, 15, 35, 38, 47, 93, 103, 112, 143, 237
Bank of Russia   190, 205, 207, 209, 216, 224, 226
Beijing   4, 81–82, 93–101, 104, 106–7, 109–10, 113–14, 118, 120, 123–26, 131–35, 141, 171, 173, 231
Belize   73, 78, 96, 167
benefits   16, 20, 36–37, 47, 57, 165, 170, 175
bilateral cooperation   66, 85, 87, 149, 186, 208–9, 211, 213–14, 218–19
bilateral dialogue   70, 104, 113, 148, 203–6, 208, 211, 215, 222, 228

bilateral relations   6, 181, 185, 197, 199–201, 203, 213, 217–18, 222, 224–25, 228
bilateral trade   21, 104, 124, 127, 165, 203, 205, 213, 216, 218, 223
bloc   2, 28, 103, 161, 164, 171–72, 186, 199, 227
Bolivia   24–25, 27, 32–33, 49–50, 60–62, 73, 112, 114–19, 149–50, 165, 183, 192, 197, 199–200, 208–11
Brazil   19–21, 24, 32–34, 49–51, 73, 79–80, 83–84, 86–88, 94–103, 112, 116, 122–29, 136–37, 139–40, 171–74, 185–93, 197–200, 211–13, 220–22, 232–33
Brazil and Argentina   12, 75, 101–3, 114, 129, 172–73
BRICS   2, 36, 98, 103, 186, 211, 220–21, 227, 235
Brussels   142, 145, 159–60, 162, 164, 174
building   33, 35, 37–40, 46, 48, 54, 96, 107, 141, 145, 162–63, 197, 199
  alliance   65

Canada   49, 51, 58, 68, 92–93, 119, 123, 185, 203
Caribbean   25–26, 42–43, 52, 54, 61, 67–68, 72–74, 77, 98–99, 146, 148, 151, 166–69, 171, 241–42
CELAC   27, 29, 33, 101, 144, 160, 179, 186, 197, 238
Central America   42–45, 52, 60–62, 64, 66, 71, 78, 83, 85, 87, 147–48, 150, 165, 168–71, 222
Chile   19–21, 23–24, 48–49, 51–52, 55–56, 61–63, 73, 95, 97–100, 103–4, 112–14, 118–21, 123–24, 135–36, 138–40, 145–46, 148–49, 162–64, 178–79, 222–24
  northern   26
China   4–6, 35–39, 50–59, 62–63, 81–82, 88, 92–141, 152, 156–58, 164, 166, 168, 170–71, 178–80, 185–86, 220, 231–32, 234, 236–44, 248
Chinese   93–94, 96, 98–100, 102, 104, 108–9, 111–18, 120, 124–25, 127–28, 130–33, 136, 139
Chinese companies   117, 120, 122, 124, 127–28, 133, 135–36, 138, 140, 207
Chinese investment   55, 63, 103–4, 121, 124–25, 127–30, 132–35, 138, 141, 171, 173

citizens   3, 33, 53, 127, 131, 191, 197, 233
Colombia   23–24, 34, 50, 52–53, 61–62, 65–67, 70–73, 83–84, 87, 88–89, 112, 121–23, 147, 149–50, 164–66, 187–88, 192–93, 198, 224–25, 246–47
concept   8–11, 21–31, 34–36, 39, 41, 46–47, 63–65, 72, 88, 90, 92–93, 96, 178, 181–82
confrontation   4–5, 19–20, 22, 29–30, 37, 39, 41, 195–96, 232
consensus   23, 42, 44, 75, 101, 148, 163, 176–77
construction   37–38, 41, 44, 113, 116–17, 129–31, 136–38, 168, 171, 205, 207, 209, 212
contacts   83, 95, 113, 147, 181, 186, 189, 208, 223, 234
contract   116, 126, 136, 138, 188, 202, 209, 216
control   11, 22, 35, 67, 72, 76, 93, 136, 208
cooperation   25, 71–72, 75–76, 78–79, 87–88, 90–91, 96–99, 105–14, 116–17, 132–35, 141–43, 161–63, 169, 183–86, 201–3, 205–7, 211–12, 216, 219, 226–30
Costa Rica   58, 62, 73, 78, 99–100, 119–21, 130–31, 149, 154, 169–71, 193
COVID-19 pandemic   2, 29, 57–58, 154, 160, 164, 168, 175, 192, 200, 205
creation   15, 20, 23, 25–26, 28, 37–38, 40, 45–46, 48, 71, 100–101, 108, 127–29, 160–61, 165–66
crisis   17, 19, 32, 36, 41, 57–59, 148, 153–54, 173, 175–76, 196–97, 242–43, 245–47
Cuba   33, 41–42, 47, 52–54, 56–57, 59–60, 77, 85–86, 94–95, 98–100, 105, 145, 184, 186–89

defense   42, 46, 65, 67, 72, 79, 82, 86, 91, 182, 187–89, 220–21
democracy   46–47, 51, 58, 65, 88, 91–93, 144, 147, 157, 169, 171
dependence   10, 17, 38, 55, 168, 183, 215, 230
developing countries   2–3, 7, 15–16, 92–94, 96, 100, 150, 153, 165, 170, 178, 181
dialogue   76, 81, 86, 97, 100, 106–7, 110–11, 142–48, 169, 171, 176, 183, 185
diplomatic relations   53, 94, 96, 105, 210, 227, 233
document   21, 47, 88, 100, 106, 113, 148–49, 163–64, 173–75, 179, 227
Dominica   25, 167
Dominican Republic   12, 43, 52, 58, 73, 167, 171

drug trafficking   53, 60, 62, 66–67, 71, 79, 85, 87, 91, 225, 227–28, 235

economic cooperation   96, 98, 100, 107, 146, 151, 157, 160–61, 215, 217–18, 221, 223, 228
economic development   9, 18, 38–39, 53, 149, 189, 191, 203, 218
economics   13, 15, 25, 66, 72, 93, 101, 157, 159, 230, 232–33
Ecuador   24–25, 49–50, 58, 61–62, 72–73, 95, 114, 116–17, 119–20, 147, 149–50, 164–66, 189, 192–93, 199–200, 207, 215–17, 221
El Salvador   43–45, 53, 56, 59, 62, 73, 78, 85, 89, 145, 149–50, 169–71, 226–29
emergence   21, 24, 27–29, 31, 36–37, 40–41, 44, 48–49, 63, 139, 142, 147, 172–73
energy   25–26, 31, 127–28, 133, 135, 177, 185, 191, 201, 214–15, 223
Europe   89, 91–93, 142, 150, 156, 159, 162, 175, 180, 237, 244
European Union   142–79, 185, 242
exchange   56, 76, 95, 107–9, 112, 121, 126, 130, 187, 217, 225
expansion   111–12, 127, 130, 148, 151, 153, 180, 182–83, 186, 189, 194–95, 212, 214, 218, 220
exports   61–62, 95, 100, 104, 116–17, 120–24, 127, 151–52, 167, 173, 175, 190–91

fight   46, 49, 57, 60, 66–67, 69–71, 78–79, 82–83, 87, 91, 154, 160, 227–28
foreign policy   3–7, 9, 13–14, 19–26, 29–30, 33–36, 39–42, 48–49, 52–53, 65–66, 86–87, 159–62, 180–83, 194–95, 198–200, 205–6, 208, 219–21, 229–30, 232–34
foreign policy strategy   7, 20–21, 42–43, 52, 104, 111, 132, 142, 181, 230
formation   8–9, 17, 19–20, 24, 34–35, 39–40, 98, 108–11, 160, 162, 165, 167, 180, 182, 226–27
free trade agreements   46, 50, 52, 58, 63, 162, 164, 168, 176, 217, 222
free trade area   23, 45, 47, 68, 122, 161
funding   56, 78, 81, 84, 89, 106, 126, 149–50, 178, 226, 229

G-20 summits   103, 213, 219
Gazprom   191, 207, 209, 212, 219

goods   101–2, 104, 118, 120–21, 123–24, 128, 162–63, 165, 170, 189–90, 192
governments   2–3, 30, 32, 41, 45, 47–48, 56–57, 59, 70, 72, 82, 84, 233
groups   14, 112, 146, 149, 169, 174, 182, 185, 190–91, 197, 199–200
Guatemala   43–45, 53, 56, 59, 62, 78, 85, 149–50, 169–70, 226–27, 229
Guyana   24, 55, 61–62, 95, 114–15, 119, 125, 131, 167

Haiti   42, 60, 73, 96, 113, 149, 155, 167
Honduras   42–43, 53, 62, 73, 77–78, 84, 88, 149–50, 169–70, 226–27, 229
human rights   21, 28, 37, 46, 56, 58–59, 144, 146, 169–70, 174, 176–77

implementation   71, 116, 122, 131, 145, 151, 178, 182, 188, 209, 215
imports   58, 61–62, 102, 104–5, 122, 124, 136, 151–52, 212, 216, 220
inclusion   9, 13, 44, 86, 132, 142–43, 145, 169, 172, 185
independence   8, 11, 27, 29, 34, 42, 75, 184, 203–4
influence   5, 9–10, 12, 35–38, 67–68, 89–90, 94–95, 131, 143, 156–58, 173, 182, 188–89, 226
initiative   23–24, 45, 48, 52–53, 56, 59, 67, 107–8, 121–22, 128, 130, 132–33, 154–56, 186, 188
institutions   3, 15, 27, 101, 110, 142, 146, 150, 156, 161, 169
integration   3, 8–9, 12–15, 18–22, 24–31, 34, 38, 44, 144, 146, 167, 170
intensification   21–22, 26, 28, 32, 35, 98–99, 112, 118, 183, 185, 209, 215, 218
interaction   2, 5, 9, 65, 68–69, 87, 94, 96–97, 99–100, 103, 106–8, 143–48, 159
international forums   32, 51, 103, 144, 160, 185, 196, 211, 213
international relations   3–5, 8–15, 17–41, 92–93, 159–61, 172, 179, 230–31, 235, 238, 242
interregional relations   5, 142, 144, 148, 159, 162, 176–77, 234
investments   45, 62, 99–100, 103, 105, 124, 127, 129–30, 133–34, 153–54, 171, 173, 231–32

Kremlin   31, 33, 180, 182, 184–87, 192–93, 196–97, 199–202, 204, 206, 208, 210–13, 222, 229, 232

LAC   3–7, 9, 11–12, 15, 17–19, 23–26, 28–29, 31–42, 44–51, 57, 59–62, 65–66, 68–72, 75–77, 79–146, 148–56, 159–62, 168–69, 174–201, 203–36
LAC countries   2–7, 14–16, 21–24, 26–29, 49–50, 53–57, 63–66, 75–78, 82–85, 88–90, 94–98, 100–101, 106–14, 119–24, 126–28, 130–35, 149–51, 159–62, 199–201, 230–32
Latin American   9–13, 15, 17–18, 22–23, 25–36, 38–41, 46–48, 50, 52–53, 60–63, 94–95, 157–58, 175–79, 186–87, 189–94, 196–97, 199–200, 217–18, 221–23, 234–35
leaders   79, 85, 95, 101, 179, 185, 196, 204–5, 207, 211, 216
leadership   4, 14, 39, 51, 57, 65–66, 95, 139, 173–74, 226

markets   26, 100–102, 139, 147, 162, 165–66, 169–70, 173–75, 182, 188, 191
MERCOSUR   20–21, 23, 29, 32, 122, 129, 142–43, 147–48, 150, 171–76, 179, 186
Mexico   47–50, 54, 58, 60–64, 66–68, 70–71, 73, 80, 83, 87–89, 98–100, 104–5, 128–29, 162–64, 175–77, 185, 187–92, 198–200, 213–15, 221–22
military   36, 40, 43–44, 54–55, 64, 68, 76, 78–81, 83, 86–89, 111–12, 117–18
military-technical cooperation   68–69, 72, 111–12, 201, 208, 210, 216, 219, 224–25, 231
model   7, 9–10, 12–13, 15–16, 18, 39, 42, 65, 69, 177, 179, 199–201, 211
Moscow   33–34, 180–81, 183, 185, 197–210, 212, 215, 218–19, 221, 223–25, 227, 229, 232

negotiations   44–45, 48, 53, 76–77, 115, 119, 147, 165, 167, 174, 202–3, 217–18, 220
Nicaragua   25, 27, 33, 41–45, 120, 149–50, 169–71, 184, 187–89, 196–97, 199–200, 203–6, 210–11, 225–26, 232

OAS   8, 32, 46, 65–66, 72, 75–76, 91, 98, 141, 160, 197
oil   50–51, 86, 101–3, 118, 122, 125–27, 134, 190, 206–9, 220, 248

INDEX

Panama   12, 18, 45, 52, 55–56, 58, 73, 78, 117, 121, 132, 137, 169–70
Paraguay   20, 24, 32, 55, 62, 129–30, 149–50, 186, 189, 192–93, 196
parties   13, 40–41, 95, 97, 99–101, 107, 109–10, 115–16, 147–48, 163, 165, 167, 169, 172, 234
partnership   87, 93, 96–97, 100–101, 103, 109, 113, 127, 132, 203, 206, 209
Peru   18–19, 23–24, 61–62, 73, 94–95, 97–100, 103–4, 108, 112–15, 118–21, 127–29, 135–37, 149–50, 164–66, 185–87, 191–93, 222
policy   9–10, 13–15, 23, 25, 40–41, 44–45, 47, 49, 52–54, 59–60, 79, 81, 96, 180–81, 234–35
political dialogue   107, 143–48, 156, 159, 162–63, 166, 169, 176, 181, 184, 187
positions   8, 10, 13, 32–34, 36, 38, 40–41, 58, 75, 93, 144–45, 174, 184–86, 196–98, 221
power   4, 7, 9, 12–13, 27–29, 35, 37–38, 40–41, 45–47, 49–50, 63–64, 92–93, 197–99, 215–19
president   48, 51, 53–54, 57, 59–60, 175, 181, 183, 186, 208, 211, 220–21, 223–25
problems   8, 17–18, 24, 67, 71, 79, 82, 85, 98, 101, 170, 173, 177–79
project   46, 48, 53, 96–97, 115–16, 128, 130–38, 155, 171, 178, 201–2, 205, 207, 209, 219
protection   40, 78, 88, 105, 144, 146, 164–65, 169–70, 191–92, 222, 236

rapprochement   95, 97, 100–101, 142–43, 145, 147, 171, 179, 190–91, 215, 222
region   2–5, 9–12, 17–19, 21–29, 32–34, 36–42, 51–55, 63–69, 88–91, 94–98, 109–15, 117–19, 121–24, 127–35, 140–47, 149–56, 177–84, 186–200, 229–32, 234–36
relations   4–5, 7, 9–10, 26–29, 40–42, 48–50, 69–70, 80–81, 85–86, 98–100, 104–6, 129–30, 142–43, 168, 182–83, 197–200, 204–6, 213, 228–31, 234–36
Russia   2, 4–6, 31, 33–35, 37, 41, 57, 59, 81–82, 88, 112–14, 160, 180–230, 232–34, 239
Russian Federation   32, 180–81, 184–85, 189–91, 197, 202, 204, 206–7, 213, 227, 232
Russia-Ukraine conflict   31–33, 41, 87, 196, 217, 221, 223, 225, 232–33, 236

sanctions   47, 56, 58–60, 80–81, 86, 184, 188–86, 213–14, 221, 223, 226

Santiago   65, 99, 107, 119, 153, 164, 222–23, 239, 245, 247, 249
security   37, 42, 63, 65–68, 71–72, 75, 78–79, 82–83, 86–90, 106–7, 112, 147–48, 182
South America   25, 28–29, 39, 43, 47, 49–51, 67–68, 71–72, 166, 170, 172–73, 175, 205
states   2–3, 7–16, 18, 20, 22–23, 25, 28–29, 31, 33, 37–38, 40–42, 48–49, 142, 198–200, 233–34
strategy   4, 6, 22, 24, 39, 43–46, 65, 98, 118, 121, 171–72, 193, 195, 231, 233
support   32, 34, 41, 43, 45–46, 48, 50, 53, 59–60, 70–71, 169–71, 184, 192–93, 197–98, 232–33
Suriname   24, 61–62, 119, 167

trade   6–7, 24–25, 45–46, 100–102, 118, 120–21, 123–24, 133–34, 141, 143–44, 151–52, 161
trade agreements   52, 99, 120, 162, 165–66, 168, 172, 177, 179, 224
trade cooperation   99, 109, 128, 151, 168, 188
transformations   5, 27, 36, 38, 45–46, 65, 72, 75, 83, 230, 235
transition   13, 15, 33, 35–36, 39, 66, 85, 92–93, 99, 197, 203
trends   23–25, 27, 39, 42, 60, 63, 81, 230, 235, 241

Ukraine   32–34, 41, 86–87, 178–79, 196–98, 200, 205, 210, 217, 221–22, 225–26, 228
Uruguay   20, 24, 26, 30, 58, 61–62, 117–19, 124, 129, 171, 174–75
USSR   44–45, 47, 92–94, 181–82, 191, 193, 199, 201–2, 204, 206, 224, 227, 229

Venezuela   24–25, 33, 49–51, 54, 56–62, 69, 72–73, 75, 80, 84–86, 112–19, 125–27, 134, 171–72, 183–86, 196–97, 199–200, 205–8, 210, 232

Washington   4, 23–25, 42–46, 48–52, 56–60, 63–64, 66–72, 75–76, 80–81, 83, 86–88, 222, 224
Western Hemisphere   44–45, 47–48, 57–59, 63–64, 66, 72, 75, 82, 84, 86, 94, 101, 104
world politics   2, 10–11, 13–15, 21–22, 31, 34, 141–42, 180–81, 198, 200, 228, 230, 233

www.ingramcontent.com/pod-product-compliance
Lightning Source LLC
Chambersburg PA
CBHW070617030426
42337CB00020B/3827